POET UNDER A SOLDIER'S HAT

POET UNDER A SOLDIER'S HAT

AN UNWILLING OFFICER'S ADVENTURES IN THE LAST YEARS OF THE BRITISH RAJ

E.P. ROSE

Disclaimer: Though dates, facts, names of people, places, regiments and ranks gleaned from my father's journals, are accurate to the best of my knowledge, I cannot guarantee them. Colored by my personal experiences and memories of India and the Middle East, details, conversations, thoughts and interpretations are mine apart from a few pearls—such as Atlee's comment to my father on Partition during the Simon Commission, the bearded head in a rucksack, and the toast-addicted and cigarette-eating gazelles. Without these and many other rich stories included in my father's writings, Poet Under a Soldier's Hat could never have come about

Second Edition

Studio on 41 Press
Galisteo, New Mexico
www.galisteoliz.com

Cover design and illustration: Donna Brownell
Book design and layout: Donna Brownell
Photographs and illustrations: Hugh Rose
Author photo: Hal Khan

Printed in the U.S.A.

ISBN: 978-0-9861188-2-1

First Edition
Design by Susan Cohen
Edited by Jeanne Shannon
Published by Quillrunner Publishing, LLC

The Library of Congress has cataloged the first edition as follows:
Library of Congress Control Number: 2013935509
ISBN 978-0-9851157-0-8

For my father, Hugh,
and all those desert frogs
waiting until the rains to sing.

Imperial Lament

remember also on Armistice Day
the dead still potent to inspire
scattered lonely in sun-baked graves forgotten
silent hosts of a lost Empire
waiting for the muted trumpets' reminder
to think of them on Armistice Day
and thank them

UZBEKISTAN
TAJIKISTAN
CHINA
KASHMIR
KYBER PASS
ABBOTOBAD
PESHAWAR
Kabul
AFGHANISTAN
Srinagar
Gulmarg
GANGES
Razmak
TIBET
Shalshal Pass
Dhura
Kandahar
WAZIRISTAN
INDUS
NORTHWEST FRONTIER
Manasarowar Lake
Brahmaputra River
DEHRA DUN
GARWAL
LANSDOWNE
Zahidan
Quetta
MEERUT
ALMORA
Kuh-i-Taftan
Nainital
DELHI
Bareilly
PERSIA
Gonda
TERAI JUNGLE
INDIA
LUCKNOW
Fyzabad
INDUS RIVER
ARABIAN SEA
Karachi
GANGES RIVER
NEPAL

CONTENTS

PHOTOGRAPHS & ILLUSTRATIONS

ACKNOWLEDGEMENTS

How could I have got this far without support and help?
First I want to thank Bill Atkinson whose idea it was to edit and publish my father's military notes, and David de Vaux for his time and encouragement that the material would indeed convert to a book. I am grateful to my friends Catherine Ferguson and Clare Gardner, on whose feedback I relied, and to SouthWest Writers in Albuquerque, from whom I learned what writing craft I have. I am indebted to, my son, Anthony Jefferson, for his rigorous and invaluable genealogical research, to my friend Barbara Pfeiffer for her suggestions, to Gwen Feisst for her Photoshop expertise, to Bill and Ellen Dupuy at KSFR2.org, who podcast and streamed several excerpts on their station, to Jonathan Richards who read them so well, to Donna Brownell for the many patient hours she spent pulling together the final project, and last but not least to my husband, David Burk, for his patient ear.
Yes, I thank you one and all..

FOREWORD

Few people are still alive who can remember the British Empire. My father, Hugh Rose, served as a British Officer with the Gurkhas in India and in the Khyber Pass on the North West Frontier, and with the Political and Foreign Service in the British Protectorates of Aden, the Hadramat, Persia and Waziristan. I found the facts in his biographical notes too fascinating to keep hidden. I wrote this book in order to record a time in history now fading to the past, and by recording them illustrate 100 years of Colonial History through the personal stories of one family—mine.

Elizabeth Rose, Galisteo, NM, 2013

PREFACE

If I'd never met the naked colonel, never heard his ranting, "Conformity kills," and "Compromise castrates," I might have remained a soldier trapped in my father's footsteps like the wriggling worm I discovered imprisoned in a geranium urn when I was four. I might never have allowed a single poem to flower, climbed where I should not have climbed, or created an oasis in Aden's desert. I was a desert frog, voiceless, silent, lying in wait for the rains to come before I could sing and mate.

I first felt the splatter, the fat drops of rain on my upturned face trekking in the wildness of the Himalayas when I was a man. Brief moments of dreamy solitude kept me alive until then, when the rains I knew would come some day, arrived, and I could sing full-throated. Until then, poor voiceless child, I trod blindly in footprints not my own.

It's my story and my family's story that compels me to peer through the spyglass into a time that can never be again. History and details of lives caught in two World Wars, the Sepoy Rebellion, known by us British as the Indian Mutiny, the Raj and the British Empire across the breadth of India and Arabia. I want you to know of my experiences serving alongside the Gurkha Regiments and Indian Army on the North West Frontier and the Hill Stations, my four years with the Foreign Service in India, Arabia, Iran and Waziristan, and of the eventual crumbling of my military career.

Escape, capture, bandits, war lords, missionaries, officers, ordinary men and ghosts, I want a record to exist, and a record of my personal adventures and struggles, my mountain treks and mysterious encounters for which I have no explanation.

Until Partition in 1947, both branches of my family were tied to India, though by two very different strings. Father's background was traditional, military, *pukka*, British, one might say. Mother's was, well, different, starting with her birth in the ruins of a Hindu temple in the jungle, her mixed blood, her parents' narrow escape from death on the very day the Indian Mutiny–or Sepoy Rebellion–broke out in Meerut in 1857. I have my grandfather's eyewitness account.

Then there was the big secret, something taboo in my parents' past, something shocking, which if I had known and uncovered earlier, might have made it easier for me to step out of Father's footsteps. I might have become a full-time writer and a poet, not a soldier who kept poems under his hat. But I didn't.

I begin my story on August 8th, 1914, the day The Great War burst over Europe when I was nine and became a refugee.

Hugh Rose. North West Frontier.

I

BACKSTORY

1
ESCAPE

Before it was fully light, Father pulled our oak front door shut, and with a single turn of the iron key closed the Belgium chapter of our lives abandoning everything except the few pieces of family silver buried two days earlier on the golf course under the 10th tee. I had no sense of loss. I was nine. It was just another of many moves. The difference was Father. We usually moved without him, but for once he was home with us, not in India.

The words may not be exact, nor the details, but I remember. It was an August morning in the summer of 1914. As I take up my pen, my story comes vividly to life and I am nine again.

Father surprised us while we were eating breakfast round the family dining table, the six of us, seven if you count the baby. Besides baby Kathy, there was Astel, my brother, the oldest of us, then my sisters Rita and Aileen, and me, Hugh. We ate in silence. Father liked quiet at breakfast time. I held a slice of buttered toast and Mother's homemade marmalade in my hand.

"We're leaving today." We froze. He paused. "Immediately after breakfast."

Those were his very words.

"Today? My friend Henner and I planned … You never said…" I muttered under my breath. "It's not fair."

"Hugh. No argument. D'you hear me? We leave in one hour."

How little choice I had back then. Orders, especially Father's, were to be obeyed without question. Mother did sometimes venture a protest, "We're not in the Army, you know, dear," at which Father would explode, "Puppies need training, kept on a short leash."

Addressing me he would add, "Stand straight, boy. Look me in the eye when I am talking to you." If I had had a tail, I would have put it between my legs and slunk away. I was a crybaby, a namby-pamby, in his opinion. I suppose I was, and he was right. I hardly knew him, or any man for that matter, until I was sent away to boarding school. Apart from Monsieur Anton, our gentle gardener, men scared me.

Father read aloud the telegraph delivered minutes earlier.

"Telegraph, Sir." And the messenger astride his Enfield vanished in a spurt of smoke.

ONE SMALL SUITCASE PER-PERSON… DOCUMENTS… HOTEL FLANDERS.

"Children, finish your breakfast quickly. Go upstairs. Pack only what you can carry." Father looked severe. For days, both Mother and Father, grim-faced, sat chairs pulled close, shushing us quiet whenever we spoke.

"Germany…France…invasion…war." That morning, their whispered snippets were clear. "Germany has invaded Belgium."

Mother clutched Father's sleeve. They spoke urgently to one another, their voices lowered. I stared uneasily at their serious faces. I glanced at Father's Indian Ceremonial sword, and his curved *kukri* hanging on the wall behind him. Father was a soldier. Feeling reassured, I returned my attention to my half eaten toast.

Upstairs, Mother packed me a small cloth-covered cardboard case with what she called "essentials." As soon as she left the room to help my sisters, I snapped it open, pulled out my bedroom slippers, threw them under the bed and sneaked Teddy and my Boy's Own Annual in their place. I was used to moving house. We moved often. I had my own ideas of what was and was not important. It was strange though, the hurry. Mother usually warned us weeks ahead before announcing, "Father has decided…." And gathering our things we'd be off again. This move was different.

I dragged my case downstairs and followed Mother and my sisters out into the garden to wait for Father. We stood together, suitcases bulging at our feet, watching Father's every curious move. He rattled the doorknob, pushed his shoulder against the door checking and rechecking it to make sure it was locked, withdrew the iron key, and with one brief backward glance towards the house, joined us on the front path. Odd, him wearing his ceremonial sword. Strapped to his waist it hung down his left leg. Father wrapped the key in a square of yellow oilcloth, then, startled us by unsheathing his sword. The blade flashed a rainbow in the early light. Using the point, he scrabbled a hole in the lawn five paces from the left gate post closest to the rose-bed, buried his bundle, replaced the soil and grass turf over the disturbed earth, and tamped it firmly with the heel of his boot. He marked the place with a rock, rechecking heel-toe, heel-toe five times, from the front gate, and sheathed his sword.

"Ready?" It wasn't a question.

Father marshaled us into a ragged troop. Confidently, I joined the ranks "falling in" behind him–one of his soldiers. If I had understood games have a way of turning into reality, I might have been a poet, not a soldier when I grew up. But that day I played soldiers. With that step, I unwittingly sealed my fate to become a soldier, a Gurkha Officer, and place my feet in Father's footprints across the globe to India. Even my name was his. Hugh Rose.

Father picked up the two heaviest suitcases and pushed the gate open.

"Follow me."

We set off in twos behind him with Mother in the rearguard, Kathy-baby clasped in her arms.

"Quick march. Brmm. Brmm, and-aaah—left, right, left..." I continued my soldier game under my breath.

"Snap to it, Hugh. This is no time for games. Rita, keep a firm hold of him. Astel, take Aileen's hand. Keep together."

Surprisingly, the trams were still running, and almost immediately a dusty-red one trundled along the rails in the center of the street towards our stop, its wheels spewing sparks from rails embedded in the tarmac. We clambered aboard. Father twisted sharply in his window seat, pointing to small groups of men tramping in a disorderly fashion beside the tram track, exclaiming,

"I say. What the devil…? Marines. Ours." British, he meant.

Years later during a class at Military College studying the Great War, a sepia photograph of bedraggled battle-worn men, unearthed the similar sad image I had glimpsed from the tram when I was nine. The dispassionate caption read, "A small detachment of Winston Churchill's Royal Marines in Retreat, after failing their mission to cut the advancing German supply route." Another photograph, dated August 8th, 1914, showed General Alexander Von Kluck's First Army's invasion into Belgium before he marched on Paris. With a jolt, I remembered the date. It was the day we abandoned our Belgian home, the very day we escaped to England.

The gathering place, the Hotel Flanders on the north side of town, was ironically the very hotel we stayed in when we first arrived in Belgium over three years ago. Now it was also where we would spend our last hours in that country.

The hotel was eerily silent in despite of the crowd of people. Anxious foreigners stood in tight groups in the dining and lounge areas waiting helplessly for instruction. To my shame, Father pushed his way through the crush gathered in the reception hall to the foot of the wide sweeping staircase on the far side.

"Make way. Make way." To my surprise, they did.

People already sitting on the stairs shuffled sideways making space. I settled with my sisters on a stair-tread one above Mother and the baby and looked around. This move was unlike any of our other previous moves. Father and Astel stood in the hall below us separated by the banisters but close enough for me to touch them. For something to do, for nothing was happening, I stretched my arm through the banisters, tweaked Astel's hair, and snatched my arm back before he caught me.

"Brat," he yelled at me. "Enough"

There was nothing more to do but wait. After an interminably dreary couple of hours, the American Consul arrived, pale and grim faced. Without any preamble, he announced,

"Go calmly. Go immediately. Make your way to Zeebrugge Harbor with the utmost of haste. Speed is of the essence. A Naval Destroyer will take you to safety."

Then, as an afterthought, "May God go with you all."

The railway lines were still intact, and the train pulling into the station was punctual right to the minute as quoted by the timetable. With a wave of his sword, Father commandeered a carriage for us. The whole town had taken to the streets headed in the same direction. Young, old, everyone carried something, a valise, a suitcase, a misshapen parcel, a carpetbag or knotted bundles like our washerwoman's. They pushed anything with wheels, baby carriages, wheelbarrows, bicycles and even a package-laden wicker bath-chair long since vacated by its incapacitated owner. A continuous stream struggled towards the harbor. I never saw so many people. Not one person returned my cheery wave from the carriage window.

"Are they all coming too? With us? To England?" I asked.

Nobody answered. Rita told me not to be so silly. Aileen dug me in the ribs with her elbow.

Arriving at Zeebrugge, the train ground to a halt inside the wrought-iron harbor gates beyond the struggling crowds funneling through the narrow entrance. The noise and crush on the platform, the loudness of it was suddenly frightening. I fought to pull my hand out of Rita's and grab onto Mother's skirts. I was no longer one of Father's soldiers. I wanted Mother. I bit my lip, blinking back my "boys-don't-cry" tears before they spilled. Father turned and faced us. He wasn't smiling.

"Attention. Now pay good attention. Stick together. Keep a tight grip.

That's an order. Understood? Then let's go."

One behind the other, clutching hands, a jacket hem, a skirt, anything, we inched towards the dockside, carried slowly forward by the sluggish tide of the equally bewildered and disorientated. The sharp corners of my suitcase banged against my bare legs. It really hurt. I didn't cry out, though. Father turned frequently to jolly us along.

"Nearly there. That's the spirit."

"British Nationals, Shed 3. Americans, Shed 5. Belgians...French...." Father pointed towards the collection of corrugated sheds along the quayside. "Over there. Look. Number 3 painted in red."

A solitary British sergeant stood at the entrance bellowing instructions through a megaphone. He, the collie, herded us. Thankful for his guidance, we, the sheep, obeyed.

The doors were rolled open on one side. A faint sea breeze fanned the sweltering August heat. Father secured a prime spot close to the opening and set about building a defensive pen using our suitcases.

"Get inside and stay inside." Father turned the largest case on end. "For you, Mother. Sit here."

Mother perched her bottom precariously, balancing Kathy-baby on her lap. We watched the enmeshed crowd unravel itself into defined family units, then still unnaturally silent, just as the crowd gathered for rescue had stilled earlier in the day at the Hotel Flanders.

One hour. One hour and a half. Two. Fidgety, I hopped. I flapped my arms and pulled faces at Kathy-baby. I didn't even raise a giggle. I pretended stories in my head. Hopeful, I looked for the bloody battle of my favorite storybooks. But nothing. Not a ship, not a fireball, not a rocket. Fed up, and innocently indifferent to the horror I was witnessing, there was nothing for me to do but huddle beside my parents and sisters. My stomach rumbled.

"Is it lunch time yet?"

Miraculously, Mother materialized a thick sandwich for the each of us from pockets sewn beneath her skirts. Cold pork and cheese, oozing tomato chutney from two thickly buttered slabs. I was so hungry, instead of eating just the crumb and filling, as was my habit, I devoured every bit, crust and all. I looked longingly at my sisters still slowly chewing theirs, but nothing extra came my way.

I turned my attention to the harbor. Across the quay an already over-packed ferry beside one of the jetties listed alarmingly. Ignoring the announcement boarding was complete and the instruction to please step away from the gangway, increasing numbers of Belgian refugees were trying to cram themselves on board. Father had hardly finished saying out loud, "Something had better be done about the situation, that ship's in danger of sinking," when the gangplank winched upwards with people still clinging to its slope, and the Cross Channel Ferryboat pulled away from the quayside.

The chaos. The screams. The slipping, the splash after splash. So temptingly close to safety, numbers of Belgians and other refugees plunged into the waters and struck out swimming to reach her. Horrifically unstoppable, the ferry sliced through the swimmers, still bravely calling out and waving, still hopeful of rescue.

Bows rising and falling, she ploughed ahead towards the harbor's outer moles, making for the open seas. Although Father and Mother ordered us to move further inside the shed, they couldn't shield us from the dreadful scene.

The grim lottery played itself out. Too many people. Too few ships. There were ships enough for us British and Americans, we had been assured. We would be saved. But where were they? Would they ever come?

"Patience, Hughey. There's nothing to do but wait." Mother snapped.

Funny. Grownups playing the Whispering Game, the game we children sometimes played at home? Even Mother and Father played. Muttered conversations passed from mouth to ear, mouth to ear. But from the serious tight-lipped faces, I saw they were not having any fun. I strained to catch their whisperings, the horrified snatches,

"Ulhans...babies...sabers...massacre...murder."

Wildfire rumors of Prussian Uhlans on horseback, vicious killings of babies and children, circulated among the grown-ups in the shed. I pictured garish cartoon strips.

Avoiding the danger of being swamped, the remaining rescue ships rode at anchor in the middle of the harbor with their companion ladders pulled up. They drew alongside for only as long as it took to load their cargo and haul anchor. It was late afternoon by the time a grey destroyer of the Royal Naval steamed into view.

"Rose family," the megaphone blasted.

In orderly fashion, we took our place on the crowded gangplank. We had just stepped on board when I heard Father say, "Mother, take the children," and pushing his way back against the tide of people making their way along the deck, he was gone.

"Get right back here, away from the railing, Hugh."

But I was searching for Father.

"Father. Father. Don't go. Mother, he's left us. He's gone to war." I called, my stomach heavy as if I'd swallowed stones.

"He's just helping. He'll find us later." Mother's hand squeezed my shoulder.

Struggling with our packages, we followed her along the deck, clambering cautiously up the slippery metal companion ladders in search of a sheltered spot.

Mother settled us against a bulkhead on the upper deck behind a life raft where we were protected from the strong headwinds. We sat huddled close, quiet. The sun hung low, the shadows long.

"Who is calling, Mother?"

The tragic pleas of those left behind followed us over the water. My sisters clapped their hands over their ears. Mother said to look up at the sky. She moved between us and the rails.

"Keep your heads up. Take deep breaths. Don't look down at the water and you won't be seasick." Mother lied to protect us from sights too awful to imagine playing out in the harbor's foaming seas.

Then, suddenly silence, the only sound the shushhhhing salty sea.

My stomach see-sawed with the swell. Still no sign of Father. Scanning the fast-receding empty quayside, a sickening fear gripped me. We had sailed without him.

Then there he was, striding towards us along the deck and my belly-stones stilled. I sunk to the deck. I wanted Mother. Squishing close to her side, I glared at the gurgling imposter in her arms. Mother patted a place on the wooden deck.

"Come, Hughey-boy. Here." Leaning against Mother's free arm, I smiled and settled back. I walked my fingers across Mother's corseted stomach, stay by whalebone stay. I stroked Kath's pudgy hand and smiled at my baby sister. There was room for us both.

The rising, falling, rolling, lulled me. Images of mysterious "Ulhans" running bayonets through helpless babies and children peopled my dreaming, and Father too, brandishing his sword, saving us.

"Whaaa?" Mother was shaking my shoulders.

"Look, children. Look. The White Cliffs of Dover."

A spontaneous cheer went up, and our fellow refugees crowding the deck smiled and nodded to each other without having ever been introduced.

"Hurrah for Merry old England," they cried.

"Blighty. What a blessed sight for poor eyes."

Britain welcomed us to its shores with a sweet, milky British cure-all, a cup-o'-char. A veritable army of stalwart Women Volunteers pressed their mugs of comfort into our hands.

"Welcome Home. Welcome home." And so we were. Home.

2
ORIGINS

In 1896, the cool summer breeze of a Himalayan Military Hill Station fanned my parents' illicit love affair. Mother lifted her petticoats, setting the bowling ball in motion, the ball that knocked down every well-placed pin in her world.

The documents and private papers hidden in a battered tin trunk under the bed where Mother died explained her secretiveness. "That's personal," she would answer dismissing our questions about her family and childhood, and how she and father met. No wonder she never spoke of India; she couldn't, without exhuming the skeletons she'd so successfully buried. The papers spoke of a stranger, not Mother. I'd never known the Emma I unearthed—tragic, I had to wait forty years till after her death to piece together the jigsaw of her secrets. It took me forty years. Patching together overheard bits and pieces, the snippets dropped, the sudden silences, or quick change of subject, I could at last fill in details. Writing this now at the age of seventy-eight, truth has at last lost its sting.

Had the wild young Emma of then still danced inside my reserved, religious Mother all the time I was growing up and after I became a man? All the time I loved her I never saw the hidden twinkle in her eye. I can't decide if my parents' tale is a sordid one, a story of love, or simply a tragedy. It just is. Like a mole burrowing beneath the ground, I covered my face with dirt exposing them. But to understand my story, I must dig and uncover hers — and Father's. I'll try to tell their story straight.

That summer of the fateful year of their meeting, 1896, as in every summer, Father's regiment relocated from the scorching plains to the hills for the hot weather. Traditionally, women and children also summered four or even five months in the cool air of the Himalayan foothills.

Emma, my mother, left her husband sweating at his desk to set up house with her children in the hills. Husband? She had a husband? And so by reading Mother's papers after her death nearly fifty years later, I discovered Mother had been Mrs. William Harrison, a married woman when she and Father met, the wife of a Circuit Judge, with two sons. I had half-brothers I'd never known existed, William and Maitland. I gasped. Could we have served at the same time in the Indian Army, together side by side, not knowing? I scanned my regimental photographs searching for a likeness, for names to put to faces, but my memory, like the sepia photos, had faded.

Just bare facts. Mother recorded dates, places, names, no feelings, no pain, no thoughts of hers made their way onto paper. I wasn't there but I imagined. Passion, the circumstances, the scenery, their very words, I let my imagination run free.

Emma, her jade green eyes, olive skin, and a youthful beauty, hinted at a passion even the severity of her coiled hair couldn't hide. Emma and my father, Hugh, unattached, handsome, fell madly in love with each other. That summer my father carried his not so blushing princess to bed beneath the wild champa tree.

The birch and aspens turned yellow, the horse chestnuts, mountain oaks and walnut trees reddened, browned and dropped their leaves. The heat far below in the plains abated. The regiments readied to march out and down the mountain trail and abandon the Hill Station until next spring. Women pulled their Kashmir shawls tightly about their chests, and forced their children into woolies. Then all too soon the air blew white, and Emma knew it was time to leave and return home to her husband. She returned, her belly swelling, pregnant with my brother, Astel. No amount of juggling dates could make the expected baby her husband's child. Either to avoid the shame of being cuckolded and certain public scandal, or from the fear of losing her, or perhaps from kindly understanding of his young wife's needs, William forgave his wayward Emma. He told her he'd accept the baby, and bring the child up as his own as a brother to William, Junior and Maitland. My eldest brother, was born April 18th, 1897, and christened Astel Harrison with his adoptive father's last name, not Rose. Outwardly marital peace was restored.

I read on in disbelief. A year later during the following summer respite in the hills, my starchy military father got my mother, Emma, pregnant for the second time. Once again she returned to her long-suffering husband expecting her lover's child. To be cuckolded twice was too shameful, too much to bear. His heart and their marriage snapped. Though William still loved his young wife, he knew he had to let his darling Emma go.

"I think I had better give you your freedom," he wept.

Though the blue ink had faded to palest grey, William's barely legible words still screamed his tragic desolation across the years. As I read them, I felt the defiant lust that ruled my mother's heart, and her yearning to love her lover. Before Emma could wound him again, William put her on a ship bound for England and banished her from India.

Father's regiment wanted her gone too.

"Get that woman out of India or resign your commission," Father's Commanding Officer ordered.

Though liaisons were mostly condoned, Father's flagrant affair with the wife of a Circuit Judge was too public to ignore. Somehow, Father escaped being cashiered.

If Emma had recognized the symbolism of her welcome, she might have had a premonition of the rocky road ahead; the drab, dismal docks of Liverpool shrouded in drizzling rain, not a soul to greet her, and a grey biting cold she couldn't believe. Alone, pregnant with an illegitimate child, standing at the rails, Emma shivered. More for her own comfort than his, she hugged Astel tight inside her cashmere shawl. Off-loaded onto the bleak Liverpool Docks in the North of England, she hailed a porter. Although she had no nanny, no companion, no servants, not one person to help her negotiate the maze of unfamiliar pounds, shillings and pence and the transport system, she got herself and Astel to Edinburgh in Scotland and found lodgings.

Father's regiment refused him compassionate leave, so he wrote asking his many kinsmen, the Roses, Edgertons and Hutchinsons living in or around Edinburgh, for their support and to welcome his bride-to-be. Silence. He sent an urgent cablegram. A second and another. His pleas were ignored. Edwardian prejudice overrode compassion. There would be no welcome for Emma. They wanted nothing to do with her. Adulterous and unwed, she was not a woman to be "received."

Terribly alone, it was two years before my Mama, Emma, next saw her lover. Father's single Army pay wasn't enough to support two households and keep Emma in the "manner to which…," and she was reduced to unaccustomed poverty. With too many hours to grieve, too few letters, winter slowly passed its cold damp passage–time for Emma to regret her choices.

For the first time time in her life she had to be *ayah* to her children and her own housekeeper, cook and cleaner. Her soft hands cracked and roughened in a cold, unfriendly country. For two long years, Emma counted the months, weeks and days before her lover's leave fell due and they could be together. Father might have missed her. While she suffered, Father's comfortable lifestyle remained unchanged—servants still filled his bathtub, still brought his evening whisky. Ordered to remove his "woman," and keep his private affairs out of sight, I imagine he missed her at first. I imagine he felt briefly ashamed—the public humiliation, his severe reprimand, and regretted the dent he'd made in his career.

These details are just my creations, my imaginings of her misery. Poor Mother.

On April 10th, 1898, my eldest sister, Margarita, Rita we called her, arrived with spring's carpet of snowdrops, crocus, and daffodils when pink and white budded on hawthorn hedgerows. But the baby girl's birth certificate branded her Harrison, not with her father's name of Rose, forcing her to live lifelong beneath an "out of wedlock" cloud. An embarrassingly public Act of Parliament finally granted Emma's Decree Nisi and freed her to remarry. But Father was far away; she had to wait.

Sometime in the autumn of 1899 when Rita was nearly two years old, Father came home on leave and could at last make Emma "an honest woman." On a blustery December day in Edinburgh, Father placed a ring on Mother's finger promising "to love and cherish…for better for worse…" With renewed hopes their marriage would work, Emma fell pregnant with their first child to be born in wedlock. My sister Aileen-May Rose appeared nine months later on May 19th, 1900. Father, of course, had long since gone by then, back to his carefree bachelorhood and his regiment in India.

The pattern of their marriage was set. Two months together, two years apart. Father arrived on furlough, impregnated Mother, and departed. Marital bliss was impossible. The only gap, 1902, was either because she hadn't "fallen" during Father's leave, had miscarried, or delivered a still-birth.

Mother, now the respectable Mrs. Rose, wife of a serving Gurkha Officer, was ready to face society, move south to be near to his Regimental H.Q. and be "received" into military circles. Next furlough, Father relocated the family to Beaconsfield and waited and waited for the flood of calling cards that never came. Ruinous gossip preceded them. The people were no kinder, no friendlier, and no less snobbishly hide-bound. Shunned by the Army wives, Mother's silver salver in the hall remained chillingly empty.

Amusing now, but not amusing at the time, when the family first moved into their new home, one memorable anecdote illustrates the snobbery of the upper class. It became a family legend. As was customary, the "County," a member of the local gentry from one of the local manor houses, "called on" the new colonel's wife to welcome Mother. A smartly turned out carriage, drawn by a handsome pair of dappled greys, drew up in front of our gate. With one horrified glance at our modest rented house, the grand lady hastily threw her calling card over the gate, wheeled her horses about, and with a crack of the whip, galloped away never to be seen again. Mother was as "untouchable" as the shudras, the sweeper caste, in India. Accompanying Father to official functions during his bi-annual furloughs was the extent of Mother's social life.

Enforced separation was the Army's cruel, subtle punishment for my parents' sin.

More apart than together, wedded bliss for them was impossible. Relations between them strained. Hopeful of finding more to share than the same roof, Mother welcomed him home for those brief months of leave every couple of years. I don't say it was love, but after Father's visit in August 1904, Mother fell pregnant with me.

Number four. Me. I came to be.

Young Hugh Rose.

3
HUGH VINCENT ROSE

When news of my birth reached Father in India, he recorded the event with a joyless comment in his Game Journal alongside details of the day's shoot.

Presented with a new son today, April 11, 1905. Bagged six partridge, one peahen, brace of silver pheasant, and a fair-sized black buck. Fresh tiger scat.

After his death in his eighties, I scanned page upon page of neatly written entries recording his kills—tiger, duck, partridge, buck, wild boar, and peahen—searching, searching. Military expeditions featured as one-line entries in his diaries. *Skirmish. Landi K. Badmash executed. Village fined 500 rifles.* No mention of family. No mention of me. Nameless. *A new son.* Hurtful I meant so little—the impressive tome was reserved for important events.

But I existed. Hugh Vincent Rose, April 11th, 1905. I carried his name. As his first legitimate son I was named Hugh in keeping with Rose tradition. I was born in a small village in southern England in the North Church Lying-In Hospital. We never questioned why our brother, Astel, as the eldest son, wasn't called Hugh. Did he know his history? Did dim memory of another father, another family in another land disturb his dreams?

In the summer of 1906 I was already a toddler when Father and I first met. True to pattern, he was home from India on two-month furlough. Cowed by his booming, military voice, I literally clung to Mother's skirts whenever he was around. I didn't like his whiskers nor the color of his skin, sallow from long exposure to the Indian sun. His tobacco smell stuck in my throat. I didn't like the way he looked at Mother as he shooed me from my place beside her in bed. Our bed. I wanted him to go away. He mostly ignored me, seeing me for the mewling weakling I was, and just one more annoying mouth to feed.

"What do you have to say for yourself, boy? Speak up. Milksop. Namby-pamby," he'd sneer.

But not yet two, I hadn't mastered intelligible speech, so stared mutely unable to reply. I was almost four when he returned home on his next leave. I could speak by then, but around him spoke only when spoken to.

"Yes. No. Sir. Good morning. Good night, Sir." I stood when he entered the room.

Mother had coached me well. I avoided his angry hand. I feared him as I feared the giant ogre in "Jack and the Beanstalk" come to "grind my bones to make his bread."

I clung to Teddy. I sucked his paw.

"Don't let me see you again with that baby toy of yours. Take it from him, Mother."

I wept. Mother obeyed of course, but when I went to bed, Teddy was waiting for me on my pillow.

"He's happier here," she whispered. "Teddies like playing at night."

During furloughs with us, Father was miserable, we were miserable. Unused to domesticity, and hating our cramped, crowded home, he fretted impatiently for the interlude to end. Our pudding long since demolished, still "Sitting up" at table Father ate his "Angels on Horseback" or "Welsh Rabbit," a savory which only he was served. We wriggled, waiting. Then it came. "Now in India…" at which opening words, Mother tried her utmost to deflect him with constant interruptions.

"Pass the water jug to Father, Rita. Aileen, clear the plates, there's a dear. Hugh, sit up straight. Elbows off the table."

Unstoppable, ignoring Mother's pursed lips, on and endlessly on, he battered us, his captive audience, with lavish tales.

"Now in India…in the Raj...By Jove. That's the life...We *sahibs* never pick up so much as a kerchief…my personal Bearer dresses me…pulls off my boots… shaves me while I read the London Times…out of date of course, …brings a *chota* peg of whisky while I have my bath…."

At home, his orderlies were us, and Mother his "Bearer."

One furlough, three weeks before he returned to India, Father sprung one of his surprises halfway though dinner.

"Bruges. I have decided. We are moving to Belgium."

Mother's fork froze on its way to her mouth. She glared, unable to argue with him in front of us.

"A little sudden don't you think, Hugh?" The set of her lips showed her displeasure.

"Just thinking of you and the children. The exchange in the pound's favor will afford you a few luxuries, m'dear." Father tempered his pronouncement with a mollifying smile.

"What's Belgium, Mother?" I whispered later as she tucked Teddy in beside me.

"I'll sail in a pea-green boat over the water, like the Owl and the Pussycat who went to sea in a...."

Our move to Belgium was my first of many moves to come. Like Mother and my siblings, I soon learned not to put down roots. Chess pieces, moved at whim, house to house, pension to pension, back and forth between England and Belgium, with no upheaval to himself, Father disrupted us from afar. So when I became a refugee at nine, I thought of it as just another move.

Margarita Rose

4
PENSION REDLICK

"Bienvenue. Bienvenue." Bruges in Belgium welcomed us.

The Pension Redlick, a seedy residence for the forgotten, became home. Just say its name and I smell overcooked cabbage, and see before me its crumbling façade, its bilious decoration. I see its mustard-yellow doors opening onto the towpath of a stagnant canal overlooked by unseeing windows dully reflecting a weak sun that never reached the dank, limp lines of dripping washing.

"Quite unsuitable for a young family—the children surrounded by so many old folk. I insist you take on an extra private room." Mother spoke through clamped lips.

Though not the upgrade in lifestyle Father predicted, with Father gone, Belgium was far nicer, far kinder, than England and her viper whisperings.

Mother took up tatting. She no longer had to keep house for the first time since her banishment from India. Mother became a woman of leisure and allowed herself to thaw. Her hazel eyes softened. Her forehead smoothed.

Teddy, released from banishment, clung to my hand all day. I introduced him to the aged residents of the Pension. Alice and Grand-mère Lilly became my special friends.

Too pretty, too young, a flower among the withered, Alice was out of place. Tears spilled, wetting her pale cheeks whenever she saw me. She pulled me to her chest. Her sadness made me sad.

"Better now? Don't cry." I put my hands around her neck.

One morning, taking my grubby hands in hers, she reached into a pocket of her midnight-blue velvet dress, and pressed a small gilt watch into my palm. Its tiny filigree hands and face gave no hint of what tragedy Alice had suffered.

"Come, my darling child. It's yours." But next day it stopped ticking so I gave it to my sister, Aileen.

Grandmère Lilly, my other special friend, liked me because I called her Grandmère. I liked her because she gave me chocolates. "Tct. Mon petit singe."

She made a grab for her "little monkey" as I passed her chair,

If she succeeded, which I mostly allowed her to do, the penalty was a bear hug and a dry, prickly kiss. Dangling a rich Belgian chocolate just out of reach of my open mouth, she teased.

"Please, Grandmère Lilly. Please...."

"S'il vous plaît. Come...first a kiss. Bisou."

Eyes twinkling, her plump forefinger stuffed an over-sized chocolate between my lips, and then laughingly squeezed my bulging hamster-cheeks.

I avoided Grandmère's doctor husband. I was convinced he was Merlin the Magician "come to get me." One time, lying in bed sick with a fever, I opened my eyes to find him leaning over me, his piercing beady eyes too terrifyingly close to mine. The waggling end-whiskers of his snowy white beard brushed my face, covering my nose and eyes and smothering me. Fighting for breath and recoiling in terror, I pulled my wrist from his grip.

"Vi-chy-Wa-ter. Vi-chy-Wa-ter." He boomed his magician's cure.

"Go outside and play, Hughey dear. Fresh air will do you good."

The internal courtyard made for a dismal playground. Mold-stained paving stones, a few straggly shrubs, and geraniums planted awkwardly in stone basins struggled for survival. A marble boy, unclothed, posed on a pedestal in the courtyard aiming his bow and a broken arrow at the grey sky.

"Cupid," Mother called him.

I told him stories, sang nursery rhymes to cheer him up.

"I promise, one day a beautiful princess will come and turn you back into a real boy."

Forlorn, he stood mute in the colorless wilderness, tear-like streaks running down his pale cheeks. Me apart, his only companion was a cooing grey pigeon with pink feet that lifted its tail and splashed white deposits onto my weeping cupid's head.

"It's good luck," Mother reassured when I ran to tell her.

I was playing outside one evening when a glimmer of light caught my attention in a usually dark and shuttered part of the annex across the courtyard. Holding my breath, I peered through a slit in the shutters and a grimy pane of glass. A lone flickering candle's dancing shadows illuminated a waxen-faced old woman asleep on a brass bed. Still and beautiful, her folded hands cradled a crucifix to her breast. Wafts of arum lilies and dense feeling of peace filtered between the wooden slats. I stared for a long time. She never moved. Next day the bed was empty and the candle snuffed. I knew the angels had carried her away.

In bad weather, which was often, I stayed indoors in the side glass annex of the pension. I passed the hours watching the blue-grey heavens scud across its glass roof, listening to the thundering hooves of a million rain-drenched horses galloping over my head. My secret name for the annex was "the hen-coop." Glued to the nesting boxes of their favorite wicker chairs, the inmates sat click-clacking knitting needles, hatching balls of wool, their silence pierced only by an occasional frail voice of meaningless conversation. Flapping imaginary wings, "Cock-a-doodle-dooing," and "Chook-chooking," I ran through crowing, but not so loudly as to frighten them or be rude.

I see now the old women's pinched faces, stiff and severe as the potted aspidistras beside them, only masked despair. With nothing to do but breathe, they knitted and crocheted memories and lost dreams into tangible objects. On the hour as though on cue, the old chickens roused, froze suddenly still, before exchanging smiles and nodding some shared secret to one another as the wild music from Bruges' church bells rang out the time from the many belfries, rattling the panes and vibrating through the "henhouse" with deep echoes. And I'd leap to the wild music—a dancing puppet pulled by unseen strings.

Thin as a scraping of butter on a slice of bread, Father's meager allowance arrived sporadically, so we frequently ran out of money. But with or without funds, Mother settled our Pension account on the due date thanks to Monsieur Charles, the pawnbroker.

"Dears, just run these to Monsieur Charles… to tide us over."

She fished out a pair of candelabra from her trunk, or from the side-table in her room, a silver salver monogrammed with the Rose family motto, "Constant and True." Sometimes a silver teapot, sometimes carefully counted spoons and forks, depending on how much we were short—the heavier the piece, the greater the exchange.

"Swear not to tell," my sisters instructed fiercely on our frequent "treasure-trips," as we called them.

Unlike them, I was too young to be embarrassed. Our outings became so routine, our visits so warmly welcomed, we thought of Monsieur Charles as our friend. He kept a large glass vase on the counter filled with brightly colored bon-bons.

"Go on," he encouraged, "choose one each."

Plunging my arm up to my elbow, I scrabbled my grubby fingers in the tempting selection feeling for a favorite garish red and yellow oval lozenge smelling of cherry and butter.

Trotting beside my sisters heavily laden with lumpy, green-baize bags, tracing and retracing our steps from home to pawnbroker, pawnbroker to home, we survived our economic seesaw.

"I want to go to school. I'm a big boy." I wailed.

Smart in new grey tunics trimmed with yellow, and with ribboned straw boaters jaunty on their heads, my sisters waved goodbye. Astel, my elder brother, away at boarding school across the English Channel, came home solely for the summer holidays. Overnight I was an only child.

"I want a satchel too, Mother."

Skulking, impatient for their return, I dragged one of Mother's old handbags filled with my nursery books and played "schools" with Cupid and Teddy in the courtyard.

"Red like a poppy, blue like flax, yellow like a buttercup," I sing-songed. "One, two, three, Mother caught a flea..." Holding up my fingers, I instructed my pupils—pupils, invisible to grown-ups.

I tracked slimy trails left by snails creeping round the rims of flowerless urns standing in the Redlick's grey courtyard. Some I placed carefully on the courtyard's crazy-paving and pointed to the big wide world.

"Go on, snail. Explore."

I spent hours with my only playmate, myself, playing in a world where snails carried me on their backs to the Indian jungle I'd heard Father speak of. I talked to my monkey dream-mates and listened to their chattering. Solitude and I made friends.

Twelve long weeks I waited for the autumn and spring terms to end, for Rita's and Aileen's release from their convent in Bruges, for their step through the front door, for their squeals, our hugs and kisses.

"Mother, we're taking Hughey out for a walk."

Walking was the last thing on our minds. Holding hands we walked primly through the sickly yellow door and out along the road until Pension Redlick was out of sight.

"Race you," and we ran.

"Boo," and we jumped from behind a peeling plane tree lining the pavement.

As wild as foals let loose into a field of sweet grass, we chased each other down dark alleyways to the towpath's forbidden ground. Hurling stones and broken bricks, we competed to make the biggest splosh, throw the furthest throw. We fished with sticks, and once prodded a long-dead ginger cat trapped against a sluice gate. Feet dangling in the murky waters, my sisters talked over my head of mysterious things like girls, school and life with a capital 'L.' A Peeping Tom, I feasted on all the information they let slip, intrigued by the kaleidoscope images. Especially bath night.

"Too much bathing washes away nature's protective body oils," Edwardian Europe believed. "Invites all manner of ills...positively harmful."

My sister's school limited baths to once a fortnight. To hide the sin of nakedness, nuns insisted their girls undress in the dark before stepping cautiously into the tub of tepid water, so shallow it barely covered the bath's ice-cold enamel, let alone their "shame." Shivering in the unheated cubicles, a nun quickly placed a wooden cover over each bath leaving only the bathers' heads stuck above the covers. She remained on watch in silent prayer, eyes cast down, modestly averted.

I wanted to see for myself the severed heads on platters floating disembodied in the candle-lit gloom, their naked silhouettes leaping on the walls. It was another reason I wanted to go to school. I nagged and nagged. I got my wish in April when I turned five.

Mother's friend, the Mother Superior of St. Mary's, granted me special dispensation to attend my sister's girls-only convent. Golden-haired, pink-cheeked, the only boy, the youngest child, I was the nuns' and pupils' spoiled "little darling." Their adoration came to an abrupt end when a nun discovered me blissfully spread-eagled on my back, my tiny flag erect, being anatomically inspected by three curious girls.

"We only wanted to see if boys really were made of slugs and snails and puppy dog's tails" was their unconvincing explanation.

"It's time you made friends with boys." Neither Mother nor the Mother Superior spelled out the real reason for my sudden departure.

I knew, of course. To keep me out of mischief, a youth called Erick escorted me to and from a boys-only day school in Bruges. I associate my daily journeying with the rhythmic clack-clattering of Erick's wooden sabots on the cobblestones, his incessant, cheerful medieval Flemish, not a word of which I comprehended nor ever learned, and playing "boat-sticks" as we crossed one particular arched bridge. I remember tempting a posse of graceful swans with breadcrumbs and their gliding with us along the Dijver Canal.

School lessons being in French, I quickly became bi-lingual, though as to what I learned in the classroom, I have scant memory. Only Friday lunches remain etched, vivid. Fridays were not Fridays without fish in Catholic schools.

In silence we were forced to demolish foul-smelling boiled cod drowned in a glutinous white flour and milk sauce flecked with minute green specks of parsley. "…for which we are truly grateful. Amen," we intoned Grace, muttering "un-grateful" under our breath if we dared.

To celebrate Friday's holiness, we attended extra compulsory prayers after class, in the stone-built school chapel, not the usual Assembly Hall. Straight-backed, we were marched in crocodile formation. Perched precariously on backless wooden benches. I leaned forward....

The chapel transformed to a mysterious and magical Aladdin's cave of gilded statues breathing clouds of wafting incense. Bells rang. The head priest, materializing through a smoke-haze into the sacristy brandishing a mighty silver cross above his head, heralded the climax of the service. Chanting toneless, incomprehensible Latin, with measured step he progressed the aisle. Six altar boys, their lacy surplices billowing eerily, floated into the draughty nave from the darkness behind a man swinging a silver incense burner, and a second bearing a candle as thick as my arm. Keeping pace, the remaining four followed, eyes downcast, their hands folded piously in prayer. This was drama—nothing like the Protestant Church's plain services Mother took my sisters and me to each Sunday.

Immersed in unseen vibrations induced by resonating gongs, bells, glorious music, and meditative plainsong, I drifted to inner realms forbidden by my own religion.

Mother's belly big again, Father materialized from India, uprooted us, and like iris rhizomes, replanted us on English soil.

"So our baby will be British," Mother explained.

Our new home—a boarding house masquerading under the grander title of Residential Hotel, in London's fashionable Nevern Square.

5

LORD KITCHENER

Tea, Prophecy, Boredom

Before dematerializing back to India, Father invited Lord Kitchener to tea. Kitchener, Father's first Commanding Officer, inexplicably so admired my father he "invited" him to join the Gurkhas once he "passed out"' from Sandhurst. They remained lifelong friends.

Four o'clock, sharp, one Saturday afternoon in November 1912, Lord Kitchener descended from his carriage. Ignoring the small crowd of hovering residents hoping for a glimpse of our famous visitor, Father whisked him off to a back room overlooking the garden—the owner's personal drawing room loaned for the occasion. Chief of Staff: Boer war. Commander-in-Chief: India. Military Governor: Egypt. Father primed us with the list of his achievements.

Although dressed without his silver-buttoned uniform or familiar cap, Lord Kitchener commanded the drawing room so powerfully my tongue glued itself to the roof of my mouth, leaving me mumbling monosyllabic answers to his questions. Awed, I Yes-Sir-ed and No Sir-ed a little too frequently. My sisters, equally overwhelmed, bobbed small curtsies and smiled shyly when he addressed them. My brother, Astel, away at boarding school, missed our important visitor.

Lord Kitchener's austere figure loomed over me, his blue eyes, cold, piercing, his black moustache, heavy, waggling.

Placing one massive hand on my shoulder, he eyed me for an eternity before booming prophetically,

"Hugh, I expect you to follow in your father's footsteps…become a soldier, eh?"

To my dumb nodding, he added, "That's the spirit. Good man," and out he marched—Father with him.

A pawn, a chess piece, I had been moved one square.

Later, before the outbreak of war, Lord Kitchener's poster-image plastered every wall and billboard in town. Inescapably, his finger pointed directly at me.

"Don't imagine YOU are not wanted. Your country needs YOU," it declared fiercely. "Yes, Britain wants YOU."

But I was not to obey his call to fight for God and country until another war had come and gone.

If Lord Kitchener's visit was the bright spark of that winter, my new sister's birth was a damp squid. Christmas came and went. Father too. His new baby's British nationality secure, he fled, duty done.

Of the homes Father chose for us, Nevern Square was the worst. Father would rather have had his mouth washed out with soap than admit he'd left his family as "distressed" as those entombed inside its walls. Reality was for Mother to face. And us.

My sisters found places at a day school. Not me. I remained unschooled. My mewing new sister, Kathleen, was no play companion. Mother fussed over her all the time. No time for me.

"Hold your tongue."

"Stop your fidgeting."

"No running."

"Away with you. Find something to do."

Nobody, not the residents, not Mother, wanted me around.

Usurped, forbidden to play outside, I wandered dark, cavernous "living" quarters peopled by the half-dead, the "distressed gentlefolk." Hunched daylong, they breathed their impending demise in the large, well-proportioned withdrawing room—their and its former grandeur crumbled in the ruins of the residence.

Victorian armchairs stuffed with horsehair stood sentinel-stiff, mute, around the room, their plush-red velvet draped with startling white lace "antimacassars" as protection from Macassar hair-oil and much-feared fleas and lice migrating from unwashed heads. I crept behind each dozing resident, hoping to catch an insect jumping. I never did.

"Don't touch," Mother whispered.

I rubbed my hand across the film of condensation veiling the French windows and peered out. Through my peephole from the inner to the outside world, the manicured garden remained remote. I longed to kick the carefully raked piles of leaves into swirling chestnut-brown clouds. In my prison behind windows sealed and locked, gloom wrapped its cloak about me.

Unlike at the Pension Redlick, no Grandmère Lilly fed me chocolates or pinched my cheek. No Alice hugged me close. No Cupid wept pigeon tears. Nobody noticed or laughed at my antics, or my imitations of the mythical Greek figures carved in the black marble fireplace dominating the drawing room.

"Get away from the fire, dear."

A meager coal-fire burned every day of that long, long winter. Dead center, confined beneath a glass dome, an ornate gold ormolu clock ticked its life away on the mantelshelf over the grate. Deafening in the silence, it and I the only living things. I tick-tocked my head side to side.

"Stop your silly nonsense, dear."

It wasn't difficult to obey. I hated the room's smell and its silence. A snail had his house. My place of refuge was inside my head. It's surprising I ever developed a voice to voice. Boredom yawned.

Literally watching time, I invented a timekeeper. Depending on the time of day, I noticed shafts of multi-colored sunlight cast from stained glass fanlights above the front door, progressed downward and upward on the stairs, stair-tread by stair-tread. Beside the gleaming brass stair-rods holding down the strip of worn paisley carpet, I scratched lines into the black varnish and watched for them to fill with light. My secret sundial, together we paced the hours.

Milly, my sole friend and playmate, emerged from the back-parts into the empty hall. At her whispered, "Where's my little helper, then?" I leapt from my hiding place behind the pantry door, and pushed while she pulled. Its creaking trolley wheels heralded four o'clock sharp, the highlight of my day.

"Good afternoon, ladies. Now… who fancies a nice cup of tea?"

No gentlemen lived in Nevern Square.

At the sound of rattling teacups, the red shawl-wrapped dormouse followed by the blue, then by five more wizened dormice, roused as one from their slumbers and hobbled eagerly towards the trolley's groaning display. Watching Milly, I learned the ritual—a dash of milk, rest the silver tea strainer over the cup, and through it, pour the golden liquid.

"One for Charlie." Milly handed me a saucer.

Lowering it carefully with both hands, I never spilt a drop. Not Charlie, the manager's spaniel. Tongue lap-splashing, his milky tea spattered the carpet.

"Good for his coat d'y'know. Tea." Blue Shawl chimed on cue.

"One lump or two?"

Milly held aloft a castor sugar cube clasped in a pair of silver eagle talons.

Plop, then drop it without a splash.

"And one for…shhhh." With Mother's back turned, Milly sneaked a cube into my hand, and winked. "Here. Take my reins." Offering me the tails of the large bow holding her frilly-edged "pinny" apron to her black, imitation silk dress, Milly tossed an imaginary mane from beneath her starched white cap with a "Gee-up. Klck-Klck."

Tea time over, debris cleared away, the drawing room restored to a safe, collective womb, Milly closed the brown velvet curtains, obscuring the greying light and extinguished all signs of life but my own.

At five o'clock my sisters returned from school. Up the stairs I fled in a madcap race to the bedroom we shared. Bang, the door banged shut. Acting as silly as we dared, hurling pillows, bouncing on the bedsprings, pulling faces, playing Copycats, Blindman's Bluff and Pig-in-the-Middle, we giggled, muffling hysterical shrieks.

Father materialized when Kathy-baby turned three months.

"Pack up. We're leaving. I'm finished with India," his only explanation.

Truth was, India was finished with him. Lord Kitchener may have thought him an exceptionally good soldier. Not so the Army. Father's career was at a stalemate. Colonel was the highest rank he'd ever achieve, his last promotion. Philandering with another man's wife had its price. Rather than serve in some depressingly remote, dead-end post, Father commuted his pension, and opted for the Army's "golden bowler."

"Goodbye. Goodbye." I ran to Milly, hugged and hugged her.

"Mercy. Mercy. Lor' luv-a-duck," she pleaded, plastering my cheeks, my forehead, and my hair with kisses. Her face was damp as I tore myself away.

For the second time I was off across the channel to Belgium. My fourth move. My life headed for a major change.

6
BRUGES

Father splashed every penny of his Golden Bowler on buying our house—our very first. Money suddenly no object, he chose an ornately gabled, rambling, seven-bedroomed house on the edge of a golf course in Knocke-le-Zoute off the fashionable Louise Avenue. It was home until war broke out in 1914.

"I've engaged four servants to run the household. Can't have my wife doing servant's work."

Transparent as winter's first sliver of ice on the goldfish pond in the back garden, Father's motive was to replicate his pampered Indian existence.

Mother's mouth opened, her eyebrows raised, exploding, "Well, I'll be...." Stifling a sarcastic retort, her lips snapped together with a snort disguised as a cough. How did he imagine she'd managed these long, hard years?

We spread ourselves deliciously into every spacious corner of our new home, reveling in our rare prosperity—the only time during my childhood. Even the sterling/franc exchange swung in our favor. Both parents, five children, a family together for the first time, the walls reverberated with happy laughter. And for once, Mother was not expecting.

My bedroom, my very own, on the first floor opened off the balustrade gallery above the hall. Ill-fitting, hand-hewn mahogany doors imported from the Dutch East Indies hung, leaving a half-inch gap. Whoo-whoo, whispering draughts eerily lifted oriental rugs with unseen hands. Ghosts walked its creaking, dark wood boards. While the household slept, I woke nightly to the unmistakable scratch, scratch of a striking match followed by the flare of ignition. Creeping onto the gallery, peering through the banisters to the hall below, the hairs of my neck and arms as stiff as toothbrush bristles, I strained, fearful of discovering the source. But no person roamed that I ever saw. Scratch-scratch. A flare. Then nothing. I never told. I knew they'd laugh.

The good days were too good to last. School and war spoiled everything.

I only spent two full summers in our lovely house. Father packed me off to school in England, as he had my brother, Astel.

"For your own good. Make a man of you."

To my misery and pain, I discovered the worst of the stories of the abuse in British Public Schools were horribly and cruelly accurate. In every sense, they are too painful for me to record and best forgotten. Numbed, my feelings and tears beaten out of me, "six of the best" became my daily bread.

During the summer of 1914, in the months before the war, Germans inundated Knocke-le-Zoute. As insurance against their future, many Flemish Gendarmes about-faced and sided with the Germans against foreigners. Previously friendly shopkeepers turned surly and reluctant to serve us.

"What-d'y-want?" Their escalating unfriendliness was blatant enough for us children to notice.

Pebbles rained against our windows. Strangers bumped us off the pavement. Shunned by neighbors, my best friend from school was no longer allowed to come to play. We learned what it was to be the unpopular minority. Mother forbade us to leave the garden after a gang of Proud-to-be-pro-German-Youths attacked Astel for being British. I remember the shock of seeing my brother limping up the front steps, one eye half closed, cheeks swollen, nose streaming red, and proclaiming victory for having upheld the honor of the British Empire with no greater weapon than his fists.

"Give 'em what-for, eh? That's the spirit." Father was proud. Mother wept.

Aileen had a run-in with a farmer. Caught trying to ride one of his cows, she misread his justified hail of abuse, not as anger towards her behavior, but as a hostile attack against her country.

"Get off my land, you nasty little foreign girl. I'll have your hide for garters if I catch you here again."

Father ignored the growing insults and rumblings.

"We will not be moved," he stubbornly insisted. "We have as much right as the Germans to be in Belgium. No Bosch will push around a British subject of His Majesty."

I overheard his ranting, and Mother's tearful pleading. It was time to go.

We stayed, uneasy, increasingly unsettled, until the accumulating small incidents made it impossible for even Father to ignore. He acted barely in time to escape before the gathering storm erupted, and the volcano of violence engulfed us in the magma of war.

It was August. Carrying a long-handled spade, Father assembled us for a late evening outing to the golf course.

"Quietly, now." He handed the four of us older children a carefully wrapped bundle.

We followed him through the wicket gate in the hedge at the end of our garden beyond the rose arbor. Astel and Father dug a hole beside the 10th tee. More of a symbolic gesture than a realistic preparation for returning, we buried our bundles: silver candelabra, Mother's silver tea-set, the Rose-crested salver and family cutlery, each piece protectively wrapped in oilcloth.

"Ho. Ho. Ho. And a bottle of rum," I hummed. This was an adventure of pirates, eye patches, faded maps and buried treasure.

"The Devil take you, Hugh. Confound your nonsense," Father shushed.

Foreigners trapped in hostile, enemy territory at the wrong place, the wrong time—not the best of combinations. Perhaps a little unfairly, I maintain it was thanks to Father's pig-headedness, Father's misjudgment, we ended up penniless refugees.

Back to the beginning of my tale. Page one.

"That August morning in the summer of 1914, before it was fully light, Father pulled the front door of our home shut and closed the Belgium chapter of our lives..."

7

MY WAR YEARS

England 1914-1918

War. War. War. "Great Britain is at war" was all the boys talked of when I started at school in England two days late after the autumn term began. War meant no more than an exciting word to them.

"Rose, tell us. What was it like? Ever see a German? A gun?"

The boy-wonder refugee from Belgium, I reveled in their attention. Wide-eyed, classmates swallowed my fanciful embroidered tales—whizzing bullets, cannon fire, and saber-brandishing Ulhans.

Just as suddenly my days of glory ended. I was Rose, the misfit, the new boy who couldn't play games, the boy with foreign ways. I was forced to chase a ball, bare-kneed in biting cold and rain, the victim of a dozen flailing boots in a muddy field.

"Foul." The referee yelled.

Foul aptly described Rugger, as far I was concerned.

A wet, I refused to play.

"Afternoon Games are compulsory," the games captain ordered.

"In Belgium we played Bounce-ball. I once bounced...."

"Bouncing-ball champ. Bouncing-ball champ." The boys guffawed.

I didn't tell them how I could roll a hoop across the yard and back.

"...If Mrs. Smith bought six dozen apples, ate one on the way home, and gave away one tenth, how many...?"

Trapped at a wooden desk, ink on my fingers, struggling with pointless calculations, I was insulated from the war.

In the greyness of my uniform and depressive predictability of school routine, Miss Serpal brought the only color to our lives. Yards and yards of color.

"For The War Effort. For Our Brave Fighting Boys at the Front." Miss Sepal got us knitting.

After prep, in the period misnamed "free time," we doggedly one-plain-one-purled hideous mufflers from garish scraps of wool collected for us by the women of the Women's Institute. Miss Serpal crammed them into hamper after hamper. We penciled messages and tied labels to each completed horror. Knitting was no longer sissy. Proud. We were proud of ourselves. I imagined my scarf warm around a soldier's neck as he slept shivering in a cold, cold trench, his grateful smile as he read "Come back safely. Rose," or, another of my favorites, "Your bravery is appreciated. Rose." Miss Serpal said personal messages would bring comfort to those brave boys. Pausing when she said, "Those brave boys," she twisted a shiny ring round and round on her left finger as she gazed far over our heads. Jones, next to me, whispered her "intended" had left for France... obeyed Kitchener's poster and signed up.

The headmaster concluded morning prayers with selected daily readings from the London Times.

"Lest we forget," he boomed.

Victorious battles won, territories conquered, and tales of bravery and sacrifice of the fallen remained as remote as a history lesson.

But when a new batch of soldiers marched past the school gate, their stirring songs interrupted our aged Master in mid-amo, amas, amat... or whatever the lesson was. Losing concentration, thankful for the excuse, we craned our necks to glimpse the column marching along the road to Farnborough Station.

Tramp. Tramp. Tramp. Those rhythmic steps, immortal sorrowful notes, linger forever along Farnborough's leafy lane.

Goodbye, Piccadilly, farewell Leicester Square....
It's a long way to Tipperary.... It's a long way to go...
And so it was, a long, long way to go.

Term time over, school "broke up" for the holidays. Our home gone, where to go?

Home, that holiday, was Number 5, Norfolk Road, a small flat in Cliftonville, where in the middle of the night, the very first week, an aerial torpedo whined overhead, narrowly missed our chimney, and demolished Number 10, five doors down.

Directly behind the defense lines dotting the coastal seafront, air raids and distant sounds of intermittent artillery fire constantly reminded us of war. Lewis anti-aircraft gunfire rattled from concrete pillboxes. "Big Bertha" thrumped occasional shells from across the channel to land harmlessly in Council allotment gardens among the cabbages and cauliflowers. Long grey destroyers of the Dover patrol battled ceaselessly off shore within plain sight of the seafront, smoke billowing from their funnels. The Taubs rained live bombs onto the coastal towns of Cliftonville, Margate, Lewes and Brighton on their flights back across the channel after their bombing raids on London.

"Cliftonville isn't safe," Mother snapped.

"Refugees can't be choosy," Father rounded. "With only handouts from the Army's Indigent Fund and the few pounds saved from my commuted pension...."

But for us children Cliftonville was the seaside. We found ways to wriggle round and under the rolls of barbed wire and the concrete barricades angled over the beach. Running down the road with my sisters to Mr. Petteman-the-Grocer, we watched him harness his elephant sized Shire horses to three bathing machines and trundle them onto the pebble-beach.

"So as the ladies might disrobe in private and 'ave themselves a swim. Keep their selves decent, like." He winked.

Frilly-capped, discreet in knee length, short-sleeved bathing dresses, the women tumbled squealing down the steps from the machine's back door and right into the icy Atlantic. Such splashing, such giggling fun, I longed to join them.

"Rule, Britannia." Bound by the common spirit of war, strangers greeted one another out loud. Nothing shook British morale, not bombing raids, nights spent huddled in discomfort, not death, destruction nor the shortage of food.

"No 'Hun' will starve me. No, Sir." Our butcher told his queue of customers one time as I waited in line with Mother for our allotted weekly quarter-pound of meat per person wrapped in newsprint.

"Any rabbit? Could you perchance spare some lung, Mr. Jones?"

Mother disguised lung as "mock duck `a l'orange." Rabbit and offal were also exempt from rationing. And chicken feet. I crunched exaggeratedly savoring each toe one by one so disgusting Aileen and Rita they refused to touch them, leaving seconds for Kathy-baby and me.

"Hun. Hun. Hun." I practiced the new word.

1915. It was a rare night we slept undisturbed. Heavy howitzers rained shells. Airships droned overhead. Whizzes, bangs and explosions were the norm. Our Warden became a familiar sight in his dark blue helmet and uniform, cycling determinedly up and down Norfolk Street.

"Any chance of a raid tonight, Mr. MacTaffy?" I called out.

"Don't you worry about them Huns, laddie. I got their number. Now off the street with you. Curfew. Ten minutes." As searchlights swept brilliant beams across the night skies, Mr. MacTaffy pedaled down our street, booming through a megaphone, "Inside, everybody. Clear the street. Make for your cellars."

We rarely used ours, however hard I pleaded. Mother witheringly ignored me with a dismissive, "Nasty, damp place. We'll catch our deaths in there, Hugh."

"Mother, we should go, Father said we must.... Please...." Stationed by the window, I hoped to see a real battle.

"Get away this minute, Hugh." Mother made me draw the heavy velvet, blotting out the faintest chink of light.

At the faint sound of an approaching airplane, our landlady, Miss Poynder, burst through the front door of our flat, white, hysterically twittering.

"Oh. Mrs. Rose. Mrs. Rose. Lordy. Lordy. I don't want to die alone. May I presume...?"

Mother's eyes widened and, disguising the fear she'd never admit, she shouted, "Under the table, children...Hurry...Right now...Don't panic." Her trembling voice gave her away.

"Must we, Mother?" I delayed as long as I dared.

Following Rita and Aileen with Kathy-baby, I crawled under the dining room table, dragging two tartan rugs and a bicycle lamp Mother kept on the sideboard "for emergencies." Two strips of black ribbon glued with flour paste across the lamp glass cut its beam of light to a feeble sliver.

"Come. Come now, Mrs. Poynder," Mother soothed. "We'll pray together. No harm will come."

She and Mother fell to their knees tight against the table to shield us with their thickly skirted bodies. Collapsed in giggles, we took turns peeking from under the chenille table-drape. Heads bowed, shrouded beneath makeshift veils of lace anti-macassars snatched from the parlor armchairs, their shaking hands piously clasped together, the two of them moaned their pleas until the sky fell silent.

"We beseech Thee.... Spare us.... Not for ourselves do we ask this favor, but for our innocent children."

Mrs. Poynder and Mother had recently "got religion." Prayer was Mother's lifeline, her comfort. With Father in London, God became her "very help and succor."

Each bedtime, kneeling at Mother's knee mouthing the "God Bless so-and-so-an'-make-me-a-good-boy" ritual, I thought of the German's, the enemy's Christian boys. Would God bless them too? Did they pray for our defeat as we prayed for theirs? Would God side with them? Us? It made no sense.

War followed us however many times we moved.

Astel was missing. He disappeared after we fled from Belgium during my first term at school. His name was never mentioned and I missed him. My sisters and I decided he'd run away to make his fortune.

"He's a cow puncher in Alberta, Canada," Mother said sourly, not elaborating.

Piecing together snippets, it was clear he'd got into trouble. I heard the story later. Whether for a "punch-up" or more serious crime, Astel served time in gaol. On the morning war was declared, the sheriff, accompanied by a recruiting sergeant, swung open the bared cell door with a clang. Jangling his bunch of keys, he bawled at the still sleeping Astel and his cellmates,

"Anyone wanting to join up—out. The rest of you varmints stay locked up 'ere."

Astel and his fellow felons signed. Under heavy guard, the Recruiting Sergeant marched the "free men" off to war and had them conscripted into the Army that very day.

War rewrote the rules. Father, recalled from retirement to London as a Dug-Out Officer, donned his uniform and left immediately for the War Office, ecstatic to be back in action. With Astel in Canada and Father in London, "You're the man of the family now, Hugh," Mother said. Nobody listened.

We rarely saw Father. His work at the War Office kept him in London, leaving Mother to manage on a scant three pounds a week after paying our school fees.

"The Good Lord will provide," she said.

Once more, Rita, Eileen and I were regulars at the local pawnshop "popping" whatever we could lay our hands on. Even old clothes and books, we discovered, raised a bob or two. Those few extra shillings made Mother smile. If it was hard for her, she never complained, and I never remember going hungry. Thick slabs of bread spread liberally with beef and mutton dripping begged from the butcher, a sprinkling of a little salt. My mouth waters—the tan salt-glaze jar, cold-set dripping, its layer of brown meat jelly beneath...

Treats, not hardships, stick in my mind, though how Mother scrimped extra pennies for them I cannot imagine.

"How about a treat, children?" Counting out one precious coin each, "Be off with you," she'd smile.

Ticket in hand, racing to claim the seat closest to the cinema's orchestra pit, I leaned forward watching, waiting.... In a beam of floodlight, seated at his theatre organ, the organist rose from the dark pit wheezing patriotic songs and setting the far corners of the auditorium trembling. "Tickling the ivories," the flamboyant organist danced his bony fingers over the keys. Feet and knees lifting in a wild search for the pedals, he wasted not a minute in the spotlight. An aging fixture, he entertained the audience before each show, and added sound for every film. Galloping hooves accompanied horses. Bass notes vibrated thunder, high notes twinkled stars. Rivers cascaded trickling up and down the keys. Eyes tight shut, I let his music tell the story.

But before the feature film played, it was our turn, the audience's. An off-white screen descended in front of the safety curtain, slowly unscrolled boldly printed words of familiar songs. The music struck and how we sang.

"Keep the home fires burning...."

"Goodbye, Goodbyeeeeee... I wish you all a last goodbye..."

"It's the Lilly of Laguna... the Lilly of Laguna. It's my Lilly of Ma lane..." Ma Lane? Without understanding every word, I knew them by heart.

Suddenly a hush fell. The screen flickered, Metro Goldwyn Meyer's Lion roared a great roar and burst through a paper hoop. Credits rolled: *Intolerance, Orphans in a Storm,* and *Scaramouche,* the faces of the Gish sisters, Charlie Chaplin and long-forgotten others...Tom Mix, William Hart...

Mother treated us to "Thé-musique" recitals at Bobby's Teashop. Over crumpets and teacakes, three elderly females scratched romantic melodies on two violins and an out-of-tune piano. Wrong notes and all, soaring, crumpling, I flew, I fell.

One Friday, Mother packed a small case.

"Come, children, today we visit Father," and she herded the four of us to catch the train to celebrate some long forgotten occasion. For the first time, I saw Father take Mother's arm affectionately and beam fondly at her.

"Tonight, Mrs. Emma Rose, I am taking you to the Theatre."

Mother never looked lovelier. Wearing a full-length velvet gown of deep maroon, around her slender neck a black velvet choker sown with the single pear-shaped pearl given her in India by her mother when she turned sixteen, a froth of creamy Bruges lace the color of her skin spilling from her neckline, she was the most beautiful person in the world. I adored her and understood love that evening.

Uncharacteristically, Father treated us to a "spiffing" meal at a posh restaurant, then took us to see *Going Up.* From high among the gods, a beam of dazzling floodlight shattered the darkened auditorium, revealing the majestic figure of Yvonne Arnaud. Next evening, another show—*Sealed Orders* at Drury Lane. Neither bombs nor air raids interfered with the magic of those two days.

In the middle of 1917, a Zeppelin exploded in flames over Potter's Bar. Our fortunes exploded too. Father's new job entailed raising and training the 10th Battalion of the Argyle and Sutherland Highlanders for the Front. Father shook the mothballs from his uniform and pinned on his ribbons.

In the money, a gentleman again, Father splashed the bulk of his salary on renting a large Victorian house in Ripon, Yorkshire, and hired a cook-housekeeper, a valet and a gardener-groom. After Margate, I found Yorkshire so quiet I couldn't sleep at first. No sirens, no searchlights, no scurrying under the table, I forgot the war was on. Those months in Ripon were the calm before the storm—the last time we lived together as a family.

Again a new boy in another new school, I dreaded being an outsider yet again. But this school was different, the boys allowed me to be friends. They thought of me as a war veteran, a kind of hero because of what I'd seen and heard.

Father got his troops battle-ready within the year. He fully expected to be rewarded and accompany them overseas. But the Army passed him over.

"Bloody nonsense...we need a younger man...we need a younger man." He mocked bitterly. "I can do the job of a dozen whippersnappers with my eyes closed."

Dispirited, Father lost his enthusiasm for the war.

Up down, up down, our roller coaster fortunes rose and fell, this time down. Worse was to come. By some irony, Father was sidelined as O.C. of the troopships plying between Southampton and Bombay, the beloved India he was destined to never see again.

Move number seven, or was it eight? I lost track. Father rented a dingy flat near Southampton's unattractive docks. The upheaval was not for the better. Raised voices reverberated through my parents' bedroom wall. Father moved out, and spent his days and nights quartered shipboard. A couple of months passed before he re-emerged.

"No sense staying." Mother decided.

The docks were in direct line of fire, and sirens wailed constantly as Germany did its utmost to destroy the docks and the ships in it. Mother was miserable. We were miserable. We packed our bags and were off, abandoning Father.

Herefordshire on the Welsh border in the West of England—cramped rooms over a Dairy became home.

"Nice and near your new school, Hughey," was how Mother put it.

But a boarder imprisoned within sight of home was a torture worse than if school lay a hundred miles away. Two weekends a term, I was allowed back home.

A new boy, a new syllabus, and masters who labeled me "dunderhead," my misery exceeded anything I imagined. Assigned as "fag" to a sadistic prefect, he took out on me the cruelty inflicted on him when he was a fag himself.

"Tea. Now. Too slow." Swish. His cane cut welts across my bare calves, my backside.

If I failed to shine his shoes, linseed his cricket bat the way he liked, I paid. Jokingly known as "fresh meat," a new boy was at the mercy of a prefect's hazel cane.

I was always hungry. The masters skimmed our meager meat allowance from our ration cards, leaving us with growling bellies. One egg a week, one tin of fruit, our Government allotment rarely appeared. It was small comfort "They" suffered equally. On Saturdays a master doled my precious two ounces of butter, sugar, and jam into three pale-green Bakelite screw-top jars marked "52-R." Mine. I stashed them in my locker. Sometimes I swapped my watered, generic jam for a friend's butter ration, for I preferred crunchy sugar grains pressed into the butter-smear on my bread. Milk, I never swapped. Third-pint bottles arrived sealed with tabbed cardboard discs for easy peeling. Ripping off the top, my tongue lapped its coated underside—thick, buttercup-yellow cream. I dipped my finger two digits deep. Eyes closed, I licked and sucked my finger clean. The milk, I drank last.

I never lost my taste for cream. My wife teases me about it declaring cream was the reason we retired to the Cornwall and Devonshire borders. Nothing can beat a breakfast of Scottish porridge oats, brown sugar, and thick, yellow crusty layers of Devon or Cornish clotted cream.

"Don't pass the cream to Hugh first," my second wife and children cry till this day. "He'll scarff the lot."

In the autumn term, 1918, Asian flu swept the country and my dreadful establishment was closed down. I never returned.

The war was over. On 11th November, the eleventh hour of the eleventh day, 1918, Armistice Day was declared. Normally undemonstrative, Mother fell to her knees, wept, thanked God, and uncharacteristically covered us with kisses. Munitions girls spilled from factories onto the streets waving banners, and singing.

"Long live the King. Long live the King."

Nobody worked that day. Bonfires blazed, lighting surrounding hilltops, and flared red to orange. We oohed and aahed at the magic. Caught in the erupting tide of neighbors flooding the streets, we let ourselves be swept to the village Common.

Bedtime forgotten, Rita and Aileen dragged Mother by each hand to join the uproarious singing and dancing. Mother was easily persuaded. Mother laughed a lot. We did too. I was glad Father was far away. Could he even laugh?

Men, women and children of all ages linked arms, kicked their legs in a wild "knees up." Cottage brews of beer, pear and apple cider, and dandelion, elderflower and rose-petal wines flowed from cottage cellars. Though Mother wouldn't take a sip, the villagers raised brimming glasses and tankards toasting everyone they met. All day long and into the night, unmuffled, free, the church bells rang from steeple to steeple across the valleys.

"Vic-tor-y. Vic-tor-y," cascading peals proclaimed.

I counted three different church bells talking to each other from three separate villages, and the distant deeper, muffled, answering booms from Hereford Cathedral.

"Three cheers. Hip. Hip. Hoorah." Liberation. The end of war. The end of school.

The best, the happiest day of my life, my celebration was as much for freedom from those walls of hell as for peace—the end of war. I could have inflated and drifted to heaven.

And overhead across the sky, the Milky Way spilled a myriad souls of all the fallen.

8
CRYSTAL SETS AND SCHOOLDAYS

I was about sixteen, when Crystal Sets took over my life. More than a teenage craze, from under the stairs, I tap-tapped the airwaves, raking for something other than screeches and whistles to crackle the small bakelite box to life. I beamed conversations from as far away as North Foreland and Boulogne, messages from an aircraft off Lyme and ships at sea, and snatches of orchestral music from the 2LO Radio station. My skin goose-fleshed one magical night when the pure voices of Caruso and Nellie Melba in their duet, *Soave Fanciulla* from *La Boheme*, cascaded into my headset—directly from the Royal Opera House, I convinced myself, though more probably from a recording made in 1907. The other day my grandson downloaded it onto Youtube, something as magical as my crystal set.

"Interesting hobby you have there, Hugh." Father patronized, mildly amused.

One evening, I overheard Father's friend mention a store of war-surplus wireless sets housed in derelict Margate/Etaples ferries at the nearby abandoned Army camp in Richborough. It was April, my last school holiday before my last school term. After breakfast next day I was off. Concealing my bike in the brambles edging the field I pushed my way through the hedge. Maybe a hundred derelict carriages mouldered on defunct rusting rails. I doubled low to the ground and clambered onto the closest car. Wiping a peephole in the dirty glass of the locked radio cabin, at first I could only see brown, foxed posters of pin-ups in scanty underwear clinging to the walls, then, there they were—huge copper coils, condensers, and mounds of spellbinding dials, antennas, and radio equipment cramming every inch of floor space.

My future was set—a wireless officer with the Eastern Telegraph Company. Resplendent in white uniform I saw myself telegraphing important coded signals around the world from a coral island. From my white bungalow home, rocking gently on a cane chair in the shade of a verandah, I sit gazing into a golden sunset, a peg of whisky in my hand....

I should have known better than to voice my dream.

"Out of the question. Gentry don't go in for that sort of thing. Hobby, yes. Career, never. It's all mapped out, my boy. Sandhurst. India. Family tradition. Understand? Generations of Roses expect it of you. There'll be no more nonsensical talk. Wireless operator, indeed." Father jerked me harshly to heel.

My dream crumpled, I returned to school for one last term.

Sixteen. I shone at nothing, not scholastically, not at rugger, football, cricket, nor any group activity. Way behind my peers, not yet in the 6th form, like Gulliver I towered over my classmates. Headmaster gave me special dispensation to graduate from shorts to trousers and hide my obscenely hairy legs. I was ashamed of my lack of achievement. I knew I wasn't a dullard. Lugged from school to school, I rarely completed a full year at any one of them. No wonder my education suffered. With no qualifications, my future loomed black.

Towards the middle of term after Assembly one day, to my great alarm a master pulled me aside.

"Headmaster wants to see you."

My ears flattened. My Adam's-apple rose and fell. I knocked feebly on the Headmaster's study door.

"Come in, Rose. Take a seat."

I perched uncomfortably on the edge of one of two armchairs on either side of the fireplace, averting my eyes from his massive oak desk, over which my, and many a boy's, bare bottom had painfully suffered of "six of the best." To my greater discomfort, the Headmaster proffered me a cup of steaming tea.

"Sugar, Rose?"

I silenced the rattling cup, vigorously stirring in two lumps. With mounting relief, I listened as Headmaster enthusiastically elaborated a plan.

"Well, Rose. Ah…mmmm. It seems you are not doing so well at school. No point harboring any academic ambition, what? You'll be leaving us at the end of term. Your pater and I think it in your best interest you attend the Army class at Carlisle and Gregson Crammer in London to study for your "A" certificate and civil service exam. Pass, and Sandhurst Military Academy will accept you as a cadet. Nothing to be ashamed of…you're not the first to need a little help. Many famous soldiers, including Winston Churchill crammed there. Oh. Your classmate, Dimsey, will be joining you."

Headmaster's words swam…leave school early…a career mapped out… Sandhurst…the Army…my best and only friend, Dimsey, going with me… Unable to stop the prickling, the reddening, I flushed and hated myself for it.

"I'm confident you have it in you…become an admirable career officer like your father."

"Great news. Thank you, Sir."

I left his study smiling foolishly, not because I was to be a soldier, but because I had purpose. My footsteps firmed to a march, and once safely in the corridor, my lips pursed, to a whistle.

"Hurrah. Hurrah. I'm in the Army Now. Hurrah. Hurrah. I'm in the Army now."

Back in the dorm, my cap spun from my hand out through the window high into the oak tree. School days were over.

Five days a week I commuted on the "up" train from Margate to Victoria Station on a lurching ride commonly known as the South Eastern Smash'em Railway. Manipulating pages of the London Times, I struggled daily to prevent my elbows jabbing my neighbor in the ribs and violate the British no touch, no eye contact rule. I once committed the heinous crime of sitting in a regular traveler's earmarked corner.

"I do believe you are in my seat," he hissed.

Ears reddening, I slid over to one of two middle spaces muttering,

"My mistake. Most awfully sorry, Sir."

For most "down" journeys home to Margate, I traveled by the Southeastern and Chatham Railway's Granville Express from London Bridge. Express it wasn't. As it rumbled slowly over the Thames beside the Pool of London, I pressed my face against the steamed window glass. Mysterious glimpses of floodlit ships and cranes swirled from wisps of acrid smoke. They stirred my romantic fantasies of the East so vivid, aromatic oriental spices perfumed the carriage.

My future, like my imagination, drifted. My footprints appeared faint behind Father's and my ancestors'—a soldier's boots. Mine? Me—a soldier? I had my doubts. I'd comply with Father's plan…use the Army as a stepping-stone to a career more suited to my roving spirit…wireless operator…surveyor. I closed my eyes. I'd look impressive in uniform.

I sat the Civil Service exam twice before I passed. The Officers' Military Academy offered me a place. I packed my bags, kissed Mother and Kathy-baby goodbye, and moved out from beneath my mother's skirts—a man.

Sandhurst Military Academy

9

ROYAL MILITARY ACADEMY, SANDHURST

I wasn't picked on any more than anybody else. Princes, Indian Maharajahs, Egyptians, Siamese and Nepalese suffered the powerful lash of the sergeants' tongues, the same as we more ordinary mortals. Since the Military College's founding in 1813, foreign cadets destined to be Commanders-in-Chief, Defense Ministers, Presidents and to hold other politically important posts in their own countries, enrolled from every corner of the globe. The Army's property, we were theirs for six months of hell—"square-bashing" and unmerciful sarcasm their preferred, disagreeable method of choice. Our Gods, the army sergeants, whittled their raw cadets to perfectly machined automatons.

"Scum...miserable lowlife... Think we are a gentleman, do we?"

My first parade. Sergeant Major Peters addressed us pleasantly.

"Now gentlemen, I do like to see nice smiling faces on parade."

I and three other new recruits, fooled by his warped sense of humor, smiled obediently.

"Take that gen'leman cadet's name for larfin' on parade."

Gasping from unaccustomed exercise, I dragged my poor, unfit body around the parade ground—three penalty circuits in atonement for my sin, followed by push-ups enough to kill me. Smiling was a mistake I never made again. I became faceless, but like bluebottles to raw liver, my sergeants swarmed to feed off my rotten sports ability. Basic training's endless drilling, trench digging, horsemanship, parades, marching, crawling, climbing, leaping, and other gymnastic feats normally reserved for the circus, merged into one nightmarish endurance test. The Barossa training ground was my hell where my every evasive ruse attracted attention like a magnet.

"Fearful of a little mud, are we, Sir? Now let's try that again—'ere in the mud like the miserable wriggling worm you are."

"Bastard. Ignoramuses. Sadists. Little Napoleons. Our bull mascot has more brains than those bastard R.M.C. drill instructors." We sneered retaliating safely out of earshot.

"ROSE, H. V. Ride Number One." Mistake. Not me. It wasn't possible. Twice, I checked the posted list. No doubt. There it was. My name. Me. ROSE. H.V. the novice. Below mine, the name read "ROSE, H. Ride Number Two." I'd supplanted "ROSE, H." a first-class rider, seasoned hunter and skilled polo player from the top ride to the lowest.

While horsemanship was second nature to my riding instructor, a career Rough Rider in the prestigious Kings Dragoon Guards before his posting to Sandhurst, the nearest I'd been to horses were Mr. Petterman's Shires hauling Bathing Machines to the sea during the war.

To the other cadet's sniggers and the instructor's amazement, on the order, "Mount," I put my foot in the stirrup, and with a mighty heave propelled myself up and over the saddle onto the sawdust on the far side. I don't know who was most shocked, the instructor or me. Obviously, I didn't know the back end of a horse from its front. Not surprising considering I'd never before ridden a horse. Not a man to be defeated, the instructor insisted I remained in his ride.

"'Orses and you, Sir, will 'ave to learn to get along. Look 'em in the eye so as they know 'ooze master."

Prince, my mount, and I eyed one another balefully. Many attempts later, I learned to mount, sit ramrod straight with a good seat, trot, canter, gallop, keep stationary, dismount and rein to a stop. But Prince was mean. At the word, 'Rein,' the four-legged beast, literally, took the bit between his teeth, gave a rodeo-class buck with all four hooves off the ground, then with a final rear, set off on wild laps around the ring. Lopsided astride the saddle, one stirrup flapping and one leg pedaling the air, I let go the reins and grabbed the pommel. In an unexpected instant, the beast mischievously dug in his hooves as though lassoed, and successfully catapulted me over his head. Prince knew I knew who mastered whom. I never overcame my fear.

"'Orses 'ave a nose for fear," my instructor confided.

I was not the only unfortunate cadet worthy of the instructor's attention. During the annual Horse Show, dressed in our best, excited because Royalty would be attending, the cadets assembled on the parade ground. The National Anthem struck up, we snapped smartly to our feet, shoulder blades back. Face front, eyes straining sideways, I glimpsed King George and Queen Mary take their seats. The show began.

A usually perfect horseman uncharacteristically knocked bricks and bars from the jumps, felled potted palms and geraniums, fluffed the dressage, lost a stirrup, and performed so badly, the instructor exploded for all to hear,

"Mr. Sir Peter Farquhar Bart, Sir. If J.C. rode 'is donkey into Jerusalem as you are riding that there 'orse, Sir, no wonder 'e was crucified, Sir. No wonder."

Overnight a gentleman cadet, my world was now one of Batmen, tailored clothes, cocktail parties, and formal dinners served with wine. Many of my peers complained of Spartan barracks and institutional living. Not me. After the homes, boarding schools and cramped accommodations of my childhood, my private cubicle was paradise. Jones, my batman, a retired career-soldier, made my bed, dusted, swabbed the floor, pressed my uniform, called me "Sir," and daily emptied the piss-filled "guzzunder" from under my bed. Rose, the "'orrible lowlife," remained on the parade ground outside my quarters. Rose, the gentleman cadet, drew to full height every time the batman called me "Sir."

There were a couple of us cadets whose clothes were "off the peg" and for whom tailored suits were out of reach. Appearances mattered, Mother and Father had taught me well. I watched. I learned, aping the elegant composure of those "to the manner born." But not their obnoxious arrogance.

Every night but Sunday was theatre night. At 7.30 sharp, the nightly one-act play began. Costumed in sharp-cut Mess-dress and satin cummerbunds for our walk-on roles, transformed from frogs to handsome princes, strutting into the Mess, our stage, as confidently as we dared, we sipped the permitted single glass of sherry. Dry sherry.

"Simply not done, old chap." A second-year cadet, a snob of the worst order, sneered. "Sweet sherry? For a gentleman, never—ever so lower."

Eyes fixed on a fellow new cadet, the snob extended his little finger mimicking the "lower" classes. I gripped mine firmly around the fragile stemmed sherry glass. A picture flashed—our genteel landlady, Miss Poynder in Cliftonville, little finger crooked, sipping from a dainty teacup, believing it "proper," ladylike. Haughtily, the epitome of a gentleman, I played my role until dinner was announced.

At 8:00 p.m. precisely, the principal actors, the Dinner President and Vice-president, led the assembled officers to their rank-assigned places in the dining hall. When they sat, we sat. When they ate, we ate. While they remained at table, we remained, and only retired when they retired. Eking out one glass of red wine over dinner, seated ram-rod straight, making formal small talk after a day of swinging on ropes above mud pools, clambering nets, and negotiating other obstacles, was not my idea of fun. Tradition forbade topics such as religion, women and politics. Official Guest Nights were livelier. The R.M.C. Band's artificially jolly, traditional airs entertained the high-ranking officers on the head table and prevented us from falling asleep.

"A Toast. The King. The Emperor. God save the King."

"The King."

With one voice, pushing back our chairs, we stood with glasses raised, took one sip, and sat down again. Up. Sip. Down. Yo-yos, we stood, we sat for every toast.

"Last orders, Sir."

"Six to eight" meant six to eight. Functions ended promptly at the hour indicated on the RSVP. The orderlies cleared the stage and dropped the curtain by removing glasses and bottles. Those of us not "gentlemen of means" were grateful for it we, members of the Mess, who footed the bill for the guests' drinks as well as for our own.

Boys will be boys. And we, not yet men sequestered in an all-male environment, played "silly buggers" at every opportunity. Pathetically juvenile, we sprinkled fizzy, Enos Salts into chamber pots, roped cadets to their beds while they slept, threw boots into jumbled heaps from the windows, made "apple-pie beds" with holly, and put salt in the sugar sifters. Pranks, though generations old, we still found uproarious.

One end of term, a group of us "stole" one of two bronze one-ton cannons flanking the main entrance of the Old College—a prized trophy captured at the Battle of Waterloo. A well-meaning snitch tipped off the Adjutant, who tipped off the Staff Officers, who tipped off the local police.

A dozen of us wrestled the cannon from its mount and onto a hired lorry. The plan—fire off a couple of horns of blank gunpowder over Blackwater Flats from Hartford Bridge, sneak the cannon back in the ensuing pandemonium, and enjoy the mayhem. With the cannon safely aboard, we drove through the village. A constable wheeled his bicycle across the road, and signaled, "Halt." He peered intently through each window before lifting the canvas concealing the cannon at the back. Approaching the driver's cab, notebook and pencil poised, he enquired,

"May I see your gun license, Sir?"

"Fall out R.C's, Gyppies, Wogs and Jews." The Regimental Sergeant Major roared each Sunday before marching us into chapel for Matins. No matter what a cadet's ethnicity or religious preference, Sunday Parade was compulsory.

Matins over, Dimsey and I jumped into our Bugatti—bought for ten pounds sterling between us.

"Let's tally-ho and go bunny-hunting." Women, we meant.

Our quest, though hopeless, made a perfect excuse for careening along country lanes and visiting local village pubs to "take Communion" with a pint of the local ale. The wind in my hair, the satisfying rev-rev of an engine pushed to its limit, the deprivations of my boyhood and the constraints of the College vanished in noisy clouds of exhaust. Housed in different blocks with different Companies, we spent most Sundays together. Best friends since our school years, our friendship lightened the rigors of our training.

One evening, Dimsey and I discovered Brooklands invariably left their back gate unlocked, allowing us to sneak inside the famous motor circuit and roar round full throttle counting laps.

Permitted two weekend passes a term, Dimsey and I, with a couple of other friends, clubbed together to splurge ten shillings and hire a Rolls Royce limousine from White's Garage, and drive to "Town."

"Anyone, need Ma Hart?" Ma Hart's pawnshop on the corner of Frimley Road was a must before leaving.

"How much you boys short?"

An angel, Ma Hart loaned us money against whatever valueless object we brought her—a prismatic compass, cufflinks, and books. Like Monsieur Charles the pawnbroker, she became a friend. Virgins all, our mood boisterous, pockets full, we masked our inexperience with innuendos, and hinted at conquests we had never made. With vain hope of scoring a woman, we made for two London watering holes, the fashionable Regent Palace Hotel, and Mrs. Merrick's infamous Night Club, 43, Gerrard Street.

My art collector cousin, Peter Hughes, owned a house in fashionable Smith Street, Chelsea. My cousin, Peter was single. Peter lived alone. Peter was a woman.

"I love the young around me—men, especially. There's a bed for you any time. Here." Peter handed me her house latchkey.

Drink befuddled, well past midnight, I found my key didn't fit Peter's door. I tried again. Was it even Smith Street?

"Must have the wrong house. The number? What the devil was it? Better try them all…"

House by house, starting from one end of the street, I worked my way down, trying the key in each front door. Feeling a presence behind my back, I lurched around. The impassive face of a uniformed Bobby peered sternly from beneath his helmet, tap-tapping his truncheon on his left hand.

"'Allo, 'allo, 'allo. Might hi 'henquire' what you are a-doing of, Sir?" His voice, though soft, was firm.

Swaying, speech slurred, I stumblingly explained my predicament. Without another word, the constable prized the latchkey from my hand. Guiding me by my elbow, we proceeded down the street trying every door until he found a match.

"Have a good evening, Sir." He politely handed back my key.

The house bulged with sleeping bodies. Sofa, chairs, carpets—occupied. The kitchen table—occupied, a snoring Guardee-Ensign sprawled across its surface. I crashed out on the floor beneath him, and added my snores to the cacophony.

If the Officers Mess was my finishing school, Sandhurst Military College was my university—the place where the first raindrop fell and I felt him stir—the man I wanted to be—a man with choice, voice, and power. I tested each new skill in class, arguing hotly over campaigns long gone, planning hypothetical tactical warfare, and how best to govern foreign lands.

I found direction, a new passion. I discovered the Army Survey Maps of British Empire and exchanged the headphones of my crystal set for a slide rule and compass. With them I negotiated geographical hurdles and traveled Britain's pink splashes across the globe. My world expanded. I had a dream.

10
SUMMER LOVE

I joined my parents in Bruges for the last summer break from Sandhurst, before my "Passing Out." Perhaps attempting reconciliation with my mother, Father rented a Victorian gothic house off Louise Avenue.

Louise Avenue. Louise, our housemaid's name, Louise, sexy Louise my teacher. Hunting for something or other in the basement, I accidentally bumped into Louise. I swear I never gave her more than a shy smile, and had studiously averted my eyes from the twin peaks of her peasant bodice. I must have failed.

Perhaps in response to my brief glance, or to my blushing cheeks, in a wordless second my belt buckle sprung undone and I felt her hand fumbling at my trouser buttons. Hitching her flounced skirt and lacy petticoat to her waist, she revealed not one stitch of under-clothing. With no thought but lust, belly-to-belly, surprised by the soft warmth of the other's bare skin, we clinched motionless for the barest moment before Louise pushed me backwards onto the dusty, stone floor. "Ya. Ya." she moaned, her legs astride me. Rocking back and forth, Louise made me a man.

Shivering with anticipation, creaking stair tread by creaking tread, I tiptoed past my parents' bedroom door to her attic room. "My lusty Louise," as I teasingly called her, waited sighing. Flakes of whitewash snowed from the lime-plastered beams, dislodged by the bouncing iron bedstead.

Mornings gave no hint of night. Dressed in her uniform and apron, subservient, demure, Louise curtsied to my parents, her downcast eyes studiously avoiding mine.

"Good morning, Madam. Good morning, Sir."

Daylong I replayed my night visits in my head. Sex, sex, lust, lust. We used one another for that one purpose only, even after I fell in love with a Russian girl.

I first noticed Sasha on the tennis court at the ex-pat's English Club. It wasn't her face, but her body, her bouncing buttocks and wobbling breasts that captivated me. A satyr in sunglasses, feigning indifference from the safety of a lawn chair, I feasted on her thighs and knicker-line as she bent to retrieve a ball. Every jump, and reach so aroused me, I dared not move. It took me two weeks to ask her out, then another week before I suggested more than a cup of tea. Unlike an English girl, with no thoughts of saving herself for marriage, she was as eager as I for a game of illicit "love, set and match" at every un-chaperoned opportunity.

I lied that summer and convinced my parents I was going on a lone camping trip in the Ardennes. Truth was, Sasha and I schemed to be gloriously alone. Carrying passions in our rucksacks along with our maps and provisions, we focused on each other, not where we were going, and soon were stupidly disorientated. Our canteens long dry, hot and very thirsty, we asked people on the trail if any springs were nearby, hoping they would offer us water from their canteens.

"Est-ce-qu'il y a un source ici?"

No luck. They kept walking, waving vague directional hand signals. Now anxious, seriously dehydrated and hopelessly lost in the dense forest, we miraculously stumbled upon a river after about two hours. Our thirst quenched and our bodies cooled, we followed the river's course downstream, trusting it led to a civilized somewhere. The light was fading fast.

It was a day of timely accidents. A couple of miles further on where the forest pushed back from the riverbank, stood a pair of tall wrought-iron gates and behind them, a well-kept hunting lodge camouflaged by mature rhododendron bushes. Emboldened by desperation, we rattled the gates. They were unlocked. Relief. We pushed one open and scuttled up the path through an overgrown garden to a heavy oak door. Carved with cascades of vines and leaves, it mirrored the lodge's natural setting. Boom. The black lion's-head knocker reverberated against its iron stud. We waited. Nothing. Then came the welcome sound of bolts pulling back one by one. The door opened a crack. An elderly woman, who turned out to be the caretaker, peered at us suspiciously. When my Russian girlfriend explained our woebegone tale in impeccable German, and realized we were no more than two bedraggled strays, she flung the door wide, and welcomed us inside.

"The lodge belonged to King Leopold, your late Queen Victoria's brother-in-law."

Edda proudly nodded towards me, at the same time watching the milk in the copper saucepan. Snatching it off the range, she poured it still frothing onto the chocolate. Too hot to sip, Sasha and I sat with our feet stretched towards the range at one end of a long rough-hewn pine table, cradling our mugs and listening to her chatter. My tummy rumbled.

"I don't expect you'd say no to a little something to eat?"

Frau Edda tickled the embers to flame with the riddling iron and threw in another log. Taking six brown eggs from a basket on the windowsill, she cracked them into a skillet, dropped in a handful of wild trumpet mushrooms, and cooked up the best omelet I have ever tasted, which she served with slabs of black, home baked rye bread.

"The two of you can't be a-wandering alone in the forest a-night. Take-ee shelter in the lodge till it be morn."

Exhaustion and full stomachs took their toll. We stifled yawns so as not to appear rude, but our eyelids drooped. Reaching for an oil lamp and turning up the flame, Edda pushed back from the table with a motherly, "Off to bed with you."

Under the glassy stares of a dozen stags' heads mounted on the walls of the main hall, we followed the dancing shadows thrown by Frau Edda's lamp to the absent King Leopold's bedroom. His bed, a richly carved mahogany four-poster, emblazoned with his Royal Coat of Arms, dominated the oak-paneled room. Undeterred by the royal shield, Sasha and I threw ourselves backwards, and drawing the bed's red and blue tapestry curtains, sealed ourselves inside. Enfolded in its dark cocoon, our weariness evaporated to gleeful laughter. Buried beneath the goose-down duvet, cuddled skin-to-skin, Sasha's cheek close to mine, our naked bodies sprang back to life, rising and falling into the mattress's soft feathers till we at last succumbed to the deepest, peaceful sleep.

That summer sex was on my mind.

Vetter was his name. One winter morning, I brushed the snow off a park bench and sat lost in the beauty of the fairyland. A pasty-faced youth about my age sat down beside me, and in very precise old-fashioned English started up a conversation about Edith Cavell. His purple velvet trousers, Norfolk jacket and shiny peaked cap identified him as a student. Truth was, he picked me up.

"Come. I show you Bruges."

He steered me to the famous Manneken-Pis of Brussels, frozen in mid-urination. I pretended to find it amusing, but I was shocked.

We took a liking to one another. We spent the summer rambling in the mountains. Vetter carried poetry books in his knapsack. He introduced me to the sensual music of words. He introduced me to Hafiz, Tagore, Rilke, and Heine. Love, like their poetry, came to life as clearly as the blue sky of his eyes above me, as clearly as Vetter's pasty skin tinged brown by the warm sun. Stretched naked on the bed of wildflowers on which we lay, high in a mountain meadow, his voice dreamily humming with the bees, we supped nectar from purple gentian flower and from the columbine. His fingers running in my hair, I was at peace.

Vetter invited me to supper at his parents' house. Mistake. Clearly they didn't like me, suspicious I was like their son, that our friendship was proof, and confirmed their worst fears. I liked Vetter. He made me laugh. I liked his gentleness. That didn't mean I didn't like girls. I did. Sex was sex. Sex was fun. Vetter was Vetter. I wasn't a queer. I enjoyed sex with a boy, that's all.

Manneken Pis. Brussels.

11
KITTING OUT

My bulging kit bag stared back at me from the mattress ticking of my already stripped bed. It was August 30th, 1924. No more "lasts" remained. The last of the lasts suddenly over in a blur of exams, rehearsal drills, farewell parties, interviews, medicals, and packing. Our class already formally "dined out" and disbanded, addresses and promises to keep in touch exchanged, reality hit me. Sandhurst was no longer home.

I was on a conveyor belt unable to get off. Dazed, I fell in behind my fellow cadets waiting for the bugle's signal, for the Passing Out Parade to begin. The regimental band poised silent, a tableau of red coats, shiny brass, and white gloves. The portly Drum Major twirled his baton. The bandmaster's baton descended. Instruments blasted into life. Anticipation, regret, an up-surge of emotion caught me off guard. I swallowed hard hoping my watery eyes went unnoticed.

"Attention. Byyy the Riiiight...Qu..uick March...and a Left. Right. Left."

In perfect unison we followed the pipe's trill, the drums' thump-brroom rebounding off the College buildings. The battery of guests seated beneath white canvas awnings stilled, heads turned. Self-conscious of the shiny new "pip" on my shoulder, chin tucked almost to my backbone, immaculate, trim, buttons bright, boots a mirror finish, and red stripe down my stove-pipe trousers perfectly aligned, I stepped crisply into the spotlight of the parade ground.

King George V himself took the salute. A flowing, ostrich-feather plume quivered from his spiked helmet, partially obscuring his royal, bearded face. The band played softly while he walked slowly between the lines, formally inspecting his new King's and India Cadets. He stopped and spoke briefly to each one of us. My turn came. Staring directly into my eyes, he addressed me in his guttural English.

"Your father was a fine soldier. I am sure you will be, as well."

"Yes. Sir. Your Majesty." Overcome, I croaked, "I intend to, Sir."

A soldier. A fine soldier. Yes. I would make Father proud. My eyeballs pricked.

The military band broke into *Auld Lang Syne.* The Adjutant's white charger mounted the broad marble steps between the cannon and Doric pillars of the historic main building. The massive double doors clanged shut. Gone—horse, man, adjutant, cadet, Sandhurst, from my life.

"Hip. Hip. Hurrah. Hip. Hip. Hurrah. Hip. Hip Hurrah."

Caps hurled skyward.

"Jolly good show. Congratulations. All the best."

Pumping hands, newly commissioned cadets clapped my back as I did theirs, exclaiming clichés such as "great knowing you…drop me a line sometime." My father, like most others claiming their sons, congratulated "Well done, well done," with an iron handshake and broad smile. Mother and my three sisters pulled me close and kissed me, their lace kerchiefs dabbing at their eyes. So feminine, so pretty, their dresses in delicate shades of leaf-green, powder blues, and softest greys, their feathered hats so frivolous, they outshone every guest. I loved them, as I never had before.

Following the reception line, we joined the milling guests who were excitedly introducing their friends to family, family to friends. A highlight of the social calendar, Sandhurst's Passing Out ceremony and Garden Party was the place every London débutante vied to be.

"May I introduce my son, Rose?" Father, bulging from his old uniform, beamed.

Son, Second Lieutenant Hugh Rose, commissioned officer. Father. Colonel Hugh Rose. Retired. Walking proudly by his side, I tingled with the weight of ancestry, recognized my step in Father's footprint, as he'd stepped into his father's—the same print trodden by his father's father. I was a Rose.

Searching the crowd of visitors over Father's shoulder, sadness briefly clouded the day. Astel, wasn't with them. Was he overseas? I can't recall. I remember missing him, wanting him to share my rite of passage, and see me stepping firm.

My posting: India to my father's old Gurkha Regiment, the 3rd. Queen Alexandria's Own Gurkha Rifles.

Five weeks remained before my ship sailed, barely time to get kitted-out. I had no idea how, and no money of my own.

"Glad to be of help. Stay at my flat, Hugh. We'll use my tailors. Do the rounds. Introduce you. I know the ropes." Father came to my rescue.

He didn't mention money, or its lack. We needed each other at that moment and I was grateful. By helping me, Father claimed back a little of what he was no longer a part, the Army. India.

Mother and my sisters returned to the house they'd taken in France for the winter, leaving me with Father for the first time in our lives—no mother, no sisters, just the two of us, Hugh senior, Hugh junior, father, son. Before Sandhurst, Father never had much to say to me, a mother's boy, in his eyes. I kept my distance and spoke little.

Close-quartered in Father's cramped bachelor-pad, we struggled uncomfortably formal, I awkwardly polite, he, haltingly companionable and overly solicitous.

"Ready for a snifter, Hugh?" he asked, pouring an evening's whisky.

Our reserve softened, Father started talking. Hunting, shooting, sport of every kind, he would have talked of them forever. But I wanted him to tell his military experiences, to tell me how he and Mother met.

I leaned forward, alert, steering him to relive his memories, to bring his India to life. "Father, what was… tell me about…" and Father leaned back in his leather chair, sucked on his pipe, blew a smokescreen and retreated into his private world. I, England, his poky flat, the present faded. With him, I crawled on my belly along dry river *nullahs*, scrambled through thorn bushes, marched wearily over mountainous passes and scrub land on a military campaign, thirsty and sweating in the humid jungle of an inhospitable terrain. Spinning yarns, he held me hostage in all-night vigils as side by side, crouched motionless in *machans*, we waited for tiger, cornered a *tusker*, rode out pigsticking for wild boar, tracked bear and panther, and lurching through tall grasses, went g*hooming* on an elephant's back.

"Lord Kitchener," Father proudly confided one evening, "personally invited me to join the Gurkhas. 'A darned good soldier,' Kitchener called me."

I saw a shadow, regret between his words. I glimpsed a man unfulfilled.

"Gets under your skin. India." He concluded, his voice wistful. "My country," Father called India, and I knew, then, India would become mine too.

Mother and Father no longer lived under the same roof. The word separation was taboo. Longing to pry, I tiptoed around any mention of Mother or any personal topic, waiting for Father to seize the opportunity and open up the cobra pit. He didn't. My question, "Father, how did you and Mamma meet?" hung between us like a Christmas bauble dangling on a thread. I had to wait thirty years to discover Mother was a married woman with two boys when she and Father met and fell in love, she abandoned them, my half-brothers, William, Maitland in India to run off with him. It was thirty years before I discovered my own brother and eldest sister, Astel and Rita, were both bastards. Not a mention of his secrets slithering below the surface beyond reach.

Those three weeks were the closest we ever got, father and son. Sadly, I liked him none-the-better. Too many memories—Father's self-indulgences, his neglectful unconcern for us, his family, the financial hardship, and lonely misery he caused Mother—the selfish, arrogant bugger. Though I played the part of the respectful, dutiful son he always hoped for, I couldn't forget.

Over our regular whisky peg one evening, he clumsily attempted to instruct me in ways of the world.

"Now you are a man, a bit of fatherly advice won't go amiss, I trust." He gruffly announced a mystifying aphorism.

"Keep your mouth shut and your bowels open." To what he referred exactly, escaped me.

"Absolutely, Sir," my answer, equally obscure.

That was it, not another word. End of subject. In silence we both reached for our whiskey.

Meticulously itemized, the kit I needed ran five pages. Father and I scrutinized the thick wad of paper, "Inventory Required." Barathea uniform, Mess kit, issue combat fatigues, trousers—whites, and mysterious items such as puttees, sam-browns and a *topee.* Six sets of uniforms for every possible military occasion, unimaginable numbers of socks, underwear, jackets, suits and shirts had to conform in every perfect detail. Six white, six khaki shorts—compulsory.

The shorts stood starched, voluminous, indecently wide-legged, and I swore to glue my legs together and wear them over underpants. "I'm told prickly heat is a problem in that area, Sir. Helps keep a man's hmm… cool." Within a week of my arrival in India, heat won, modesty lost. Like every seated man wearing gaping shorts, I spread my knees to cool my privates and learned to ignore a soldier's exposed crinkly flesh-red balloons if no ladies were present, .

From "John Lobb, bespoke Bootmakers since 1849, Number 9, St. James Street," I ordered two pairs of black, one pair of brown lace-up shoes, a pair of riding boots and a pair of slippers.

"You'll be needing these, Sir, shoe and boot trees. I recommend Beech, Sir. Beech never warps."

Made-to-measure footwear was one more expensive item on the list. Father enjoyed spending. I gave up worrying.

"Start on the right foot, my boy. First impressions and all that."

As always, Father's funds fell short. He paid for everything "on tick" without any complaint or reference to the "red" pit he was burying himself in.

"Put it on my account." Father scrawled his signature to countless I.O.U.'s at a horrifying number of establishments, for horrifying amounts. Appearances counted, we both agreed. Correctness. Looking the part. That much I'd learned, and accepted all he offered.

"Thanks most awfully, Sir."

Each day, nine sharp, with a wave of his rolled "brolly," Father hailed a cab to the outfitters listed.

"Turn you into a *pukka-sahib* in no time."

He liked the word *pukka*, and repeated it every time the taxi drew up to the doors of yet another "approved" merchant.

"Damned important to pass muster, make a *pukka* impression." I counted up the many precious pounds a *pukka* impression cost, and how many times he used the phrase.

"Can't have my son wearing clothes off the peg like a commercial salesman."

We drew up at Hawkes Bespoke Tailors, Number One, Saville Row.

"Had my own uniform made here when I was first commissioned. The place has been in business since 1771. Served emperors and kings." Father's eyes gleamed.

Father oversaw, checking every calculation. "Nip the seam in a little. Shorten the cuffs..."

Stuck with pins, arms wide, stiff as a scarecrow's, I spent hours draped in partially cut cloth, scissors snipping along the tailor's chalk, as tape measures were stretched across my anatomy as though I was a tailor's dummy. Neck, fifteen and a half...shoulders, twenty-six and an eighth...shoulder to wrist, armpit to elbow, elbow to wrist, wrists, chest, expanded, at rest, inside leg, outside leg, waist, waist to shoulder—every conceivable part of me was measured and entered into the tailor's ledger, "so Sir can be confident of an impeccable fit reordering from any part of the globe. Just drop us a line, Sir. We'll send your requirement as per our records."

Prodded, primped and preened, twisting this way and that, I gradually took on the guise of a soldier.

"'Civvies' are as strictly regulated as uniform, and your social obligations as important as military duties," Father instructed.

According to Father, India was one endless round of partying, each event requiring specific clothes—casual, semi-formal, formal, then sport-specific outfits –polo, tennis, cricket, shooting, and hunting. I let him ramble on. My head reeled.

Kitting-out completed, Father patted me on the back, satisfied with his picture-perfect image of an officer and gentleman. I admired myself in the looking glass more than once. Pith helmet on my head, an officer's baton under my arm, I marched a dusty road heading an imaginary regiment.

"For a small consideration," Hawkes sewed yards of red-embroidered Cash's nametapes marking every item with "H.V. Rose." Neatly folded, wrapped in tissue paper, sprinkled liberally with mothballs, packed into drawers and hanging space of my new brassbound cabin trunk, and an insect-proof tin trunk, my kit was delivered by Hawkes to Southampton Docks. That black tin trunk trucked the world with me for 30 years—a treasured personal relic I associate with the stinging smell of naphtha and the East. Battered. Together. We survived.

"Captain Hugh Vincent Rose. Bombay. India. *S.S. Castle.*" Proclaimed white letters painted both lid and sides. My helmet in a helmet-shaped case, my sword and spurs, traveled separately. Kitting-out was over.

"Time to introduce you around. I'll stand you lunch at the Club."

With a twirl of my new, tightly rolled silk umbrella, bowler on my head, I hailed a taxicab, "The Senior."

The Senior Service Club, the Army and Navy, the Oriental, we dined at each in turn.

"Tío Pepe. Dry." Over pre-luncheon sherry Father showed me off, his trophy son.

"I'd like to present my son…."

"Make a good impression. Important chappie, my boy." He prompted in stage whispers, hand over his mouth.

"Make the difference to your career. He's a decent sort. Help you out in a spot of bother."

Father's tiny flat, inseparable for three whole weeks, my smile frozen…I was glad the end of my visit was in sight.

On our last day, Father treated me to the "wonders of the world" ruled by Britain, displayed at the British Empire Exhibition over two hundred and sixteen acres in Wembley—Egypt's reconstructed tomb of Tutankhamen, the Chinese Lacquer Room, the Burmese Pavilion, an African village in a mock jungle, Maltese ruins, and other wonders of the British Colonies and Dominions covering twenty percent of the globe. Father and I were two of the twenty million people who attended the exhibition during its twelve months.

Father kept the final stop of his itinerary a surprise.

"There. Go on. Look closely, Hugh."

In front of us stood a commanding bronze equestrian statue outside Scotch House in Knightsbridge, galloping hungrily towards Hyde Park's green grass. I looked at the horseman, haughty, his seat firm astride his prancing steed, poised, and was glad Father knew nothing of my shameful horsemanship at Sandhurst.

Father smiled as I read the plaque, "Field Marshal, Sir Hugh Rose."

"It's in our blood, d'ye see, India, the Army, history—and now, you, my son, playing your part. Your great-uncle, Sir Hugh, served with Field Marshall Sir John Campbell, Commander-in-Chief of India, and helped suppress the 1857 Indian Mutiny. Great soldier. Put safety of his men first. Sir Hugh was knighted for masterminding the capture of Jhansi Rani, India's Warrior Queen. Later his peerage was raised to Baron. Baron Strathnairn, and he became Commander-in-Chief in India after Lord Clyde. Never married and the title died with him. Shame." Father coveted a peerage.

I studied the likeness of the statue's delicate slender face to Father's. Both shared the Rose chin—weak, in my opinion, not the chin of the hero my father painted. I ran my fingers along my strong jaw line, grateful I took after Mother. Later, I read his fellow officers thought Sir Hugh a snob, a terrible bore, they dreaded his coming to the Mess.

The statue is all I have to judge my ancestor by—that, and a military portrait of him, grand in full uniform, sword in hand, sash and insignia of his Knighthood across his chest, boasting of a brave and clever soldier.

I remembered studying his battle strategies at Sandhurst. Still on the curriculum in the twenties, my son, Michael, tells me they were still considered classic battle tactics in the 1950s when he was a cadet there.

If it hadn't been for Father I'd never have seen my ancestor's statue. In 1938, before the outbreak of World War II, it was removed and put ignominiously into cold storage in Westminster Abby's crypt. Unless it was melted down for the war effort, it may still be frozen in mid-gallop, horse and rider staring fixedly into space. A public lavatory now stands in its place.

Statue of Sir Hugh Rose.

12
LAST FLING

Still not admitting marital defeat, Mother and my sisters stayed on in Le Touquet, leaving father to fend for himself in London. It was their way of saving face. But we knew. Their marriage was over.

Ostensibly my visit to France was to spend time with Mother before sailing for India, but really I wanted a fling and selfishly spent only a token time being companionable. Poor Mother.

"Off you go, dear boy. Enjoy yourself." She indulged her Hughey without complaint.

I had three glorious weeks to worm into the so-called called highlife—become one of the "in" people in a game of see-and-be-seen. Aileen, my closest sister, knew exactly how to hit the fashionable resort of the Paris Plage, a broad seafront promenade peppered with elegant hotels and casinos.

With feigned indifference, we people-watched. On the promenade, sipping Turkish coffee, we stared through elegant smoke rings rising from Aileen's ivory cigarette holder. We blew away our hangovers with a round of golf beside the sparkling Mediterranean. We frequented Chemin de Fer and Baccarat tables at the Casino de la Floret, playing down to our last *sou*. We made a solitary glass of the cheapest bubbly last the evening, so our empty pockets went unnoticed. Aileen hit the jackpot, winning all of twenty pounds. As rich as any high roller, we ordered Dom Perignon.

"Appearances matter. Remember?" We giggled, picturing our childhood trips to Monsieur Charles' pawnshop.

Though under age, I brazened my way into the Salle de Jeux's hallowed ground—not to gamble, but to shamelessly ogle its dazzling clientele throwing high-value chips like marbles onto the tables, and possibly glimpse the Prince of Wales. Aileen on my arm flashing her clear green eyes, great figure and seductive smile, the bouncer never gave me a second look. One evening, the Prince himself, his lady we called "the Scarlet Woman," and his Equerry, swept past, acknowledging us with a brief nod—our posturing and nightly dress-up for the evening's charade rewarded.

In a cruel game of snakes and ladders, the elite meticulously scrutinized each guest to decide their social fate. Would-be socialites, Aileen and I, "fresh meat-on-the-hoof," crept up the social ladder rung by precious rung. Once we had been approved, our program cards quickly filled. A handsome couple—Aileen, outrageous in a skimpy shimmy, kid gloves and sequined hat, I, in black tie and tails—we vied to be the most alluring. Young fools. Ridiculous either of us cared whether "they" approved or disapproved. I knew my days of frivolous make-believe ended with my leave. Adulthood loomed.

The day came. I put on my uniform and caught the Dover Ferry. Mother and Father, temporarily reunited in London solely for the event, accompanied me to Southampton. Secretly I was relieved seeing them together, arm in arm, knowing Father would step up and help Mother if she needed him once I wasn't around.

"It's a momentous family occasion, Hugh. No argument, we're seeing you off. No. Not another word."

Though I protested, Mother and my three sisters insisted.

The normally grey Southampton Docks swirled with a riot of colored frocks and lacy parasols relieving the men's austere khaki. Sweethearts, wives, parents and children, the mood, music faked the frenetic energy of a party in full swing. Straining to hear ourselves speak, we shouted over beloved traditional British favorites blasting from the Marine Band.

"De ye ken John Peel with his coat so grey…"

"I belong to London, dear old London town….".

Familiar tunes rose above the crescendo of excited voices.

"Goodbyeeee Goodbyeee I wish you all a last goodbye…."

In confirmation, the megaphone boomed, "Passengers are requested to embark."

Parting, a sudden reality, I gripped Father's hand.

"Goodbye, Sir. Thanks most awfully for everything. I won't let you down."

"That's the spirit. Do your stuff, my boy. All the best." He thumped my back, looking wistful. "I sailed in the *S.S. Assaye*...first time to India."

I found voice enough to croak farewell.

"Goodbye, Mother. Goodbye, Aileen. Goodbye, Kathy-Baby. Tell Rita goodbye for me, would you? Look after each other till I return."

I embraced each in turn for one last time ignoring their sniffs and tears. Swallowing hard, I turned abruptly and headed for the gangplank without a backward glance.

"Buck up. Shoulders back. Stiff upper lip. Mustn't pipe the eye." I commanded myself, conscious suddenly it might be forever.

From the gangplank I studied His Majesty's troop ship, the former *S.S. Assaye.* Still wearing the old P&O Company's drab black and yellow faded paint, she'd been recently resurrected from the mothball fleet. Despite her appearance there was plenty of life left in the old lady's sturdy, well-trodden decks. Worn out as a liner, she was no beauty, but to me her lines could not have been more stately. His Majesty's colors fluttering, she lay dwarfed between the spanking *S.S. Berengaria* afore-ship, and the *S.S. Majestic* aft. Commandeered as a troop ship in the Boer War in Africa immediately after her maiden voyage, she only reverted to her true calling as a cruise liner after peace was declared. Now here she was again, a dowdy troop ship.

I joined the jostling uniformed men on the gangplank and pushed my way through the throng crowding the portside rails. The *S.S. Assaye's* alarming list flashed an un-nerving boyhood image from Belgium. I saw again the desperate refugees struggling to escape and heard their cries.

"Let me stow that for you, Sir." Startled to the present, I surrendered my canvas grip into the capable hands of an orderly.

I made for the rail, hoping for one last glimpse of my family. Freed from the capstans, the hawsers were hauled on board, and the anchors weighed. The deck shuddered beneath my feet. The engines coughed into the throbbing low-pitched hum that stayed with us all voyage long.

Before the *H.M.S. Assaye* pulled away from the quayside, a hail of colored paper-streamers rained to the deck catching the railings and festooning us like so many Christmas trees. Some landed overboard in the ever-widening span of water separating ship and shore. We were umbilically connected, we on board, families on the quayside. Though we delayed severing the cord, there was no stopping the inevitable snap and the unraveling of our guts. Relentless, turning slowly, the ship pulled away, hooting her deep farewell. Whooping sirens competed victoriously with the now barely audible strains of *Auld Lang Syne* still bravely playing on the quay. I leaned over the rails as far as I dared and waved until my arms ached. Separation, anticipation and apprehension took turns as I watched my parents and sisters shrink to dots on the ever-diminishing quay, blur, and then disappear. A trail of soggy streamers, souvenirs, marked our bittersweet parting.

I lurched, unsteadied, as the water's faint swell caught the ship's keel and Southampton was swallowed by the Solent. The famed choppy seas of the English Channel hit full force, wetting my eyes and my cheeks with spray. My chest and the ship's bows heaved and fell in unison. Free of England's shores, tossing her mane, she ploughed full steam ahead through the bucking seas—my voyage and the *Assaye's* under way.

13
VOYAGE TO INDIA

Walking through the *S.S. Assaye's* staterooms and descending below decks to my cabin, my cruise fantasy evaporated. With her chandeliers and rich trappings gone, any grand notion of traveling "P.O.S.H"—scuppered. Dark, my three-berth cabin just above the water line boasted a salt-crusted porthole and a cupboard-sized bathroom reeking of oily paint. My cabin mates, already unpacked, watched me from their perches on the upper and middle bunks.

"Left you the lower, old chap."

Rose, Rawlings, and Rathbone. We introduced ourselves, laughing at the coincidence of our initials. Our first time at sea, our first posting, first time to India, everything a discovery, we bonded fast friends.

"Hey fellars, soap won't lather—ditto shaving cream."

The urinal became "the head," or more peculiarly, the "pig's ear." The Mess was now the Wardroom; stairs were companionways and doors were hatches. We renamed ourselves too. "The Three Rs," we called ourselves. The label stuck.

"Ring for the attendant," we joshed, pretending our batman was a cruise cabin attendant in disguise. Officer training schooled us well. "A gentlemen never 'did' for himself." Spoiled, un-housetrained teenagers, we never dreamed of doing chores. Like a mother, our batman cleaned, pressed our uniforms, ran our baths, and laundered shirts, streaked underwear and odiferous socks.

Pre-dawn, I awoke, my stomach rolling with the sea. "This is it, Hugh. Queasy or no, time to go," I muttered, clinging to the rim of the metal basin and checking my image in the cabin's bathroom mirror. Pale, sweaty, its skin broadcast my nervousness. My racing heart proclaimed I was a fraud. Taking a deep breath, I struggled upright, closed the cabin's hatch, and stepped into the oily-smelling narrow passage heading for the fresh air and my first command—Drill Officer in charge of P.T. One hand pressed against either wall to keep the Atlantic swell from throwing me from side to side, I clawed my way up the companion ladder and lurched onto the upper deck to face a wall of twenty stone-faced seasoned gunners, all of whom had seen active service. Their sour expressions declared they hated P.T. as much as I did. Puppet-like, they flapped their arms and hopped in languorous obedience to my strangled, "…and a One. Two. Arms wide. Legs together. Knees…"

I didn't blame their resentment—a youth new to shaving, in charge of men with years of military experience behind them. Those first timorous days, I was never sure whether my orders would be obeyed, or if the men would toss me over the side.

In recurring nightmares leering men rudely gesturing "up your Kyber," their faces an inch from mine, lip-synced my soundless mouthing. From my bunk, awake, restless, I envisioned myself confidently bellowing orders, and men jumping to my every command. Repetition whittled at my stage fright. Barked orders became masterful.

I was surprised—the ship being run as an Army Base. I still had hopes of lounging in a deck chair all day, book in hand, sipping a Pimm's and staring out to sea. I should have known. The Army was the Army. Drill. Muster on Parade. Battle Stations. Abandon Ship. Eat. Stand Down. Sleep. Jarring bugle calls again governed my day. Reveille's first shattering call levitated me so fast I hit my head on the overhead bunk. Perhaps the bugler ran out of puff by nightfall, because Last Post's "lights-out," so hauntingly beautiful, soothed me to sleep.

As at Sandhurst, we dined formally in full Mess dress at 7.30 sharp, following the prerequisite sherry. Luckier than many, I found my sea legs stabilized after a couple of days. However ill, to be excused required a doctor's chit. Men were expected to control fluttering stomachs and remain at table, however turbulent the Bay of Biscay off Spain. As a teller across a Ouija board, plates slid from guardrail to guardrail, slopping soup, stews onto white damask cloths. Stemmed glasses snapped. Crockery crashed. Uniformed men careened towards and away from the table, cutlery in hand, napkins on laps—too busy holding onto the food in our stomachs, we couldn't laugh at the slapstick scene.

Violent waves lifted, dropped, rolled, swilled men's guts side to side, and bow to stern. I pitied our men, the poor buggers, strung below decks, squeezed into crowded airless holds with barely five and a half inches of headroom above their swaying hammocks. Green-faced inmates lay there, too nauseated to protest such grim conditions. I, and other junior officers were assigned to be in charge of Rounds below decks—the worst of the worst duties. Descending to that smelly, awful place twice a day took all my willpower to avoid emptying the contents of my own stomach.

Two days later, the Bay of Biscay and the stench of vomit mixed with cleaning fluid vanished in our wake. Instead, the far sweeter odor of dirty socks and unwashed skin wafted from below decks,

The clouds rolled away. The pitching grey Atlantic seas smoothed calm. Life took on the color of the Mediterranean, as did the weather. Cool, open-necked tropical khakis replaced our wool. Senior officers relaxed. Routine slackened. Troops erected a boxing ring and a makeshift canvas swimming pool on the aft deck. Officers and enlisted men splashed and played together, building a trusting camaraderie. Roughhouse deck games and silly horseplay cooled our cabin fever.

"Your turn, Sir." Gunners I drilled at sun-up tossed me into the pool fully clothed.

Spluttered protests ignored, I lost count how many times. A few days more of lazy fun, a suntanned and happier crew steamed into Port Said.

As the *S.S. Assaye* slid closer to shore, a gagging whiff of heat-stewed rubbish blasted across the shrinking span of water flaring my nostrils with the distinctive Eastern aroma of spice-n-refuse. Strange guttural cries, horns, bleating goats, braying asses and a medley of other unidentifiable sounds assailed me, then hesitated, suddenly silent. Minaret by minaret, each took up the Moslem's holy call to prayer.

"*Allah-Wah-Allah-al-Allah.*" Notes reminiscent of Rimsky-Korsakov's Scheherazade, floated over the water enveloping me in its tide. Even now, Scheherazade brings to mind those first Port Said images, sounds and smells—an East such as I never imagined.

I stretched my arms wide, resting their weight on air so heavy it felt like thick pea soup. I leaned forward, careful not to touch the burning rail as I had the first time. Dazzled by the whiteness of the buildings, I shaded my eyes and stepped backwards into a narrow stripe of shade to join Rathbone and Rawlings.

"Look. Look." We jabbed towards shore, hardly knowing where next to point.

High-prowed wooden dhows with curious raised platforms aft cut swaths through the salt water, their patched rust-red and off-white sails mirrored taut and billowed in the emerald-green sea. Bare-chested men wearing strips of cloth pulled between their legs shinned at lizard-speed up masts and crawled along booms high above the water. A group of six or seven hauled their fishing nets onto the deck.

"*Wahid-Ithnane-Thelatha.*" A sing-songed count of 1-2-3 and a chant of what I guessed was something like our "and a heave-ho-heave," accompanied each pull.

Ashore, slender minarets thrust above and between shimmering mirages of strange cat-eared buildings and low mud huts. A tangle of donkeys, camels, herds of goats, wooden pushcarts and turbaned men in grubby checkered sarongs and nightshirts flowed along the quay. The ship anchored some distance offshore.

"Any closer, men might jump ship, and we would be swamped by stowaways and rats," a seasoned officer from our Mess explained.

The *Assaye's* engines muted to a low hum, and for the first time since we left Southampton, the throb beneath our feet stilled strangely quiet as the anchor dropped, chains rattling, and reined her to a stop. With the stillness, a wildfire, lung-searing heat hit me full face, burning my nostrils. Gasping like a beached goldfish fighting to extract oxygen from an alien environment, I licked my lips and opened my mouth, wondering how a human body could survive temperatures "hot enough to fry an egg on."

"Cook a bloody joint of beef on the deck, more like," we Three R's joked.

My shirt quickly darkened with sweat, and my shorts stuck uncomfortably between my legs. I wasn't the only one. Foreheads dripped. Damp stains spread under every armpit, outlined backbones and buttocks, and wet-glued our khaki shirts and shorts to our bodies. Not a pretty sight. "Get used to it, Hugh. Adapt and ignore," I lectured myself, and forced my attention to the time-old scenes unfolding in the sea.

Before we even dropped anchor, a swarm of craft crowded the ship, the men and boys on board shouting and waving, "*Sahib. Sahib.* Cheap-cheap price."

Merchants rowed alongside, fobbing off crudely carved camels, glass beads and fake antiquities with mock broken hearts, until the asking price dropped and then halved and quartered to seal a sale. Carpet sellers unfurled rolls of carpet the length of their narrow craft, silk shawls, bolts of cloth splashed a myriad of color without ever getting wet. I threw a handful of change overboard and laughed admiringly as young boys plunged into the murky harbor water, disappearing and reappearing like so many glistening cormorants. Not a coin escaped. Exploding from the water, clutching their shiny silver trophies, "*Shukrun. Felus.* Please, thank you. More," they called, and upending, vanished again into the oily, shark-infested depths.

The *Assaye* stayed in port just long enough to refuel and replenish her larders. Two days of freedom for everyone but the Purser and his crew. Their job was to buy and oversee the loading and unloading of supplies from coal-lighters and barges, and to ferry local laborers ship to shore. Kickbacks were the Purser's accepted and unbegrudged right as long as he kept our bellies full. Discreetly juggling the budget to line his pockets, he soon completed his business. Pretending insult and starvation, suppliers in the *suqs* and hardtack stores didn't put up much of a fight. His patronage was far too valuable to lose.

Tinned bully beef and Spam vanished from the table, and we gorged instead on *channard,* king mackerel, swordfish, tuna, prawns and "safe"' peelable fruit and vegetables such as bananas, oranges, limes, mangos, green beans and cucumbers. Though we complained about the unappetizing fresh produce discolored by an hour's compulsory soaking in *pinky-pani,* a solution of potash permanganate, we wolfed it just the same. Watermelon, plumped up with typhoid, hepatitis or cholera-carrying human waste was forbidden. Local camel and goat meat never appeared. Too flyblown. Too worm-riddled. With local rice and flour came weevils and rat droppings. Though the Mess cooks did their best to sort the rice before cooking, I sniffed every mouthful for the unique musty smell and searched for telltale black specks.

Sailing Dhow

14
PORT SAID

Cabin-fevered, I counted the hours to jump ship for a day's long overdue R&R with my friends. Another monotonous evening of gin rummy lay ahead till Shore leave the following morning. In mid-deal, my name boomed over the tannoy.

"Lieutenant Rose. Calling Lieutenant Rose. Report immediately to the Duty Officer."

"For you. A signal from the Fleet Admiral." The Duty Officer handed me the signal with a-who-is-he-to-have-been-singled-out look on his face. '

Admiral de Welt requests Lieutenant Hugh Rose to dine informally this evening at Admiralty House. 1900 hours. Launch detailed.

Momentarily puzzled, I hesitated before remembering. The Palais d'Egmont. Le Tourquet. Admiral De Welt's twin daughters. Pretty girls. I'd danced and kissed each one in turn, but—their faces? I had no memory. I must have made a better impression than I imagined if they remembered both me and when the *S.S. Assaye* had docked in Port Said.

I hurriedly changed from khakis into my tropical whites and waited on deck. White Ensign and pennants flying, the barge pushed away from the Admiral's private jetty and drew alongside. The ship's hull below me dropped steep as the rappel cliffs of Sandhurst's Barossa training ground. Fifty pairs of eyes bored from the deck. I swung my leg over the side onto the rope ladder praying I looked more confident than I felt.

Balancing on the top rung, I fumbled for stable footholds rung by rung. In mid step, my unsuitable dress shoes slipped leaving me dangling by my left hand. I grappled a rung with my right. Aping a trapeze artist, I pushed both feet against the ship's side, swung far out over the water, and twisted 180 degrees before swinging back and regaining my foothold. A cheer went up. I flushed red struggling to regain my composure. I cursed my clumsiness and wished I could evaporate as shrill whistles piped me aboard the launch. When I reached the lowest rung a Petty Officer saluted and grappled me to safety with his free arm. My composure somewhat regained, I returned the salute lopsidedly with my right hand.

The transition from the *Assaye's* floating world to the civilian's on dry land was too sudden for the evening to be much fun. I entered a surreal civilization of silks and women, or was it the other way round and mine the unreal? I became wooden and oaf-like. Speech dried. To my relief, the evening was over as suddenly as it began and I could sink back into the womb of the ship's bowels. Ballooning breasts, shadow-legs beneath flimsy silk swirled through cigar dreamclouds until I finally slept.

Up at first light, I joined the line of fidgety men by the gangplank waiting to scuttle ship. Exchanging tales of wicked vice, the chatter was of how to best sample Port Said's forbidden fruit. We fueled our imaginations over many evenings with celluloid descriptions of scantily clad cinnamon-skinned beauties, tinkling ankle bells, twirling breast tassels, and enticing undulating bellies.

"Looky. No touchy."

Sickened by gruesome tales of rotting male private parts, we firmly agreed any other activity was out of the question.

At last, the announcement came, "Permission to go ashore."

The three of us bought smutty postcards, paid to watch a show of unspeakable depravity, gawked at the famous Indian rope trick, were mesmerized at the swaying cobra piped from a basket, watched the *gully-gully* men produce live chickens out of thin air, and ate rose-scented Turkish Delight. We wandered the cavernous Simon Artz Emporium, looking at everything from gold and rubies to lampshades made from camel's skin. Finally we settled on impossibly theatrical white straw-stuffed *topees*, and stepped into the sunlight, proud—'*pukka*' gentlemen of the Raj. As with every ship hoving into view, as the *Assaye* tipped the horizon, the dark emporium exploded to a fairground blaze of electric illumination and brassy music, springing staff from their sleeping mats under the dusty counters. Straightening none too spruce clothes, they readied to charm the last rupee from the pockets of their *Sahib* prey.

Rawlins hailed a horse-drawn *droshki,* and with crudely graphic gestures, settled on a price to take the three of us to a brothel. The *droshki* stopped before a seedy house with a limp, faded, red Chinese lantern above the door. It was too late to change our minds. A fearsome bare-chested pimp dragged us in, preventing our escape. Inside—a storybook illustration; gold-turbaned, a man with a waxed moustache wearing red baggy trousers, silver scimitar and scarlet sash around his bulging waistline, bowed and pointed.

"Very lovelies. Good clean girls. Delight you much delight." He followed us inside.

The room was dimly lit and oppressively curtained. A lone ceiling fan stirred just enough air to ruffle my hair. The pimp snapped his fingers, summoning a couple of girls to fan us with peacock feathers. Across the room, six dull-eyed girls, rouged and lipsticked as painted dolls, puckered their scarlet lips and swayed alluringly to a stringed instrument.

"Which you like? Dance Seven Veils? Belly Dance? Sex now?" The pimp demanded, listing the price for each service.

We settled for "Seven Veils and Belly," at which he clapped his hands, signaling the girls to begin.

Feigning manly sophistication, we lounged languidly against the garish red, pink and orange satin cushions expectant. After downing a couple of beers, sucking on a hubble-bubble, a hookah, the girls' lackluster performance collapsed us in a fit of coughing and helpless sniggering. When it became apparent we didn't mean business, and were just "there for the beer," the chief pimp harangued us for insulting his "lovelies," then cursing us in Arabic, called over two murderous-looking eunuchs to throw us out.

Scimitars waving, yelling abuse, they came at us, whether to rob or harm we weren't waiting to discover. Hurling a handful of rupees to divert them, we fled. Rawlings and I catapulted into the waiting *droshki.* Rathbone dislodging the dozing driver from his seat, took up the reins himself, and whipped the bony horse into a madcap gallop. Out of reach, and only then, we burst onto tear-jerking laughter.

That evening, safe in the Wardroom, pink gins in hand, we embroidered our tale to a rapt but unconvinced audience.

"We escaped within an inch of our lives."

15
SUEZ CANAL

In the early light before dawn's sky blazed blue, and while the air still held its coolness, the smooth sea shone grey as a sheet of steel. The ship's engines shuddered into life at 0500 hours, shattering the calm. The *S.S. Assaye* pulled from her moorings, carefully navigating her prow through the narrow entrance into the Suez Canal.

Men lined the rails to watch. The lock gates groaned shut behind us. The forward gates cracked apart, allowing the gushing flood to lift us gently to the higher level of the canal's 120 miles linking the Mediterranean to the Red Sea. The banks pressed so close I felt if I stretched, my hands could scoop up handfuls of its sand. Boys running beside us on the towpath and others slowly pedaling their bikes kept easy pace with the ship. Despite the early hour, the path was lively with *dish-dash* robed Arabs in nightshirts perched sideways on the bony donkeys' rumps, their bare feet swinging to the dainty trit-trot of their mounts. Sticks in hand, they urged their beasts to keep moving. In one last desperate attempt to attract a final transaction from their fast-vanishing market, a couple of merchants laden with heavy bundles of tourist knick-knacks ran panting beside the ship, shaking carvings and fake antiquities, calling, "*Sahib. Sahib.* Best price. Rock bottom."

We overtook a languid camel caravan slung with bulging orange, red and indigo woolen saddlebags. Groups of men walked, trailing strings of three or four camels tied nose to tail by twine looped through nose-rings. A mile beyond, we drew level with a smaller group of shrouded tribesman in black. Some sat, others knelt behind their camel's hump. Backward, forward, backward and forward, rhythmic, they rocked in unison with the camel's motion. And I understood why camels got their name—"Ships of the desert."

"Bedu," a fellow spectator informed me.

A flock of bleating long-eared goats herded by a boy of no more than ten caught my attention, and by the time I looked back, the Bedu had turned, headed for the empty landscape.

Soon they and all living things evaporated. We were alone, gliding in a pale sea of dunes and blue shadow-waves. While I strained to see them, the sun rose and scorched dawn's soft light to the bleached glare of day. Such beauty. I wished I were a poet, or, like my Belgian friend, Vetter, could quote a poem to describe my feelings. Quietly watching, imagining, words tumbled to mind—my first poem:

beyond the point where objects can be no longer seen
capsized by shadows indigo
six "ships of the desert" drown swallowed by sand's pale sea—
spiral eddies as from an oarsman's paddles mark their passage
then vanish with the breath of even' tide

I scanned the desert for the Bedouin tribesmen, but they had vanished, merged into the sand. What clues did they use to map their way from one horizon to the next, each a replica of the one before? I stared transfixed, unable to move.

Faint, desperate cries seemingly coming from a fast-approaching dust cloud shattered my reverie. At first I couldn't quite make out the cause. To my amazement, an open-topped yellow taxicab bearing two of our subalterns drew level beside the moving ship. Disheveled, they stood unsteadily in the back waving a bottle, and clutching the cab's doors to keep from being thrown out.

"Stop. Stop. Wait. Wait. Don't leave us. Hello. Hello, there. Hold up, I beg you. Stop." Their shouts, rising, panicked.

The ship's captain swung his binoculars in the opposite direction, studiously ignoring them. The ship moved relentlessly forward. The men, red-faced and panting fell back silent. The taxi bucketed along the rough terrain keeping pace. One…three…hours passed. Finally, the ship veered towards a quivering mirage of date palms and a lone towering mosque. Gradually the oasis solidified to Ismailia's crowded port halfway between Port Said and Suez. We stopped only to take on sweet water and the shamefaced subalterns.

Two very miserable men scampered up the gangplank to our jeers and cheers. A.W.O.L., they were instantly arrested and escorted below before a court martial under armed guard. Lucky for them, its panel members saw the funny side. Rather than charging them with desertion and ruining their careers, the panel reduced their rank to Orderly Officer for the remainder of the voyage, and let them off with a severe scolding.

A dhow laden with dates going in the other direction waited in the wider passing place at Ballah. I saw no other ships until we reached Lake Timsa, where the canal opened briefly. With Ismailia long gone, nothing remained to fill the dreamy days but Egypt's mesmerizing infinity on the western bank, and the barren Sinai Peninsular on the eastern. The next scheduled stop, Aden, lay far ahead with the Bitter Lakes still to cross, the Gulf of Suez and the Red Sea.

Now with the *Assaye's* engines' lowered hum, her slower pace, I had to double check to make sure we were moving. No breeze, too hot to do much of anything, and with not much of anything to do. No drill since our arrival in Port Said three days before. The ship's routine disintegrated. Officers, men, we slopped about in shorts, our shirts unbuttoned, and some men shirtless.

The heat more tolerable on the shade side, I found a vacant deck chair and dragged it aft to distance myself from a group of chattering men. I wanted silence. I wanted to enjoy the emptiness alone. The relentless sun, suffocating air, and slight rocking of the ship lulled me near comatose. I moved only to keep my chair in the ever-shifting strip of shade, or lift a glass of *limu*, limewater, to my lips. Foggy, I drifted in and out of wakefulness, wandered paths chosen by my mind.

Reality far away, I rode the backs of elephants, confronted fierce tigers, cooled in marble palaces and temples, and skied the Himalayan snows. Ceaselessly pressing onward, caught in dream's tide, I walked, face upturned into hydrating rain. The desert frog stirred.

With a jolt, I plummeted back. Uneasy. I was a fraud. What the hell was I doing on this ship headed to India? For that matter, why was I in the Army at all? I abhorred violence. I positively disliked "square-bashing". I resented being ordered about. I hated the physicality of sports and horses. As for crawling on my belly in the mud, the lack of freedom, and the jolly Rah-Rah camaraderie.... Why? Certainly not for the glory of military action. I ranted on inside my head, searching for answers. Perhaps the Army was all I was good for. Perhaps I really was the weakling Father thought me, that I had allowed him to push me into his shoes. I had neither stood my ground, nor chosen my own career.

"Out of the question," Father had decreed. Dutiful, I had obeyed.

I resumed my self-enquiry.

Too late now, Hugh. What's done is done. You don't have to stay a soldier. Not forever. You can transfer to specialist departments. Develop your own career. Make the Army your instrument, your vehicle. Meanwhile, Hugh, enjoy your all-expenses-paid adventure. See the world.

I sat up. Confident. Determined. Though it might be my destiny to step into my ancestors' shoes, my Rose footprint would be unique.

Before I left England, Mother had repeated the oh-so-familiar story of her birth.

"Father and Mother, missionaries in the small jungle village of Gonda in the Terai beyond Barielly, devoted their lives to the Taroo Indians. It was there I was born, in the ruins of a Hindu Temple." She spoke of people she'd never spoken of till then.

I scribbled place-names. Terai, Gonda, Bareilly, Naini Tal.

Mother paused.

"….and I still have family in India. Here—my favorite brother's name for you. Jimmy Knowles. He's a magistrate and a hunter."

Wistful, reluctant, she handed me a fat envelope.

"Promise, Hughey, you won't open it until you're gone."

"Promise. I'll look up Jimmy first chance I get." I held her hand.

Wordless, we scanned each other's eyes, hers pleading, so forlorn, I hadn't the heart to press her further. A brother, other siblings, her village in India…?

I kept my word. One leave during my first year, I took the train to Gonda. I found the place where she was born. And I met Jimmy.

Now for Mother's story as I know it now some forty years later, secrets she kept hidden in a tin trunk beneath her bed, secrets I wish I had uncovered before her death. I would have understood and loved the all of her—the woman she came to be, the woman she had been, the one I knew, the one I had never glimpsed.

16

EMMA KNOWLES

My Mother

"I was born in the ruins of a Hindu temple." The way Mother began her story with that bald statement was meaningless without describing the lives of her parents, Isabella Keilly and Samuel Knowles, grandparents I never met—missionaries caught up in the Indian Mutiny. But she had given no details. Nothing. I wanted more.

Whenever I tried squeezing information from her, Mother pursed her lips.

"It's too long ago. Best forgotten, Hughey boy."

I unfolded the papers Mother handed me before I left England. At last I had time to absorb every historic word, and piece together some facts.

The word "illegitimate" jumped from a page. I flushed from either astonishment or shame, I couldn't tell which. Reverend Samuel Knowles, my grandfather, was a bastard—his father, my nameless great-grandfather, too. The illegitimate son of an Earl, he "loved" a baker's daughter and got her pregnant with my grandfather, Samuel Knowles. Attempting to legitimize their baby, they altered the birth entry in the parochial register, were caught, charged with forgery, a capital offence back then, and dragged to prison in irons. Thanks only to his friendship with the Prince of Wales himself, the pages read, my great-grandfather and the baker's daughter were saved from prison and the noose.

It was 1849. With the label "bastard son of criminals" about his neck, seventeen-year-old Samuel's future loomed bleak. "Taking the Queen's Shilling" as an indentured soldier, he was assigned to the Third Gurkha Rifle Regiment, and put on a ship for India. The price for his fresh start was seven years' Army service, severance from his parents, and from England. Strange. I read the sentence a second time—the Third Gurkhas were both my father's regiment and mine—and smiled at the coincidence.

Samuel arrived in India in the 1850s during the rebellious, edgy, pre-mutiny atmosphere, when British military garrisons redoubled their patrols and requested more troops be shipped from "Home." The Army, desperately needing manpower to swell the ranks, coerced as many men as they could to join up and ship out regardless of age or suitability, Samuel included.

"Are you willing to fight?" the Recruiting Sergeant's only question.

"Yes," the only answer. Samuel signed his name.

On landing in India, Samuel, sweltering in a heavy woolen uniform, was marched immediately to join his regiment in Meerut, near Delhi. How my pale-complexioned grandfather survived his cruel induction to such heat…I dabbed the sweat running down my face. My own shipboard discomfort on the Suez Canal was nothing by comparison.

After the briefest basic training, Samuel and fellow survivors of the ordeal were sent to hone their soldiering skills on the frontline, with instructions to kill or be killed. Samuel killed, reluctant soldier though he was, I imagine from self-defense rather than genuine loyalty to his country. The Army records state he fought many local skirmishes "honorably and bravely," and earned himself a medal and a ribbon. But trophies for killing weren't honorable to him. He was a soldier only to repay the Army for his passage from England.

I wonder about the letters he sent home. Did they say, "Dearest Mamma, I have killed today…." I think not, for killing weighed heavy on his conscience and featured in his prayers. Violence was against his gentle nature and against his religion. From childhood he shared his mother's love of the Bible, her stories of saints' lives and miracles. Inside the Chapel's cold stone walls, on Sundays he escaped to God's arms and forgot the shame of his parentage. On the frontline there was no such haven.

The spilled lives and gory battles finally got to him. God's command, "Thou shalt not kill," reverberated so loudly in Samuel's head it became impossible to ignore. He transferred to the Army's Education Department to work off the remainder of his seven years. Army life became less odious.

There, Samuel noticed Isabella, a young widow in her twenties. Although not exactly beautiful, her face glowed strong and handsome. When she permitted herself a smile, her green eyes had a warmth and twinkle that touched him in a way he hadn't felt since he left home five years earlier. Like him, she was deeply religious. With so much in common, it was inevitable they fell in love. They married in 1856.

I lowered the letter to absorb the information. I closed my eyes. But what of my grandmother Isabella, how had she come to be in India?

Flash. The answer—India was her native country. Her mother was Indian, her father, British. So there it was. I had Indian blood. Eight parts. I never questioned my mix of Scots and English. I was British through and through. I paused to feel the Indian in me running in my veins. It was obvious now, mother's sallow skin, her pale Brahmin eyes, and features reflected the same strong beauty of India's Eurasian women.

Three years later, when I was next home on leave, I studied the sepia photos in the family album.

"Mother," I pointed, teasing, "Don't you think Grandmother Isabella's and Great Grandmother's dark skin, heavy eyebrows and black hair make her look Indian?"

"Suntan. Inevitable in the East." Rising to the bait, Mother snapped.

It made sense—Grandmother Isabella being Eurasian. In the early 1800s when the East India Company first traded in India, unions between lonely British troops and local women were commonplace. It was socially acceptable for a man to choose an Indian woman wife or lover—until the descent of class-conscious Victorian wives on India's shores, who brought their tight-laced "Little England" with them. Overnight, mixed relationships were taboo. Labeled, "Mixed. Eurasian. Chi-Chi," my great-grandparents and their children were not received by exclusive British society.

Status was of no consequence to my grandparents, but the label made their daughter, Isabella, less desirable as a wife. It took some time, but at last they scored an Englishman, and married off their dutiful Isabella to Charles Reid in 1846. She was barely seventeen, poor girl, while her husband, Charles, was a withered old man of eighty-six. I shudder thinking of their union, of his groping wrinkled flesh dulling her soft virginal bloom. Thankfully, Isabella bore no children during their seven year marriage. Charles died at the age of ninety-four. India is, nor ever was, a country kind to widows, however young and beautiful. Condemned as outcasts, forced from their homes, shrouded in widow's white of mourning, they wandered penniless, beggars, until death freed them. Isabella was luckier than her Indian sisters. Because her father's and husband's British nationality classified her as white, Isabella evaded their cruel fate, kept her marital home, and found employment in the Army's Education Department in Meerut.

So it was my grandparents met—a runaway bastard, Samuel Knowles, and a young Eurasian widow, Isabella. Fate. Two outcasts. Both alone, both devotees of God, they fell happily in love with no thought to the other's lineage or past.

They married in 1856. Whether they married for convenience or from loneliness, they grew to love each other deeply, so deeply Isabella fell pregnant twenty-one times and bore him fourteen babies, though only seven made it to adulthood, one of them being my mother, Emma. Mother. One of seven siblings. Another revelation to digest. Parted only by Samuel's death in 1913, Grandmother Isabella wore widow's weeds for eleven long years. United in 1924, their graves lie beside each other in Naini Tal. Sad, we never met.

I paused, letter in hand. I wished I had known her, and heard her stories.

"I'll place some flowers there some day," I promised, before reading on.

Within a year of their marriage Samuel's indentured service was up. The "Queen's Shilling" repaid in full, Samuel was at last free to resign his commission, free to follow his true vocation—serve God, become a missionary in the Episcopalian Church, free to spend every available minute of every day, and night with his beloved bride. Isabella fell pregnant. Samuel, now The Reverend Samuel Knowles, affectionately called Brother Knowles, took up his first appointment at the garrison chapel on the outskirts of Meerut, one of Britain's largest garrison towns in India.

Just before the birth of their first child, a boy they named Arthur, they moved from the shelter of the Army Lines to a European Compound in the Civilian Lines across town a couple of miles away. Isabella and Samuel were too engrossed in their work, their charitable projects with the poor, their marriage, a new home, and their darling baby Arthur, to notice the rumbling volcano about to erupt and engulf them in its violence.

An isolated bungalow away from the Army Lines in pre-mutiny Meerut was an unfortunate place to be in May 1857. Sprawled over five miles, the town and cantonment were too large to be enclosed. Laid out in a grid, Meerut's Civilian, Military and "Native" districts were carved into separate sections, known as Lines, each meticulously segregated by race, color, and rank. Civilization ended on the far side of the Race Course abutting a no-man's land which in turn held back a wasteland of smoldering rubbish where pie dogs and orphan children competed for the decaying waste. Beyond lay the local native township's warren of narrow alleyways, shanty homes, shops, and markets, where no foreigner dared venture without an armed guard.

For many months, wild talk of a "chapatti"—an unleavened flat bread—and strange rumors circulated through Meerut's bazaars that the one-hundred-year British rule was over.

"When chapatti come—time Ferengez die. Raj, finished."

"All become red," the servants whispered.

Like the other foreigners, the British, both civilian and military, ignored the omens with a dismissive "Preposterous. Unthinkable. What? Leave

India? Never, by Jove."

Unfortunately for them, Samuel and Isabella weren't listening either. There'd been rumors before. There'd be rumors again. Rumors, though disturbing, were "just talk," Samuel reassured Isabella. "Just another regional uprising, easily quashed."

But there was no containing the tinderbox when it exploded on May 9th, 1857.

A consignment of grease-wrapped bullets for the new issue Enfield rifles arrived from England. Rumors spread, even before the shipment was unpacked from the crates and issued to the *sepoy* troops.

"The Christian pigs, the British dogs deliberately mixed pork and beef fat and coated the bullets to defile both Hindus and Muslims. By unwrapping the bullets with our teeth and handling them to load our rifles, the purity of our caste will be destroyed, and we'll become unclean, untouchable."

"A sacrilegious plot." The *sepoys'* outrage exploded.

Falling like dominoes, the unstoppable chatter spread from one horrified ear to another.

Explanations came too late. Reassurance of no avail, the damage was done.

At parade on May 8th, the Commanding Officer, Colonel Carmichael-Smyth ordered the ninety *sepoys* of the Bengal Native Infantry to load the new grease-wrapped bullets into their muskets for firing drill. Once. Twice, and for a final third time. Only five men obeyed.

At first loud whisperings passed between the men, then confused shouts of horror. Their anger rose to fever pitch. All eighty-five men laid down their muskets on the dusty ground in a final act of defiance to protect God's laws, their caste, their culture.

Even at this stage, tragedy could have been averted. Instead, the British Command compounded the insult with unsurpassed stupidity.

"Downright mutiny. Insubordination will not be tolerated. I'll show those blackie-natives who is master. Make an example of the wretches."

Grossly misreading what was at stake, and with a complete lack of understanding of cultural and religious taboos, the short-sighted Colonel decided on a public Court Martial, a public humiliation.

Punishment was harsh, swift and grossly unjust. Next day, on May 9th, the Colonel ordered the entire Garrison to the parade ground. Forced to witness the mutineers' disgrace, over 2,000 British soldiers and nearly 3,000 stone-faced native *sepoys* and men from other Indian regiments stood at attention ringing the parade ground. The eighty-five mutineers marched onto the ground under armed guard to face the huge assembly.

Drums rolling, in full view of the assembled Garrison, Colonel Carmichael-Smyth stripped each man ritually of his rank by physically ripping off buttons and stripes from his prized uniform, cashiering him from the Army.

Worse was to come. A cart equipped with implements of a forge creaked onto the parade ground. Ignoring the mutineers' faithful service (and some had given twenty years) the Colonel meted out prison sentences of from five to ten years. One by one, loyal *sepoy* by loyal *sepoy*, each man in turn stepped forward to be shackled. An iron ring hammered onto each hand and ankle.

There was no compassion. A few months shy of retirement, one lifetime soldier lost his meager pension. The injustice, the degradation, the distressing sight, and the reverberating sound of metal on metal, instead of being the deterrent the Colonel planned, inflamed such anger, an audible roar rippled across the parade ground as the eighty-five men were literally carted away to prison, dishonored, humiliated, clapped in irons. Within hours, every native in every surrounding township knew every detail of the outrage. Boiling fury against the British overflowed, spilling into village after village. Though outright mutiny had not yet broken out, it was this incident, on May 9th, that precipitated it. And the very next day, Sunday, the revolt exploded.

The Indian Mutiny. May 10th, 1857. The First War of Independence. The chapatti arrived.

"Whoa. What a story."

I sat back in my deck chair and my mind, struggling to the present, met the unsettling thought that we, the British, and I myself, might be looked on with resentment as an enemy conqueror, an oppressor even. I had never thought of our British colonies that way. India was part of Britain's history. I always assumed we were welcome benefactors, bringers of progress. I pushed away my doubts. Too late to worry now, I was committed. I looked at the next bundle in my lap neatly tied with blue ribbon. It contained Grandfather's personal account of the outbreak of the Indian Mutiny, the very day and hour. I pulled the bow, took out its precious hand-written pages to read my grandfather's compelling eyewitness account.

Emma Knowles

17

IN HIS OWN WORDS

"The Outbreak of the Indian Mutiny"

Meerut, May 10th, 1857
That fatal Sunday on May 10th 1857 woke us to one of the hottest days in our remembrance. It seemed too hot for the doves to coo, the crows to wrangle, the starlings to wrangle or the monkeys to chatter. The Sadar Bazaar at our back and the native lines in our front seemed as still as the graveyards, while the dust-laden air outside remained as calm and as quiet as when preceding a mighty storm or earthquake. The first intimation we had of coming trouble was that there was no cook to give us our "little Breakfast" and no syce to get our buggy ready for morning service. They had both taken "French Leave" or like rats had run from a doomed house. We found only two servants who proved faithful, our waterman and our sweeper. The former, a young Mohammeden, (sic.) was a son of my father-in law's old water-carrier. This sturdy young fellow rendered me in the field in the most trying circumstances, invaluable service. And so the day wore on past the fierce heat of noon till the bells of old St. John's Church awoke to send their sharp, shrill sound over the Cantonment and reach us in the native lines and there turn into ominous meaning.

We were dressing for church service when we heard firing from the 20th lines and our water-carrier rushed in saying that the 3rd Cavalry had broken from their quarters, primed with native drugs and liquor, some on the bare backs of their horses like so many demons, brandishing their sabers and crying, "Religion. Religion. Kill all the English pigs" and that some of them were wildly galloping our way; and that the whole of the native troops had mutinied and were joined by the city rabble and the riff-raff of the bazaars, burning houses and murdering their European and Eurasian occupants; and then on his knees he said: " I have eaten your salt and cannot betray you. For God's sake, Sir take the Memsahiba and children and fly for your lives to the British lines." Hastily telling my wife to quickly finish dressing and the Christian native nurse to get our baby boy, Arthur, ready, I rushed out onto the verandah that looked towards the huts of the 20th and 11th native regiments to try and see what was really going on. There was a dull, lingering glow in the western sky, and in the gathering dusk I could distinguish that brave gallant veteran, Colonel Pinnis of the 11th mounted, in front of the grim line of the 20th haranguing the mutinous men, when a volley of flame leapt out, and I saw this good soldier fall riddled with bullets and his horse gallop with its empty saddle back to his stable. Then I knew for a certainty that the Great Sepoy war had begun. Running back into the rooms we knelt together, offered a brief prayer, and fled from our house across the fire swept road running through the native lines to the bungalow of Mr. Cootes, bandmaster of the 11th in the compound of which we found timely shelter from the flying bullets and flashing swords of the mutineers. Here we found others collected who had wonderfully escaped cruel death from the sabers of the infuriated 3rd Calvary rebels. The only weapons of defence we had were a muzzle loading shotgun and an infantry officer's sword. We consulted together which way would be the better to take in order to reach the European lines quickly and safely from the pandemonium of rapine and slaughter going on about us. We decided to try and cross the deep, wide ditch at the back of the house and make our way over the plain that stretches on past one of the regimental bazaars to the Carabineer Quarters in the direction of where the railway station now stands. We could hear the shouting and firing drawing forebodingly near, so climbing over the mud wall of the compound among some scrubby bushes, which hid our way of retreat from our searching foes. Two of the women after we got them on top of the mud wall, refused to go down into the yawning trench but danger was too near to stand on any ceremony; so giving each a shove they rolled down like barrels into the shallow water below. They acknowledged afterwards the necessity of such treatment, as they realized how they had been saved from becoming helpless victims to the savage lust and cruelty of maddened mutineers. Our fears now were that we should be attacked or overwhelmed by the armed rabble from the different posts in Cantonments and the Gujars, robbers, let loose from the surrounding ill-affected villages. But we found we had timed our escape before the above-mentioned enemies had full converted the Mutiny from an imaginary thing into an actual fact, though they stood ready for any deed of devilish nature. So it happened that when we passed, in the deepening dusk, a lane that led into a crowded bazaar, an armed mob at its head that seemed prepared to mischief of any kind, allowed us to pass on our way though not without insulting us by calling us Christian Pigs and other vile names; so when we met another ruffian band armed to the teeth coming in from the village for their night's work of murder and plunder, they let us go on without in any way abusing or molesting us; and in like manner, when weary and tired from the journey and depressed by the heat and uncertainty of our condition, we reached the compound of Captain Cookson, Cantonoment magistrate, and saw in the incipient obscurity the guard of sepoys belonging to the 20th Corps turn out. We fully expected them to fire on us and then attempt to bayonet us to death but God's power restrained them as it had mercifully held in check the other gangs intent on our destruction, and we trudged on under our Heavenly Father's protection till we saw the joyful sight of the Carabineer vedettes thrown out for the protection of their own lines and we were passed on into the quarters of the 6th Dragoon where we found kind hospitable shelter for the night.

I wish I could say the same of the next company of fugitives who untimely took our line of retreat, for sad and pitiful to write they were met by a frantic band of rebels and cruelly done to death…

…And so the blood of European men, women and children pitilessly shed by the bazaar rabble, the murder of English women outraged and mutilated, the slaughter of little children impaled on sepoy bayonets or hacked to pieces by police swords, all went unavenged that night… Oh how the heroic officers of the Carabineers and Rifles fumed, fretting on the parade ground restless and eager to be led against the wretches whose hands were red with the blood of their slaughtered countrymen, pleaded for an order to pursue the mutineers, but all in vain. Nothing in heaven or hell could move the two indolent, incapable officers on command to timely action; one old, obese, stereotyped old General and his equally apathetic, terrified Brigadier. It was more than a fatal blunder. It was a shameful crime. So said everyone in Meerut Military Quarters that night; except the two responsible commanders, the one taking refuge in his easy chair and the other behind his piles of red tape.

But we must return to our helpless selves in the Carabineers' lines, outcast from our comfortable home and deprived of all the usual means of making the excessive heat bearable and life tolerable; and though the Quarter master and his good wife who gave us shelter and all the help they could under the circumstances; but everything and everybody were unsettled and restless, and all night long there were noisy commotions and firing of native guns and mines all round the Cantonments and frequent alarms that thousands of gujars were about to attack the lines while the great body of troops were absent, and murder all left irrespective of age or sex…

So on the early morning of the 11th we determined to try and make our way to the Artillery lines at the extreme end of the Cantonments to the east where we had dear, religious friends and whom we knew would gladly take us in and give us shelter if they possibly could. We started from the Carbineer quarters and found our way to the wide, beautiful Mall that runs for three miles under a fine avenue of trees east and west through the station. Leading off this promenade are a number of roads and when we reached the end of the Mall out of one of them, two badmaashes armed with talwars, a kind of sword, sprang over the mud wall of a compound on the opposite side of the road and rushed to assail us. I had the Infantry officer's sword ready in my hand, and springing in front of my wife and nurse with my child, I stood on the defensive. I felt quite cool as I warded off a blow of the ruffian and ran him through the breast. The other brute had made a cut at the nurse and baby but the brave woman guarded the child with an umbrella and saved our baby and herself from the full effects of the savage stroke, but they were both slightly wounded. As this badmaash turned to come at me, providentially a shout quite near was heard and the rebel rolled in the dust with a bullet through his brain. A rifle patrol had come up just in time to rescue us. After the gallant sergeant and his men had cast the corpses of the two would be assassins into an adjoining ditch, they escorted us to our destination. When we arrived, we found the house empty but their loyal chaukidar, watchman, told us where to find them in the greater safety of the Artillery hospital. By this time we were all hungry, sick and sore, the dear wife utterly tired out, the poor nurse crying from the cut on her hand and our darling boy, Arthur was in high fever, not so much from the gash on his little shoulder which we had bound up the best way we could, but we fear in the fight with the two badmaashes his head must have been exposed to the fierce morning rays of an Indian May sun. However we rested in the cool verandah of the house and sought comfort in prayer and were fed on milk and hot baked cakes by the generous, chaukidar from his morning meal. Then we took courage and finding the hospital was not far away we again started forth to reach it. We arrived there in a short time, though we suffered much from the excessive heat on the way… But that night of the 11th was a sorrowful night for us. We found that our darling boy had received a baneful touch of the sun, and this combined with his lack of proper nourishment and the trying night before, his exposure to the noxious air and his inflamed wound, brought on high fever that could not be lowered. At midnight our precious boy passed away from his mother's loving arms to rest forever in his Great Redeemer's bosom.

My hand holding the account dropped to my lap. Saddened by the enormity of such a tragedy, my eyes escaped into infinity along the lengthening shadows between the dunes beyond the canal's reddening waters in the sunset. Though seventy years had passed, I felt my grandparents' pain. Baby Arthur would have been Mother's eldest brother had he lived. I sat awhile, before peering inside the envelope hoping to find something of Mother herself—but there was nothing, not one scrap of information.

With nothing left of the lives they'd known before their harrowing escape, their baby Arthur dead, their home and church destroyed, staying on in Meerut was too painful to bear. My grandparents Samuel and Isabella left. For the next seven or eight years they moved from one Episcopal posting to another within the area northeast of Delhi, and replaced their "darling boy" with as many children as nature allowed. Some died, some lived, and by the time they decided to found their own Mission, the count was five. Isabella was pregnant again and the birth imminent.

It was time to put down roots, settle in one place and devote themselves to their missionary work in earnest. So with Horace, Elizabeth, Percival, Katharine, and Jimmy in tow, they set off for the Terai foothills in the wild Gonda district to bring God to the Taroo people.

They planned to entice the Taroo Indians from the Terai jungle with promises of education, a clinic, and "Angleezi" medicine. In exchange, the Taroo would agree to convert to Christianity and build a House for God. That complete, and only then, my grandparents would build a house for themselves. They stayed for twenty years, until they retired to nearby Bareilly.

"Samuel Knowles, beloved and respected, Brother." His glowing obituaries recount his achievement, devotion and scholarship.

Visiting Gonda at the end of my first year's posting to Fyzabad, I discovered the church he built still bore his name.

Isabella and Rev. Samuel Knowles

18
SKELETONS

"A missionary's daughter born in the ruins of a Hindu Temple on the outskirts of the Terai jungle in a small village called Gonda in 1866."

Yes, yes, yes, I knew the family legend backwards. I'd heard it all my life—that, and that her missionary father, Samuel, built a church and devoted his life to the Taroo people.

My grandfather was known as Brother Knowles by the time he and my heavily pregnant grandmother rode into the mud village of Gonda with all thier worldly goods, trailing a string of five children. Perhaps from compassion, the Taroo headsman allowed them to set up a makeshift home in the abandoned ruins of a temple on the outskirts of the village. After sweeping out mounds of bat droppings and untidy rodent nests, the family spread their belongings deep inside the thick walls beyond reach of the monsoon rains, under a corner still covered by a fragment of roof, just two days before Isabella went into labor.

"Like Our Lord Jesus in his stable," they joked.

On May 6th, 1866, Emma May, my mother, keened her arrival with a searing cry on the ruins of the temple's floor. Healthy and strong, unaffected by dirt, heat, scorpions and poisonous snakes, Emma lived the rest of her life as it began—a survivor.

The mud courtyards and narrow alleyways of Gonda, its fields, its irrigation ditches hacked from the surrounding jungle, and the spreading branches of the giant banyan near her home became Emma's playgrounds. Despite her parents' disapproval, Emma shook out her thick, jet-black hair, kicked off her shoes, and ran with the unclothed children of the Taroo. She was more circumspect around her parents and her siblings, demure even.

Visitors were rare. The few local Anglos and foreigners lived clustered around Bareilly and Naini Tal over fifty miles away. With no society dinner parties or recitals to dress for, and with nowhere to practice social skills, Emma spurned the crinolines and bonnets of her English peers. She was seventeen, suntanned, unladylike and fast growing too unruly to be marriageable. Her parents intensified their search for a suitable mate from the small pool of men with what little money they could afford for her dowry. They landed a perfect match.

William Harrison, a judge in the Indian Political Service, contracted to marry Emma. Though he was older and set in his ways, he was kindly, good looking, and a "gentleman of means." Emma couldn't say it was love, but she liked him well enough, and his flattering attention made her blush.

"Passion will come later as it did for your father and me," her mother, Isabella, reassured her.

Liking him would do for the present. Emma married him.

Mrs. William Harrison, the Judge's wife. Emma role-played Mistress of the House and quickly mastered how to manage his large bungalow with its sixteen servants, and play the accomplished hostess to his friends. She played dress-up and filled her wardrobe with clothes and jewels. She "did her duty," her arms about him. Staring at the ceiling from beneath her sweating husband, she counted flies above their bed while sighing fake pleasure, glad he could not see the passion missing in her eyes.

Though William showered her with whatever she fancied, Emma was bored. When William was gone, she had no one to talk to. When he came home, she had to play the wife rather than be herself.

"If I sit one more evening listening to your stuffy friends, I'll scream," she threatened.

He took her for carriage drives in the evenings hoping to amuse her. He gave her Chestnut, a two-year-old mare from his stable. But her sparkle stayed dimmed. It wasn't until her boys, William Junior and Maitland, were born, that the walls of her house brightened with the noisy happiness she'd known in her own childhood.

"It's not seemly, Emma, for a *memsahib* to look after her children. *Ayahs* are hired for that." Her husband admonished after she shooed the *ayahs* away for wanting to play with her children alone. Emma didn't embroider, wasn't allowed to cook, to garden, or groom Chestnut. Every task of interest to her was either unsuitable or the servants' job.

"I'm no more than an ornament to you. In future I shall accompany you on Judicial Circuit and take an interest in your work," Emma declared one morning at breakfast. "Besides, Chestnut and I both need the exercise."

Emma spoke so fiercely, William caved in.

"I haven't said I agree, but if I do," he evaded, "then I expect you to ride sidesaddle and appropriately attired like a lady."

"Yes, William." It was a small price to pay.

Emma, William's perfect queen, primly seated on Chestnut, trotted beside him, prettily veiled against the flies, ladylike in a striking, well-tailored dark green habit, button boots, a jaunty hat and white kid gloves, and sporting an ivory-handled riding crop and silver spurs. William, her proud knight on his lively Arabian stallion, pranced beside his bride.

The great distances between village courts on William's Circuit meant journeying weeks at a time. Lack of home comforts didn't bother a country girl from Gonda like Emma. The countryside and small villages reminded her of home.

"Oh. Look, William…do you see…?"

Emma pointed out the minutest details; pug marks of panther and tiger impressed in the dust or river mud, cloven tracks of deer, upturned divots of earth where a boar had grubbed for roots, the flash of blue as a peacock trailed his magnificent feathers across an open clearing, or a movement of the grasses where a shy snake slithered out of sight. She named the trees and flowers, mahogany, teak, mango, flame, deodar, golden datura with its dangling bells, and scented jasmine's tumbling vines. Away from home Emma bubbled.

The two figureheads and their retinue emerged from the dusty heat haze—plumed, turbaned house-servants, *syces* for the horses, cooks, and a cavalcade of mules laden with the paraphernalia of an *angreezi* camp orchestrated to command awe. Bowing to greet them stood the *thulsidar*, the village headman, offering heavy scented garlands, glasses of hot buffalo milky tea and sweetmeats.

The ritual over, with much stick waving to show his authority, the *thulsidar* thrust back the inquisitive villagers. He escorted the procession to their campsite under the village banyan tree's multi-pillared cathedral created by earthward seeking roots sprouting from its outstretched limbs. In minutes, the servants had the main tent up, its carpet laid and furniture arranged—beds, chairs, table, lamp—and a separate washroom tent complete with thunder-box, bath and washbasin.

"Away with you. Step back." William dismissed the crowd of onlookers, ushered Emma inside, firmly securing the flaps.

Since the 1700s when the East India Company first set foot in India and imposed Colonial law, the system of open-air courtrooms had remained unchanged. There was the British Judge, representing the Might of Imperial Justice in a curly grey wig and red robe, with two servants beside him, one flicking a horsetail whisk to keep insects from settling on the important *Sahib*'s face, and the other waving a wand of peacock-feathers to cool his temper in the sultry air. Seated in the shade of the majestic tree at a wooden table, quoting the Magna Carta, William, like his predecessors, pronounced judgment on land disputes, petty theft, and broken vows, and put right the honor of dishonored husbands and abused women. Petitioners sometimes walked for days, and spent unending hours patiently squatting, waiting to have their cases heard.

"All stand. Court in session."

It was Emma's chance—a few hours to herself. Like a greyhound let from a trap, she loosened her stays, jumped astride Chestnut and streaked for the jungle before the servants could follow. Out of sight she dismounted, and discarding her hat and boots leaned against a tree, face tipped, drinking the light dappling through the leaves. Solitude. Inhaling long and deep, she sighed her dreams and longings for her Gonda. She missed her parents and her siblings. She missed her Taroo friends. William limited her visits to once a year. Other than during that brief visit, and accompanying William on occasional Circuit, she was homebound until her annual hot-weather escape to the hills with her boys for the season.

From May to September, work shimmered to a stop. Only men stayed put in the plains. Believing the cauldron heat dangerous for the "fairer sex," leaving them prone to heatstroke, cholera, malaria, jaundice and other debilitating diseases, even death, the men packed off their women and children to the hills. Born and brought up in the humid jungle heat, Emma was used to that. Her problem was the contraint of William's four walls.

Never dry, their bodies ran with sweat. Blocks of ice in iceboxes melted to useless puddles. The eyelids of the *punka-wallahs* fluttered closed, their hands, feet and toes attached by string to the *punka* stilled, and the wet grass mats drooped motionless from the ceiling, until angry shouts from William and Emma startled the heat-drowsy *punka-wallahs* at their posts outside the windows along the verandah to get pulling again. Her own, her husband's, the servants' tempers flared.

"I declare," said Emma, "it's time I took the children to the hills."

Summerhouses in the Himalayan foothills were only partly furnished. Besides her vast personal wardrobe, Emma needed a complete set of household items. For weeks their bungalow erupted into a chaotic sea—blue tissue paper, green baize bags, and Emma fussing overseeing the servants liberally sprinkling cloves, cinnamon sticks and black peppercorns into each crate, trunk and bag to deter moths and bugs. Vicious curved sewing needles stitched shut countless flaps of hemp-burlap. Globs of red wax, impressed with the Judge's crest, doubly ensured everything tamper-proof. Only then did Emma permit the crates out of her sight in the charge of a small contingent of servants who traveled ahead to unpack them and ready the bungalow for their arrival. The annual upheaval was a part of a *memsahib's* life.

With a wave to her husband, Emma and her children settled into their private carriage on the train. An *ayah* for each boy, a maid for the *memsahib*, a cook and a sweeper-boy, the servants traveled separately behind their *angreezi* charges on slatted wooden benches in an interconnecting, open-sided compartment. Massive blocks of ice sprinkled with sawdust to slow evaporation were loaded in wooden crates into Emma's carriage at each station. Though the feeble vapor rising from them barely lowered the inferno's temperature, somehow, their very presence cooled the sun's cruel rays probing between the wooden slats of the darkened carriage. The glazed-cotton blinds remained buttoned to the lower windowsill by a leather tab.

The train rides of my mother's time, and my own thirty years later, were virtually the same; the ineffectual ice-blocks, heat, soot, the sweat-drenched nights on a bedding roll, the lurching train stop-starting taking on water and coal, the third-class passengers clamoring for a place, the hourly disturbance of the Station Master's shrill whistle, the hooting of the engine, and being nearly catapulted onto the carriage floor each time the train lurched to a grinding halt, made sleep impossible—flavors of the Indian Railways to treasure.

The train chugged laboriously upwards through pine-covered slopes towards its final destination. The scented air told Emma journey's end was in sight. Late afternoon the second day, the train struck the railhead buffers with one last jolt before disgorging its travel-worn passengers onto the wooden platform that served as a station.

A disheveled Emma and the boys dismounted to the welcoming *salaams* of their servants. An open pony-rickshaw stood ready for the final leg of the journey.

The station behind them, and the bustling bazaar gone, the cooler air and the scent of fir cones sparked them alert. Twisting excitedly left and right, the boys and Emma took in their new surroundings—the row of hotels and guest-houses teetering on the edge of a seven-thousand-foot drop, the towering Himalayan peaks floating unseen in heavy cloud on the "up" side of the dirt track hidden above them, and the bungalows nestled in the rhododendron and deodar tree-lined suburb clustered about the gates of the Third Gurkha's Hill Station. The *rickshaw-wallah* turned into the driveway of their summer bungalow. Emma read out the name nailed to the gatepost, "Shangri-La."

I am not certain which Hill Station my mother went to that year in 1896—either Lansdowne, Raniket or Almora—each one built by Central Command half a century earlier to give the mountainous Nepalese Gurkhas a feel of home. Abandoned for five, six, sometimes seven months of winter, the Hill Stations slept beneath deep snow until spring, until the wail of regimental bagpipes roused them from their slumber. Every hotel, shop and business flung wide its shutters. A fairy ring of shanty market stalls mushroomed round the railhead. *Memsahibs*, their children, *ayahs,* servants, and the ever-hopeful "fishing fleet" of unmarried girls tagged close behind. Music, balls, dinners, polo, cricket, picnic, card and children's parties, sprung the Hill Station into an endless round of merrymaking.

Emma protected her reputation as a respectable married woman by taking a friend, Mrs. Hannah Marshall, with her as chaperone to parties. But Mrs. M., either blind, complicit, or having too good a time herself, failed to keep Emma in check. Trouble loomed in the guise of my father, Hugh Rose, a handsome young officer of the Third Gurkha Rifles.

If Emma had only known her future, she might have resisted temptation and clung more faithfully to her marriage vows. But she was headstrong and thirsty for life. She nipped in her waist, lowered her neckline and donned her prettiest dresses. She wanted fun, a lot of fun. My father did too. A young man, a young woman, both on the loose hoping for romance, the dangerous equation resulted in the inevitable. They found ways to be alone together.

I turn the picture to the wall, the picture of my mother hurriedly unlacing her stays, the flurry of falling silks, the lifting of petticoats, their wild, passionate affair. It is nothing I want to dwell on. My mother, the mother I knew, was a rather joyless, fanatically religious Victorian, not the fun-loving young Emma of then. Mother kept that woman locked out of sight. I wish I'd glimpsed her.

The heat of the plains abated, heralding the end of the season. Emma returned to her husband—her belly swollen with a child who could not be his.

What passed between William and Emma when William discovered she was pregnant remains private. Perhaps their marriage floundered—became one in name only. Maybe young Emma pined for her lover, my father. Maybe she swore undying love in passionate letters with stories of their expected child. Maybe her husband and she rebuilt trust in their marriage again. History doesn't relate what painful struggles raged behind their bedroom door, only that William forgave his Emma and agreed to bring up Astel as his son and to be a brother to William Junior and Maitland.

The following hot season, Emma went to the hills. Her lover happened there too. She fell pregnant again—conceived my sister Rita. Cuckolded twice—no. This, her poor husband could not forgive.

"I must give you your freedom. Go." He locked himself inside his study.

William put her on a ship bound for England before Emma could shame him again, and banished her from India.

"No letters, no presents, no messages. You no longer exist. Your name will never again be uttered in this house. Any contact with the boys, I forbid," he added, his face iron hard.

Her parents, as harsh, stuck to their unforgiving religious principles. Isabella and Samuel excised their daughter from their lives, never to contact her again.

"Gangrene. The limb must be amputated." And Emma was.

And so in 1898, Emma kissed her beloved sons, Maitland and William Junior for the last time. Wrenched from her home and all she had ever loved, her children, her parents, her siblings, and the sun-kissed land of her birth, she sailed for England with two year-old Astel by her side and a baby in her belly. All her life a refugee, separated from her lover, she pined for her lost India, her own family, her boys from her first marriage, the kindly adoring husband William whom she had abandoned, the easy life she once enjoyed, with its wealth of servants, its carriages, her horse Chestnut, the sun—all sacrificed for love of a man who, hating domesticity, abandoned her. Though their enforced two-year separations unglued their passion, Father did finally make her an "honest woman."

Motherless in India. William Junior and Maitland, the half-brothers I never knew—their story.

There one day. Gone the next. No preparation. No goodbyes. Their darling mother, Emma, vanished—her abandonment never explained, nor the reason for their father's locked study door shutting them out.

"You have no mother now. I forbid you to speak her name."

Obedient, Maitland and William Junior never did. Bereft, their private agony, their unspoken grieving unstoppable, love froze. Loss, abandonment, grief claimed their toll in different ways.

Emma's betrayal festered like a mortal wound. William's health deteriorated so seriously and rapidly he was unable, or unwilling to look after his two sons. He reluctantly placed them in an Indian orphanage. Two years passed before William's unmarried sister, Caroline, rescued them and took them to live with her in British Columbia, Canada.

William Junior and Maitland both returned to India briefly as officers with the Gurkha Rifles, the very same regiment as both mine and Father's.

That we had likely served side by side and met unaware, that we shared our mother's womb not knowing we were half-brothers, disturbs me still today. Was shame so powerful it overruled Mother's acknowledging their existence to us, her second family? So many years had passed after leaving India, by the time I discovered their existence, faces and places had long since blurred. Though I've scoured my regimental photographs for a likeness, I cannot be certain we met. I like to think we did, and posed unsuspecting, proudly side-by-side. I so wish we could have known each other, had exchanged letters, healed the wounds, and embraced.

After Mother died, a letter arrived from a stranger, asking if the Emma Rose, née Knowles, listed in the London Times "Deaths" column could be her husband's long-lost grandmother. And so, through the telephone and letters, we both discovered the jigsaw piece that completed our family's puzzle.

"I don't even know her name." The woman's sadness whispered down the wire.

"Emma May. It's Emma." I told her.

No one in the family could imagine what terrible event had made William Harrison place his sons in an orphanage. Neither Maitland nor William would speak of her, the woman confided.

"Great Uncle Bill, and Maitland, my mother-in-law, Mary's step-father-in-law, stiffen, looking haunted when we probe. It's awful seeing them so sad. I've taken it upon myself to unravel the mystery, the explanation for their cruel abandonment. Was their—your—mother so bad a woman—a victim herself? I ask, not to make her wrong but to understand. Uncle Bill, William Junior, never married. There were rumors, suspicions.... A sensitive man, a wonderful and skilled watercolorist." The word homosexual hung unuttered.

She paused, "Maitland never had children of his own. He married my husband's grandmother, Daisy, a widow he met in Kootenay's National Park in Canada in 1932, and brought up her child, my mother-in-law, as his daughter."

Together we shared the specters rising from Mother's journals and papers hidden in the tin trunk under her bed. Her careful spidery gothic script corroborated the new revelations. My how-why-who-questions spilled, begging answers, details of my mother's first husband, William Harrison, the judge.

"His grief was so great William's health suffered, and he was unable to function. That's why he put William and Maitland in the Indian orphanage. He retired soon after and returned home to England. He died a few years later in 1903...in Ramsgate." The stranger's voice continued down the phone, excusing him.

"Ramsgate? My mother, Emma, lived out her last years in Eastbourne barely fifty miles from him."

We both fell silent. So near and yet so far, both of them so old and lonely, both mourning, perhaps regretting lives that could have been, neither knowing of the other's proximity. If only.... What if they had reunited? But they never did. Perhaps luckily for Mother, she died ignorant of how her first-borns', Maitland's and William's, suffering had been compounded.

Did Father comprehend what ruin he caused? Fury rising, I slammed the exclamation key and caused my Remington typewriter to seize. Surely, he must have recognized their names, "Harrison," seen Mother's face mirrored in theirs, and realized whose sons they were. Did remorse trouble the philandering cad—guilt, for having robbed them of their mother, for orphaning two boys? Sipping his evening *burra* peg, two fingers of whisky served on a silver salver by a bowing, turbaned bearer, did he give their tragedies a thought, the glaring disparity between his life—theirs—ours, his family, juggling francs and cents?

Tight-lipped, I took a deep breath, changed the ribbon on my typewriter. Ink flowed, anger gradually diminished. Perhaps merely spoiled, selfish, Father never meant deliberate harm. I caught myself. I too had dragged my own young children from their mother's arms, forbade mention of her name. Who was I to judge? No different—my footprint, his—uncomfortably similar. I was more like him than I cared to admit, my behavior, lifestyle—the Colonial way. Lifting glass to lip was all a *sahib* was expected to do. If I dropped my hankie in India, I never picked it up, I wanted a drink, a servant fetched it. Was I as callous, cavalier and arrogant?

Strange—history cruelly repeated itself in me way along my time line. My mother, my first wife—adulterers both. Towards one I felt sympathy, the other, none. Cuckolded, my wife's lover sired a child during our marriage. Was abandonment encoded in our family genes? Mother's first husband kept his boys, then placed them in an orphanage, I, too, kept my children from their mother then placed them in a Holiday Home, a "paying orphanage," for almost five years.

By some ironic karmic twist, I atoned for my mother's sin.

Wedding of George Knowles. Bareilly.

19

"CONSTANT AND TRUE"

Rose Clan Motto

The dinner bugle catapulted me from my deck chair. It was already dark; I must have snoozed. I groped my way to the Mess and joined my friends already seated.

"Here comes the recluse," they joshed me.

Too caught up in my grandfather's account of the Indian Mutiny and Mother's secrets, I didn't reply. Curled up on my bunk that night, sleepless, open-eyed, I ran my father's reel, my mind running.

"Constant and True." The Rose coat of arms proclaims.

I though back to the generations of Roses who served in India. I was the fifth. All firstborn sons are christened Hugh or Hew, all firstborn daughters, Elizabeth. If I had children, I vowed to name my daughter Elizabeth, and my son, Hugh Michael. I am Hugh, my father is Hugh, his father was Hugh and his father before him and so on, back and back to the time of Robert the Bruce, according to myth.

I took the train to Inverness, Scotland, to see the Rose Clan's Family Seat for myself.

Protruding from the high tower, the scraggy stems of Kilravock's fabled rosebush struggled from the mortar between the granite stones below me.

"If the rosebush blooms, the heir will die. Is that true?" I asked Elizabeth, the current Laird showing me around the castle.

"Superstitious nonsense, nothing more." She looked at me sharply, and pointed out the beautiful gardens and the parkland around the lake to later explore on my own.

Elizabeth Rose had taken to religion like my mother and converted Kilravock Castle to a Guest House for Christian Women.

I gazed over Kilravock's crenellated battlements to Cawdor Castle, of Macbeth fame, brooding darkly in the distance above a stand of trees. Just then a gust of wind flapped my Hunting Rose tartan tie against my face. Straightening it in place, it struck me how its woven greens mirrored the surrounding parkland. Similarly, I supposed, the red and oranges of our dress tartan were reflections of Scotland's blazing summer sunsets and her purple moorland heathers. I traced my finger along the tartan's double white lines that told our ancient origins. Laird of all, surveying my fiefdom, I fantasized. But my line of the Roses descended from a minor offshoot of a younger son. I once half-heartedly tried to prove the true line of descent was through my father, and so upset Elizabeth she has treated me as an upstart ever since.

As a child trapped in the circle around the dining table, I listened as Father regaled the family with tales of his ancestors to teach us the clan's history.

"The Roses are Highland people, different, more bloodthirsty than their lowland brethren. Roses have occupied Kilravock Castle continuously since the 11th century."

Despite its impenetrable tower, deep dungeon and beautiful grounds, the castle is no more than a large fortified house.

"Our family seat," he would boast and then recount the family legend.

"The Roses hid King Charles I in a hollow oak tree on the grounds, I'll have you know. Saved him from the Roundheads, and in gratitude he gave the Laird his signet ring."

Another legend told of Queen Mary's visit from Balmoral, and of her commandeering a family snuffbox by deliberately admiring it, which protocol demanded must then be presented to her as a gift. Before each subsequent visit, the Laird made sure the most precious of his heirlooms were carefully out of sight. Stories. Stories. Embroidered or true, no matter, we lapped them up and I eagerly looked forward to Father's after-dinner tales.

Mellow with a brandy and cigar, Father leaned back in his chair staring, not at us around the table, but through a cloud of smoke blown towards the ceiling.

"It is our heritage. It's for to you to pass our stories on to each generation.

Now my great-uncle, Sir Hugh Rose, was a brave soldier who saved his family from death by saber, from being run through and left hanging pinned to the wall like coats on hooks."

And so he'd begin. Shivering at his graphic description, I imagined blood dripping, pooling to the floor. Though I knew every word by heart, I could never hear the legend too often. I resolved to be a hero, an adventurer too. But that was then when I was seven or eight. A child's fantasy—I tramped behind my forefathers, my feet firmly implanted in theirs.

Father boomed. An orator couldn't have proclaimed his stories better.

"When Sir Hugh took command of the East Indian Company's army of *sepoys*, a battle of the Indian Mutiny raged. The siege stretched long. The enemy closing in, the Cawnpore massacre was imminent, food and water scarce. People groaned from untended wounds. The stench, the heat…you can only imagine. Capture and death were inevitable. Escape or die. Sir Hugh devised a plan to save his family—disguise. Now, servants caught helping India's *ferengi* enemy risked violent death. Notwithstanding, many remained loyal to their *Sahib* and *Memsahib*, and loved their *sahib*'s children as their own. Hurriedly dressing their charges in native dress, the servants smeared the children's fair skins with boot polish. But their white eyeballs shone and gave them away.

"Stain the *memsahib's* and the children's eyeballs with walnut juice and they will pass as natives," he ordered, "and on no account must they utter a sound."

I imagined the fierce, stinging pain, the terrified silence. Father continued,

"When the sun sank behind the mango trees, and night fell, two servants smuggled family from the battered residence. Laughing and clapping in fake celebration, they processed barefoot, dancing to a hut in the native village. For many fearful days they traveled by foot and bullock cart from safe house to safe house, passing horrifying body after body of the butchered rotting in the sun, before at last reaching safety of the undefeated lines."

How much was truth, how much was fable didn't matter, I swallowed every word. Fact was—Sir Hugh never married, so who the *memsahib* and children were remains a mystery.

Father emphasized not all the British were hated and many servants remained strongly loyal.

"Depended on us, d'y see. Security. A man's employment meant a home for his wife, children and extended family. 'My *memsahib*,' my children, my baby—*hamara baba,* servants vied with neighboring servants as to whose family was the grandest, the best. Kind *ferengi-sahibs,* they protected, the hated they killed. Servants repaid unfairness and brutality with revenge."

Father embarked on another oration—another favorite tale of his and mine.

"Four years after the Maharajah of Jhansi married a beautiful fourteen year-old girl, he died, widowing his bride-queen before she could bear him a child. To keep her throne, the Rani, the queen, quickly adopted a son, and declared him rightful heir of Jhansi. However, the British Governor General of India, Lord Dalhousie, long coveting Jhansi for the British Empire, ruled her claim invalid. He ordered her from Jhansi Fort promising a generous pension. Defiant, the Rani refused, and barricaded herself and her people inside the fortified town, determined to fight to the death and drive the British from their land. Armed with sticks and stones and any weapons they could find, Hindus, Muslims, men, and women, both high and low caste, united to join her rabble army. Attacked and besieged by two brigades, out of water and food, the Jhansi Rani and her band of brave warriors refused to surrender. Two terrible blood-spilled weeks followed in one of the last major battles of the Indian Mutiny."

I waited breathless for the part I liked the best—her escape.

"Then Rani Jhansi, the 'Warrior Queen,' garbed as a man, galloped forth from the fort astride a white horse—bridle reins between her teeth, a scimitar in her hand, her baby strapped to her back. For three years or more, Jhansi Rani evaded capture. Raiding and killing, so invincible was she, the British Native troops believed the gods had sent her to punish them. Her daring deeds reached every ear. India acclaimed her a national heroine, a goddess even, protected by divine powers. Sightings became more and more fanciful. She was seen astride or standing on her white stallion, her long black hair streaking behind her as she rode across the sky. Still only twenty-three, on June 17th, 1858, your great-uncle led his regiment, sabers waving, and cut her down. As she lay wounded, some say she crawled onto her own funeral pyre and lit it herself. Sir Hugh Rose reported she was buried beneath a tamarind tree under the rock of Gwalior where he swore he saw her bones and ashes."

Father ended her story here without mentioning the British wanted no memorial, or that the Warrior Queen's followers stole her body and placed it reverently on a funeral pyre to free her soul. A shrine marks the spot where India's beloved 'Jhansi-Ki-Bai,' an icon of India's independence, fell. Books, films, plays and even a T.V. series celebrate her heroic life, casting Sir Hugh Rose as the archenemy. Supposedly, the dastardly Flashman depicted in George MacDonald Fraser's novels was loosely based on him.

Listening to Father as a child, I glowed with pride, but now I am regretful it was my ancestor who masterminded the capture of India's most flamboyant heroine. Jhansi Rani. The Warrior Queen.

"Remarkable for her beauty, cleverness and perseverance...the most dangerous of all the rebel leaders." I read his report. Rewarded with a knighthood, first promoted to General, Sir Hugh Rose eventually rose to Field Marshal.

I never did get to know my father well, and the little I did, I didn't much like, despite his respected military skills. If Lord Kitchener thought him a brilliant soldier, then I suppose he was. But the Army arrested his career, freezing his promotion—punishment for "behavior unbecoming."

Father's brief, disruptive visits every two years, his disregard for our welfare, and his treatment of Mother were hard for me to forgive. I'd be naïve to suppose he even remained faithful to her.

"Constant and True," the Rose Clan's motto, are not words descriptive of my father.

"Egocentric Philanderer," is the label I pin on his chest.

Perhaps I judge him harshly.

Rose Clan Crest

20

ADEN

"The Arsehole of the British Empire"
Everything Has To Pass Through It

"Whooop. Whooop."

My two days of doing nothing more strenuous than lazing on the deck thinking about my family ended in gentle bump as the *S.S. Assaye* docked in Aden's noisy port, secured by ropes the circumference of a man's leg. Two coal lighters, their Plimsoll marks barely above the waterline, sat anchored nearby waiting for the laborers to swarm aboard and relieve them of their burden. I made out the faded lettering "Cory Brothers." Groups of Somalis stood ready for a day of hot, dirty work of humping heavy sacks, baskets, and buckets to refill our hold with coal. I found the ebony-dark Somalis taller and more handsome than the people in Port Said.

It was just seven in the morning. Everyone already dripped sweat. There was no respite from the heat neither on or below deck. The majority of those who could do so headed for the cooling fans of nearest beer hall in hotels clustered around Aden's Steamer Point. But we Three R's had different plans. We wanted to see an oasis. The very word conjured romantic visions of palms, camels and deep wells. It was a mere forty miles away by train across the desert, we learned. We made for the gangplank. I paused to peer at the now familiar scene of overloaded merchant craft and naked youths shouting from the water, "*Sahib. Sahib. Felus.* Please to throw." Stopping, I searched my pockets for some change.

"Do come along, Rose. You've seen it all before. Buck up." My friends called out. I dragged myself away and hurried to the gangplank.

The beat up taxi-rickshaw we hailed was soon weaving crazily across Steamer Point's crowded streets, somehow skirting the crazy tangle of lorries, bicycles, rickshaws and people. Though the traffic chose whichever side of the road it preferred, by some unwritten law, to which we were not privy, people escaped death by inches. I recoiled from the bombardment of noise, pungent smells, persistent flies and desperate beggars clawing through the open rickshaw. Young and old barefoot human beasts of burden, with nothing or only a ragged shirt to protect their backs, pulled and pushed teetering loads alongside camels, donkeys and mules. Faring better than their human competitors, their bony backbones were protected by blankets.

The train rescued us from Steamer Point's Hieronymus Bosch-like hell, and headed into the silence of Hadramat.

Apart from flocks of goats stripping the thorny scrub and a couple of camels with young herders, there was nothing much to look at. Then nearing Lahej, as though we had crossed a line drawn in the arid ground, we were suddenly in clusters of carefully tended date palms dissected by grids of silver lines where the channeled water caught the light. A yoked ass, poor beast, blindfolded to keep him from getting dizzy, walked from nowhere to nowhere in an endless circle round a well, drawing water. I saw some villagers using makeshift seesaws counterbalanced by heavy rocks tied to one end of a long pole. Rhythmically tipping upwards and down scooping and lifting bucket after bucket of water, the goatskins spilled into the channels. I'd read of wells like these, wells unchanged since Biblical times, but never expected to see them.

Out of a jumble of pink and red bougainvilleas and spindly date palms, the crenellated skyline of the Sultan's magnificent four-storied mud palace rose in classic Arab architectural style, sprouting wind towers and fox-ear corners in a disorderly abstraction of alcoves and carved pillars. White lime-framed windows, the soft brown of the palace's baked mud walls and fan-shaped colored glass panes above the doors, created a strangely beautiful composition, haphazardly unschooled as a child's painting. I had no idea the towers were more than ornamental, and the downdraft they created made even the hottest day bearable.

"Not quite Buckingham Palace." Rathbone opened a slim volume he'd borrowed from the ship's library, *Major Granby's Guide to the History of the East.*

"The palace is the principal residence of His Highness, the Sultan of Lahej. As such, he is awarded a thirteen-gun salute at ceremonial functions," he read.

"Must be an important chap to warrant such a prestigious salute," he added.

"Or Britain badly needs something from him," Rawlings responded sardonically.

Lahej. A hand-painted sign announced we had arrived. No platform; we jumped from our carriage to the dusty ground. The thermometer read 115 degrees Fahrenheit. Colors unified the sun's glare. We had a couple of hours to kill before the down train.

I am not sure how I expected an oasis to be. Not this. No stalls, no hotel, no nomadic caravans of camels. In one glance, I took in the small vegetable market, the palace, and the sun-bleached square. Flies swarmed the sticky dates, and goats roamed among the vendors gleaning anything and everything. Women selling meager produce from baskets on the ground squatted monkey-like, obscured beneath black burqas with only their lower arms and hands visible. We made for the only café, an open-sided *barasti,* a hut of woven palm, and settled on a bench in its shade. Bearded men looked up from their green and red tasseled hookahs, more curious than welcoming as we joined them, but the proprietor was friendly enough. We were intruding, we knew, but it was preferable to wandering aimlessly, being stared at. Mint tea was a safe bet. Hot and sweet, served in tiny gold-rimmed glasses, it was surprisingly refreshing. I ordered a plate of aromatic *samosas* sizzling in coconut oil, but my less adventurous friends refused to even try one, fearing their unseasoned digestions would flip cartwheels. Not mine. *Samosas* stuffed with potato, chili, cumin seed reminded me of Mother's fiery Indian meals at home. My mouth watered.

Neighboring the café, a baker flung discs of dough against the sides of the domed mud oven. Unfazed by its heat, leaning towards the flames he pealed off blackened unleavened flatbread for his customers. Looking at him made me stream with sweat and grab for the sweat-rag round my neck.

An date palm lined avenue led to the palace gates at the top end of the square. Half a dozen men armed with antique rifles lounged beside a pair of bronze cannon observing us from a narrow strip of shade, curved silver swords in their belts. I thought of the Sultan's harem, his women slaves, locked in their stifling, dusty quarters on the other side. Gone–my nineteen-year-old fantasies of gauzy clothing, black eunuchs, and fountains splashing delightfully in flowered gardens scented with jasmine. Nor did the Sultan's famed cavalcade of gold-caped retainers bearing hooded falcons, wearing belts with silver *Kunjis* appear.

Turning back to the square, we were taken aback at the number of men telling amber "worry beads" with one hand, and engrossed as lovers holding hands with the other. It was difficult not to stare.

"Bit over the top, what. Public display and all that...unnatural practices, do you suppose?" Rathbone muttered.

My skin threatened a blush prickling with images of me with Vetter naked in the mountains, and of my boarding school games.

"Train's due. Time to go." I blinkered my memories.

As we walked towards the halt, the ethereal "Scheherazade" call to prayer drifted from the twin minarets of the mosque across the square, softening the oasis. Every man dropped to his knees, head to the ground facing Mecca. Ramrod still, we three the only people standing, I gazed up, blinded by the turquoise-blue tiled dome catching the sun.

No train in sight. To take my mind off the burning heat, I walked over to a monolith standing inside a circle of whitewashed stones. Some kind of memorial, I supposed. Chiseled on a flattened surface, I read, *"To the fallen and the missing in action. To The brave men of the 4th South Wales Borderers Territorial Army. 1915. Lest We Forget."*

I relayed the quote to Rawlings and Rathbone, before joining them in the feathered fringe of shade under a palm tree. I knew little of Aden's and the railway's history. Rawlings opened his guidebook. Finding an entry under *"British Protectorates, Aden and Environs,"* he read, *"Aden was administered from Delhi..."* That was news to me.

Rawlins continued, *"and was first linked to the Lahej Oasis when the Turks built a narrow-gauge railway during the Great War of 1914. In the hopes of liberating Aden from the British, the Turks laid 2,000 miles of rail across the burning desert from Turkey to the Yemen then continued on to Lahej where they set up camp and claimed sovereignty but the welcome they expected was not forthcoming. The Sultan and his people were indifferent to becoming a protectorate of Great Britain. The Sultan ruled his people as he always had. Exhausted from their stupendous effort, and unwilling to struggle further, the Turks gave up any serious attempt of occupation of Aden."*

"Does your guide have anything on the campaign itself? How many lives were lost," I asked.

"Here. *The Aden Campaign. The Brecknocks, the 4th South Wales Borderers,*" Rawlings read on.

"The Aden Campaign, the Phony War, as it was known. The British Garrison and the Turks hatched a gentleman's truce. No fighting weekends. Saber-rattling weekdays. The Turks sent fresh vegetables to their British enemies. The British returned the favor with tinned goods and fresh fish. Both sides saved face and no lives were lost. Britain's politicians put an end to the amicable arrangement, fearing loss of control of the strategic corridor between Lahej and the port of Aden. A batch of raw troops from the Territorial Army were hurriedly dispatched them to reclaim Lahej from the Turks, and end the Gentleman's Truce."

No mention of the death march from which few survived. The minimal reference covered the blunder hiding the shameful waste of lives. The account continued, telling of the pale young men who landed at Steamer Point in the hottest, most humid month when temperatures soared 140 degrees Fahrenheit in the midday sun. Even the Somalis melted. But London ordered the new recruits to march the 40 miles of burning desert to Lahej. Totally unused to either action or the heat, without proper training or protective head gear, and with little back-up support or adequate medical facilities, they fell victim to the horrific heatstroke, searing thirst and fevers.

The needless tragedy, the disgraceful loss of life, the mismanagement by our distant government provoked us into a lively discussion.

"Meddling from the comfort of their armchairs with no notion of what conditions men faced on the ground. What if we were ordered to do something stupid, would we meekly obey, refuse, choose mutiny, risking the brig and even death?" We argued the difficult dilemma. One I hoped never to face.

I marked my mental list to visit the memorial in the walled British Cemetery in Aden.

Ten years later when I was posted to Aden, grisly reminders were still being uncovered by the tide of shifting sand; discarded army boots, empty water canteens, and the brittle, sun-dried carcasses of soldiers, their hands claw-like, their eyes hollow sockets long since picked empty of their succulent morsels.

When the train halted briefly at Khormaksar's small collection of mud dwellings in the middle of nowhere to allow passengers to jump on and off, a herd of wild gazelle crowded the open-sided carriages, cadging cigarettes. Impatient for their tobacco-fix, they tossed their heads and butted their horns against the train's sides, greedily chewing any smokes fed them by the passengers. Trains = people = cigarettes. A Pavlovian response gone haywire, we said.

Back in Aden, we downed a couple of warm beers at the Crescent Hotel before heading to Crater and King Solomon's Reservoirs.

Crater, its very name described itself. Entombed in the bowels of the natural fortress, suddenly cut off from the West, we were defenseless. A series of narrow tunnels cut through the volcanic cone opening to an alien world, the clip-clop of our horse-taxi the only noise. The eerie padding of unshod feet of both camels and men on the beaten earth had me glancing nervously over my shoulder. We were the only Westerners. Unfriendly. People grew quiet and stared. Our exposed knees, our tight clothes were offensively out of place. It was an unpleasant initiation to being a minority resented purely because of my race and what I represented. A quick look around convinced the three of us there was nothing more to interest us and absolutely nothing we wanted to buy. We were ready to leave. But I am glad I saw Crater while it was still raw and unspoiled. Uncivilized, some might say.

On the way back to the dock, our Somali taxi driver regaled us with local legends in broken English.

"Crater was the center of the earth, the Garden of Eden, the site of the

Great Flood, the very spot where Noah in his Ark sailed over the volcano's rim." He rattled on and on. "Ark in very secret place only I know," before slyly questioning, "You like see? Fifty dinars, very cheap price."

"Yes. Take us." Trapped, our raconteur became suddenly vague and uncomprehending.

"Tomorrow. Today no possible." He backed off.

Leaving Crater, he reined the horse-taxi to a sudden halt in the middle of the long, dark tunnel.

"Not move, fifty dinar more. Pay now."

He tried the old trick and refused to go any further. His "Stand and Deliver" scenario was no match for us. We dragged him roughly from the driver's seat, dumped him unceremoniously into the dark passageway, and left him uselessly waving, hurling imaginary rocks, and cursing, "Sons of the devil's mother. Fry in hell." or something of the sort. As in Port Said after our brothel escapade, Rathbone snatched up the reins. Furious echoed curses bounced off the tunnel's walls.

"So-n-s-o'-dev-ils- mo-thererrr fuckeeeer."

My dreams that night were a confusion of grown men in white, *dish-dash* nightshirts holding hands, *Imams* calling the faithful to prayer, and of struggling for a resting place in the Ark between a hundred animal legs, while Noah shook his finger warning of unnatural practices, and quoted an Arab saying, (or was it Persian?) I'd overheard in the Mess. Even as I slept I blushed.

"A woman for duty, a boy for pleasure, but for sheer delight, a ripe watermelon."

If my dreams had been prophetic I would have seen myself back in Aden within ten years, seconded from the Army into the Political Foreign Service. I would have seen the Admiral's walled garden I created during my posting there, heard the cooling fountains splashing, and inhaled the vibrant scented jasmine, gardenias, and roses of its refuge. I'd have seen...But no, I was in the desolate present, tossing sleepless in my bunk, unaware of what kind of footprint I'd add to my forefathers'.

Throbbing engines disturbed my sleep. The *S.S. Assaye* picked up speed and turned her bow east. The last leg of my journey began. Next morning I awoke to find myself far out to sea. India would soon be a reality.

Hadramat

Sultan's Palace. Mukullah.

II

THE SECOND CHAPTER IN MY LIFE

1920-1930

PROLOGUE

with scant hope of material gain we went
because our fathers served before us
because we had heard the stories of their achievements
in campaigns long forgotten
within the crumbled magnificence of the sub-continent
and of the loyal companionship of her people
the fighting races of India and Nepal
far from home we suffered exile—
dumb witness of our sojourn
broken statues in British graveyards bear testimony
to the children the brides and young men
snatched from life before their natural time
who lie below the barren earth scattered
along the frontiers of an Empire that is no more
the old order submerged now by the new—
we cannot ever tread that road again
but a little honor remains
a few friends may come to speak for us
the few still proud survivors of Imperial India
perhaps it may one day be said we bore ourselves honorably
mankind can only follow the path of its beliefs
we could not do otherwise"

Hugh Vincent Rose

21

BOMBAY

Unsure of my way, I followed faint footprints in the dry earth left by a single line of people trudging relentlessly ahead across a scrubland. I hurried to catch up with them before they disappeared into the tall elephant grass on the far side of the open ground. Before the grasses closed behind them, one by one, each person turned, stretching their open hands towards me, their mouths moving with no sound I could hear. Brandishing an unsheathed sword, their leader, a uniformed soldier, urged them forward. Now closer, I startled, recognizing Grandfathers Hugh and Samuel, Grandmother Isabella, Father, Rita, Aileen, Kathy and Astel with two boys I'd never seen. Lastly, a young woman, her hair unpinned, turned, retracing her steps, her arms out towards me. Before she could touch me, the young woman evaporated, and Mother stood in her place, her green eyes fixed on mine.

Reveille blasting louder than usual brought me out of the dream.

Sweating, I leapt from my bunk. Reveille subsided. Silence. The ship's throbbing engines cut. Bombay. I'd arrived. "All packed, Sir?" An orderly's head appeared round the cabin door.

From the porthole, hurricane lamplight pinpricked the darkness. It was not yet dawn. Hastily pulling on a pair of knife-creased khaki shorts and a freshly ironed shirt, I scurried to join Rathbone and Rawlings breakfasting in the Mess, now eerily silent, the only sounds the slurp-slurping and the rattling teacups.

We checked the cabin one last time. It was time to leave the ship, to disembark. Embark into the real world. Disembark. Embark. I smiled nervously at the play of words, almost sick with anticipation. The others felt the same, I imagined, because as we shook hands and clapped each other roughly on the back agreeing to meet up on our first leave, our voices boomed a little too loud, a little too hearty.

"Splendid idea, old chap. Not seen the last of us yet, Rose."

"The bar at noon, then? Majestic Hotel."

Two orderlies arrived and collected our baggage,

"Ready, Sir?"

A stream of khaki-clad troops pushing and shuffling down the gangway disappeared into the chaotic whirlpool of men searching for their groups on Ballard Pier. Hesitantly, with no idea of how to assemble or how to find my own draft of men, I made for my platoon sergeant who was bellowing directions.

"Enlisted men; assembly-point C7. Leave the men to me, Sir. Officers transport… that sign, there. D. Majestic Hotel." Saluting, pointing, he shooed me out of his way.

As an officer in transit, I was allocated two nights orientation leave on arrival and five days journey leave to get to my posting. A Sapper, a Lancer, and a Gurkha, scattered across the continent from India's most northern frontier bordering China and Afghanistan, to Kaniyakumari, India's southernmost tip—it was unlikely the career paths of us Three R's would cross again.

"Last days of freedom." We joked. "Two days sightseeing to go."

My Majestic Hotel room, though not luxurious by European standards, lived up to the name majestic. In the muted light filtering through the wooden shutters, I made out a single bed beneath a mosquito net, marooned as a ship in a sea of a pink marble, a small mahogany table, two hard-backed chairs, a pair of cane loungers, and isolated on the far wall, a tallboy and a clotheshorse. No hole in the floor, no bucket for bathing, my bathroom boasted a Western lavatory complete with a packet of scratchy interleaved "Jeyes" toilet paper, a porcelain bath, and basin with brass-plated taps that actually produced hot water. A hotel valet carried in my bags, unpacked, and laid out a change of clothes. As soon as the door closed behind him, I checked under the bed—scorpions? snakes?—all eight corners of my suite and bathtub—clear. My first day in India, I excuse myself such silliness.

Downstairs in the hotel lounge I found Rawlings and Rathbone, pink gins in hand.

"Bit of luck, what? Two days courtesy of the Army."

We feigned nonchalance puffing smoke rings, when in truth we were overawed by the grandeur of its marble-pillared lobby, wide sweep of marble staircase, and sensuous statues of dancing women, potted banana trees, and translucent alabaster bowls where gardenia blossoms and lotus flowers floated. A pair of carved basalt elephants guarded the hotel's entrance. A turbaned servant, immaculate in scarlet tunics, hovered to second-guess our every need.

"This is the life," I exclaimed.

"Rather." Rathbone agreed.

Though still hot, we were champing to be off. The doorman hailed a horseless *gharri* to take us to The Gateway of India, the new architectural wonder built in 1924 for King George V's visit. I recognized it from the clipping Father had shown me of its inauguration from the London Times. Moored below its steps, rows of boats bobbed, waiting to ferry visitors across the bay to Elephanta Island. No time, the holy monolith would have to wait.

The driver, clearly new to his motorized vehicle, brass-horned an opening through Bombay's tangled traffic. Honking and hee-hawing at nerve-wracking speed, buses, lorries, rickshaws—everything that moved—"horned," forcing individual passages through the melee leaving no sliver of light showing between oncoming vehicles and our *gharri.*

"Slow. Driver. Slow down."

"Yes, please to horn, *Sahib.*" Misunderstanding our commands he pointed to a lorry. A sign on the back read, "Horn Please."

Deciding he didn't plan on dying, I surrendered.

Unsavory smells and dust enveloped me as we turned into the back streets and made for the fabled Grant Road to see its native and Eurasian prostitutes in cages advertising their favors. I was not prepared for their dull apathy, or the sad, pleading eyes of such young girls. I was ashamed for having thought of them as a sideshow. A beggar reached into the *gharri,* clawing my arm and thrusting his stump and sores. To add to my shame I flinched—with revulsion, not sympathy.

"Turn around, driver."

A few roads distant, the heady scented flowers and salt air of Bombay's Millionaire's Row expunged the foul air of Grant Road and its desperation So this was India, where the wealthy and poor lived within sight of each other.

Next stop Malabar Hill. The car ground up Corniche Road towards the tourist attraction, the Tower of Silence, a ghoulish place of funeral pyres and vultures picking flesh from the bones of the dead. My head swam. With a sudden sense of *déjà vu,* the closer we got, the stronger my certainty I had been there before. Impossible, I knew. Maybe the stench of smoldering corpses misfired my brain cells. Maybe Mother's vivid descriptions of India played so brilliantly in my mind that every detail was familiar.

Reeling from the dreadful scene, we left without stopping.

Rounding a bend, our *gharri* all but slammed into a Rolls Royce skewed across the road, one door hanging by its hinges. Two heavily bejeweled ladies in expensive silk *sarees* were screaming from the back seat and pointing hysterically to a burly Englishman bleeding profusely from several knife wounds. He stood with a golf club raised over three rough-looking men sprawled semi-conscious on the edge of the road. At the very moment we rushed to help, a car of Europeans came up behind us, jumped out and went to calm the women. Rawlings and I staunched the sergeant's wounds with sweat rags snatched from our necks and the driver's *puggri*, turban. Rathbone grabbed the golf club from the wounded Englishman and took over guard.

"Oh. Thank you. Oh. Thank you."

Still trembling and sobbing, the women related how six *badmashes* jumped in front of the car, stunned the driver, yanked the door open and came at them with knives.

"They wanted to drag us out, but he rescued us," they sobbed, pointing to the club-wielding man, Sergeant Kitch, who had happened on the hold-up while driving to the club for a round of golf.

Grabbing a seven iron he had felled three of the gang, and the others had fled.

More help arrived. A lorry transporting a relief shift of constables to the Malabar Hill police appeared. With one glance at the scene, they leapt onto the road, whacked the bewildered criminals unconscious with their bamboo *lathies,* threw them roughly into the back of the lorry, and chained them to its sides. Rathbone and Rawlings drove the hero Sergeant Kitch to hospital in the *gharri*, while I escorted the women home in their Rolls. Home turned out to be a palatial mansion, and the two ladies, Her Royal Highness, the Begum of Indore and her lady-in-waiting.

We spent a couple of hours at the police station next day giving endless statements. The story was, the Begum's husband, the Maharaja, was such a despotic, jealous man, he decided to disfigure his wife to prevent her from ever being unfaithful. He hired the six *badmashes* to waylay her and cut off her nose, the recognized penalty for adultery. The Maharaja's outlandish behavior so enraged the Viceroy and Governor General of India, Lord Reading, he instantly deposed him and installed the Begum's son on the throne.

In gratitude, the Begum sent Sergeant Kitch a Lakh of one hundred thousand rupees. When she discovered Army regulations forbade him accepting such a gift, instead, she presented him with a solid gold cigarette case embossed with the State Coat of Arms and inscribed, *"To my Rescuer, Kitch from his Grateful*

Damsel in Distress. H.R.H. The Begum of Indore."

So ended my first day in India, jangling my sleep with unfamiliar images, flesh-eating vultures, captured maidens, heroic rescuers, and flashing knives. This was no England.

Goddess Durga.

Gateway of India. Bombay.

22
TRAIN TO FYZABAD

Fyzabad? *The 5th Northumberland Fusiliers.* I read my orders again. They were clear: Fyzabad in the United Provinces for a year's attachment to the 5th Northumberland Fusiliers. Not my own Gurkha Regiment? It must be a mistake I supposed. Not so. It was policy, the army's way to allow greenhorns to cut their teeth in relative obscurity and after a year present themselves to their regiment. What did it really matter where I went since everything was a new adventure. And what better introduction to India than a five-day, fifteen-hundred-mile train ride on the Great Indian Peninsula Railway? No. A year with the Northumberland Fusiliers. I could cut my teeth and to boot, they would knock me into a passably professional officer by the time I joined my own regiment, the Queen's Own Alexandra Rifles..

The Delhi train pulled out at six next morning. I settled in a corner by the window, I flinched when two loud-mouthed junior officers stormed my carriage. Nothing Indian escaped their ignorant distain. Pretending a hangover, I pressed my forehead against the glass and stared out of the carriage window. I would see only India's magic. An old-timer, Major Athill, occupied the fourth bunk.

He, too, studiously buried himself in his own thoughts, but noticing me turning to catch every passing scene, he began calling out major features rolling through my moving screen—geography, religion, agriculture, anthropology, architecture and the caste system. Barelegged women, breasts partially exposed, worked alongside men. Others so shy, they covered their faces as the train passed.

I rarely saw an unkempt house or yard. Swept and sprinkled with water, even the poorest dwelling looked tended. Appearing, disappearing, village after village flashed by, oases of mango and palm groves, ruins of ancient cities choked by jungle vines, remnants of large gardens, "Kampani *Baghs,*" Major Athill called them. Ponds of pink lotus blossoms...herons, egrets, hindu temples, mosques and minarets...garish twenty-foot painted effigies of gods and goddesses.

"Lord Shiva. See his trident," Major Athill called. "There, that's Durga, fierce Mother goddess riding her tiger. Now, her, she's a fearsome one. Black Kali—her neck hung with skulls."

A towering Hanuman, the monkey god holding his tail, a bright blue male figure, Krishna, then elephant-headed Ganesh, Nandi, a seated bull calf turned with its face toward a temple. Major Athill reeled off a jumble of names and myths too strange for me to get my head around...the Remover of Obstacles, Ganesh, clasping the tip of his broken tusk.

For the next five days I surrendered to my role of voyeur. The countryside a kaleidoscope, my vision blurred, sharpened, blurred, in forever-changing patterns—I was never bored.

An electric fan blowing onto an open-crated block of ice wafted a faint cooling vapor into the carriage. I thought of Mother's annual train journeys half a century earlier, of her suffering in layered, tightly laced long-sleeved gowns with a servant fanning the cool vapor from blocks of fast-melting ice.

Like Mother, I traveled with a personal servant—she, with a whole entourage to serve her, I, with a quarter-share of Major Athill's Pathan bearer, Ahmed.

Ahmed let down and made up our bunks, laid out fresh clothes, served us *chai* and ensured his *Sahib*'s comfort. Fighting a losing battle against the soot blowing back into our carriage, he leapt, slam shutting the window blinds, whenever the train entered a tunnel. However vigilant his guard, glowing smuts pinpricked our skin and clothing and covered every surface with gritty soot, till by evening we looked like coalminers after a long shift underground.

Ahmed served breakfast—cold *dhal, chappati* and *chai*—bought from rail track vendors running beside the slow-moving train. But for dinner, the train stopped. My companions and I headed for the grand Victorian dining car. Raj-style at its best, it was a mix of elegance and tawdry, ornate rococo gilt and mahogany, velvet curtains, and pink etched glass candelabra. With silver knives and forks, we ate off monogrammed plates set on double damask, and sipped wine served from decanters cradled in silver coasters. Outside through the window lace, I watched sweaty Second Class passengers and coal-smudged British engine drivers dash for the station's refreshment rooms. Third Class fended for themselves on the contents of their *tiffins*, lunch boxes. No meal break for the Indian stokers, no respite for them. They continued shoveling coal and taking on water.

The platforms overflowed with family groups sleeping, cooking, and feasting, surrounded by goats and chickens. Women washed themselves and their naked children from standpipes. Men arced yellow, and defecated onto the rails. Adding to the chaos, food vendors, *chai-wallahs*, and *pani-wallahs* jostled for space weaved in and out of the the crowds toward their frantic, signaling customers. Some carried baskets of banana-leaf wrapped snacks and peanuts. Another balanced a tray of spicy-smelling *samosas* on his head, another juggled a tea-urn, milk, sugar and tin cups. Three men passed my carriage window with *tiffins* of curries, rice and condiments stacked ten, twelve, even fifteen high.

"Pani-wallah."

"Chai-wallah."

"Dood-hai."

Water, tea and milk.

Hypnotic. A bewildering intermingling of color and sound, India exceeded every description I'd ever read.

Ahmed jumped from the train intent on some private mission. I tracked his distinctive khaki turban until he vanished, swallowed by the crowd. An irrational hurry-hurry-the-train-will-leave-without-you-oh-whatever-shall-I-do panic gripped me. The same nine-year-old's terror I experienced in 1914 the time Father disappeared leaving us alone on our rescue ship in Zebrugge. It came again, my fear of being left behind. Anxiety mounting, I kept my eye on the Guard's raised green flag.

"Cutting it a bit fine, Bearer." I grunted disguising my relief.

"Plenty time, *Sahib*, Sir." He smiled, parting red, beetle-nut stained lips and teeth, swinging onto the footplate as the engines, whistling sharp and long, pulled slowly from the station belching warning plumes of smoke.

Major Athill, deep in a book, didn't look up. The two subalterns were wedged into their corners, one, head bowed to his chest, and the other purring, mouth open, head back. Back in my seat, I closed my eyes, lulled by the babble fading from the receding station, and the carriage wheels' "rattle-rat-rattle-rat."

An alarming grinding metal against metal and hiss of steam startled me awake. Suspended in mid-air, the locomotives' powerful engines inched slowly out over a breath-stopping ravine on a wooden bridge so flimsy I expected to be pitched into the raging river far below.

With much shouting and commotion, two extra engines were coupled behind the last carriage before tackling the Western Ghats. Groaning engines' pistons struggled to crank their snaking burden up the zig-zag track towards the mountain pass. We moved so slowly some adventurous passengers jumped off on one arm of the Z-bend, walked across the open ground, and remounted the train on the other.

A group of teenage students leapt from their carriage, and using the train as their wicket, competed to score the most "runs," by touching first a carriage on one side of the bend and then a carriage on the other, egged on by cheering passengers. I was tempted to join them, but no–too un-officer-like I decided.

At last the train topped out. Rock face blasted by Welsh miners half a century earlier hemmed us in a narrow pass, squeezing us through the final tunnel. On the edge of the world we paused, then hurtled down to the plains. Next minute rumbling over the river Dot, we pulled into Delhi's redbrick Victorian Gothic station.

The still-moving carriage door flew open and a horde of coolies stormed our carriage fighting to porter our baggage. Having neither Hindi nor Urdu to control such a crowd, my protests went ignored.

"Whoah. Arret. Basta. Stop." Italian, French, English—horse commands even, I shouted in vain.

My bags vanished. Every piece. Gone too, Major Athill and the two subalterns swallowed in the melee. I was on my own. The railway police came to my rescue, brandishing vicious metal-tipped bamboo *lathies*. In a masterful matter of minutes, I learned my bags were safely stowed on the Calcutta Mail across the platform where its iron engine stood belching sooty smoke getting up steam. I searched for Major Athill. No sight of him, though he was also booked on the Calcutta Mail to Lucknow. I decided to fill my five hours wait and my stomach with a stupendous meal and made my way to the "First Class Only" station restaurant.

Entering, I was surprised to see Major Athill already seated, engrossed in conversation with two companions. He acknowledged me with a nod and smile, but didn't invite me to join him. I would dine alone.

Waiters in traditional shirts-to-the-knees belted with maroon cummerbunds, wearing matching grey pantaloons and turbans displaying a pleated cock's-comb of the same fabric, plied me with coconut fish wrapped in banana leaves, ground mutton *korma*, ladies' fingers, snake-gourd in turmeric sauce, *ghee*-soaked *chapattis*, *dhal* and steaming basmati rice speckled with black mustard seeds, cumin, and cardamom. Cold tankards of beer soothed the spice-fire in my throat. Stuffed, a proper *sahib*, I smiled at the *double entendre.*

Delhi's temples, slums, and mogul Red Fort built in the 1600's disappeared from view. Back on the Calcutta-Lucknow train, I propped my eyes open long enough to take in the red sandstone Qutb Minar Islamic minaret's seventy-two meters, before succumbing. Slumped in the half-light of the shutter-darkened carriage, I snored my way across the plain, and woke only as the train began its slow climb towards the horizon.

For the first time, I saw them, the mountains of my dreams. Craning my neck from the carriage window, I viewed the heavy clouds dissecting the dark Himalayan Range, 200 miles distant. Behind the clouds, invisible, the smell of snow.

It was mid-October. Autumnal mist shrouded the lower foothills and the farmlands. Smoke billowed from boiling sugar-cane vats hugging the fields, signaling the cold weather. Major Athill shared my carriage once again.

"Major, Sir, any idea of the religious significance of the pyramidal cones in the fields?" I questioned.

"Stacked cowpats." Major Athill guffawed. "Local cooking fuel."

To my eye, the sculptural symmetry of the brown discs could grace any art gallery in the world.

"'Bareilly."

"Nainital."

I read the carefully painted signs, recognizing the names. I didn't say a word. My family history was my business. I wondered what Major Athill's reaction would be if he knew of my Indian connection, and that my grandparents, Samuel Knowles and Isabella worked as missionaries in the Terai jungle beyond Bareilly. I pictured my staid mother, her brother Jimmy and her other siblings growing up in this so foreign, foreign country. My pillar-to-post childhood was tame by comparison. I renewed my promise to visit Mother's village. I'd find the Hindu temple ruins where she was born, discover if Grandfather's church still stood, and visit Jimmy, the brother she'd so shyly mentioned before we parted. I couldn't pinpoint the feelings I experienced—the vague glimmer of some connection, a sense of being winched link by link from a mysterious depth. I was getting close. I shivered. I felt my family crowding round.

My mind spun like wheels spun in a nursery rhyme, *"On and on over the tracks, clickety clack, clickety clack..."*

Rolling into Roorkee a few hours later, the train crossed the white sands and gold-flecked waters of the Ganges' holy river sparkling crimson in the setting sun. Holy men in orange *dhotis* stood knee deep in its waters waving flickering lights to Lord Shiva and the Ganga, the Ganges river. The picture hanging in my mind, I slept peacefully until the sound like chalk screeching across a blackboard, the brakes engaged, announcing our pre-dawn arrival in Lucknow.

"All the best, Rose. Pleasure to have made your acquaintance." Major Athill shook my hand firmly. "Don't forget, now, the Pearl Palace, the Turkish Gateway,

Saadat Ali's Tomb and the Begum Hazrat's gardens. Worth a visit if you're inclined." And with a wave, my tour guide was gone.

When I dismounted, my nostrils flared in the unaccustomed higher altitude, my teeth felt cool to my tongue. The sun had not yet risen above the peaks. The Fyzabad train on the branch-line left late afternoon. I had time to explore the once ancient city of the Kings of Oudh, the Lucknow, Major Athill raved about.

"British Club, *Sahib*?" The *tonga* driver assumed. It was a statement rather than a question.

"Pearl Palace. Hurry."

"Nay," I shook my head.

The sky was brightening. I wanted to witness dawn's rays transform the inlaid pearl of Pearl Palace to pinkish gold. "Like a lotus opening petals to the sun." Major Athill had eulogized. He was right. It was a lotus. In awe I watched pearl change to pink and then to gold.

Next, with a flick of the driver's whip and dring of his hand-bell, the horse-drawn *tonga* clip-clopped through the bustling city at a good lick, though not fast enough to prevent swarms of flies from settling on my face and creeping up my nose. By ten, the mud walls edging the streets trapped the heat, and the harsh light erased the buildings' fine details. I sat stupefied under a mulberry tree in the gardens of Begum Hazrat Park too hot to move. But there was still one last stop I had to make, the ruins of the old British Residency.

I dismounted the *tonga*. My throat tightened. The siege, the screams of massacre so horrifically silenced—bullet-scarred, the Residency walls brought the bloody tragedy of 1857 to life. Reminders of the Mutiny's brutality, so visible, caught me by surprise. I stood stiffly to attention, motionless, and instinctively snapped a salute to the Union Jack fluttering over the building.

"BY COMMAND OF QUEEN VICTORIA, EMPRESS OF INDIA TO FOREVER FLY DAY AND NIGHT IN HONOR OF THE SLAIN." I read the plaque.

"Chatell Club," I croaked.

The club, once a palace of the House of Oudh, cocooned me deep within its walls. I shrank quietly into a cane lounger in the corner, recovering. New to India, new to the club, a stranger, I was left to my own company in one of the ornately scrolled and gilded rooms where courtiers had served their Kings. Too many thoughts, too many images running…

Seventy short miles north to Fyzabad, 1,500 miles west from Bombay, the train journey was over.

I stepped onto Fyzabad's platform.

And my journey began. 1924.

23

A YEAR IN FYZABAD

5th Northumberland Fusiliers

"You arrant arse."

My introduction to the 5th Northumberland Fusiliers was painfully swift.

The Senior Subaltern's words stung. Wooden faced, at attention, we new arrivals endured a severe dressing-down for our various misdemeanors.

"And you Rose, told your platoon, all of whom have at least ten years service on you, that 'never in the course of all your service,'–all of a full three weeks–'had you ever seen such a dirty platoon.'"

If my year with the Fusiliers taught me anything, it was that I was indeed an arrant arse, as the subaltern called me, or was it ass? Except for one exciting incident, I discovered soldiering to be a mundane round of parades, drill, paperwork, sports, and learning how to behave as a gentleman *pukka sahib.* Protocol and avoiding pitfalls took precedent. No battles to fight, no swashbuckling leading men to victory. Active Duty? "Inactive" better described my duties.

"Officers and Gentlemen" had much to learn, I discovered my first day.

First ripping us to shreds, the Senior Subaltern of the regiment handed out a daunting list of dos and don'ts. Immature, nineteen, and desperate to be "One of Them," I scribbled meticulously beside each rule.

"One," the Senior Subaltern barked. "White *topees* are worn by station-masters, not gentlemen."

I cringed, relieved I'd not yet worn the *topee* so carefully chosen from the Simon Artz Emporium in Suez only two weeks previously.

"Two. Bombay Bowlers—small khaki pith helmets, standard design, are to be worn at all times."

"Three. Each officer is expected to hire a bicycle and "call" upon everyone on the list provided in this order. First, all three Messes. Second, the Deputy Commissioner. Third, the Civilian policeman and his wife. Last, all other officers and their wives."

"Four. Visiting cards must be engraved, not printed, and conform to regulation size, calligraphy and format." Relief. I had one thing right at least. Father gave me a set as a parting gift.

"Five. The only clubs to be listed on your cards are the "Senior," the United Services Club in Pall Mall, and the Royal Yacht Squadron, Cowes in the Isle of Wight. Their names are to be placed bottom left corner of the card."

My peers and I exchanged glances. None of us could afford membership in either prestigious institution, though I'd occassionally lunched in them with Father.

"Six. Place your visiting cards in the small black box provided at the bottom of each drive marked, 'Not at Home.'"

Back then I knew which corner to turn up to indicate marital status, but I have long since forgotten the "shoulds and should-nots" of such useless information.

"Seven. A uniformed officer must never carry a parcel or other large object. Orderlies, not gentlemen do that."

"Eight. Officers are permitted to carry a regimental crested cane or a polo stick. Nothing else."

"Nine. Mess bills are to be paid punctually. Subalterns may not incur debt over a specified amount for hard liquor. Check your allocation."

"Ten. Never strike a Native, whatever the provocation."

We exchanged glances, shocked it needed saying.

On and on the instructor droned, listing rules governing dress, social behavior and whom we may or may not entertain.

"Eurasian and Indian communities are out of bounds. Mixing is forbidden…"

Prejudice—spoken out loud. I thought a major objective of our being in India was to win over the locals, develop friendships with people from other cultures. I pictured Mother's pale olive skin. It wasn't rosy. It wasn't milky white.

What made a person "mixed" or Eurasian? Mother was Mother. I'd never thought beyond that thought. And me? What was I? I capped my uneasy questions and screwed down the lid.

"Mess kit…must…must not…day…evening…except Sunday…black tie… dinner- jacket…officer…'dine-out'…'dine-in'…guests…ante-room."

I staggered from lunch to my siesta, reeling from too much information determined not to let down my guard. It took me weeks to move easily in my skin without fear of exposing my ignorance, lack of private means, Indian connection, and details of my background. Desperately wanting to conform, I behaved to code regretfully convincing myself I was a member of a superior class, a dominant race. Like my fellow British, I expected Indians passing me in the cantonment or bazaar to *salaam* and step aside with a 'let-me-the-*sahib*-by' attitude. A strutting, arrant arse, I never questioned my arrogance.

I settled into a peacetime soldier's life, Indian Army style. Early morning drill over with and the men dismissed, I strolled to the Mess for a four-course breakfast, pushed a pen around till lunchtime, then took a two-hour siesta to recover from my strenuous day. I wasn't complaining. It was a gentleman's, but hardly the exciting soldier's life I had imagined.

Geoffrey Vaughan, a new subaltern, and I shared one of several bungalows in a three-acre compound in the European "lines." Nestled in flowering trees and shrubs, and pleasant from the outside, it was bachelor-austere within, furnished by the Army. So unforgiving the woven jute of my native wood-framed *charpoy,* and so intrusive Fyzabad's nightly jungle sounds from across the river, I hardly slept for a week. Eerie howling jackals; loud warbling, croaking frogs; incessant, repetitive song of the brain-fever bird; the *chital's* harsh alarm; and ominous sawing of panther tightened every muscle.

At last my eyes fluttered shut. Bloodcurdling hollering and piercing whistle blasts cut the night catapulted me from the *charpoy* and reaching for my pistol.

"All safe, *Sahib.*" The *chowkidar*, the night watchman outside my window, blew his whistle and let out another yell to demonstrate his wakeful diligence in protecting the bungalow from thieves. He nodded uncomprehendingly when I ordered him to desist. He shouted again the next night and the next. It was a requirement of his job, I learned.

As in most of India in the nineteen-twenties, "running" water ran from cans. Every evening before I dined, *bhisti* placed a tin tub before a roaring fire in the living room, then filled it with kerosene tins of boiling hot water carried from the kitchen recalling Father's bath-night tales. Knees bent, belly deliciously warm, submerged in the hot water, I sipped a whisky *chota* peg while listening to the crackling of the fire's resinous pine and watching the giant flickering shadows. I lingered until soap scum settled on the surface and the increasingly tepid water wrinkled my skin forcing me out. Abdul Karim, my personal bearer, a tall, dignified, bearded Moslem, stood post at the door ready to scrub my back, then, eyes averted, handed me a thick towel followed by my clothing, and dressed me as though I was a helpless baby. Keeping conversation formal, after drawing on my socks, he vigorously massaged each foot in turn.

Together, Karim and Geoffrey Vaughan's bearer, Salem, ruled their domain, our household, with an iron hand for a price. Adding or subtracting rupees ten percent *dastur* was the going cut for hiring and firing servants, and every bazaar transaction. I thought of skimming as a fair gratuity for services rendered. One evening, Geoffrey counted we had seventeen servants between the two of us, courtesy of Karim. "Each caste one job," Karim explained. "One for carry, one sweep, one for wash, one iron, one peeling and chop, and one cook." The tasks never overlapped.

Every private house, office, and lowly "go-down," hired its own *chowkidar* night watchman. Ours spent his nights on a *charpoy* in an up-ended crate beside our bungalow. His "Lookout Post," he proudly called it. Despite his fierce looks and the vicious knife he kept pushed into his belt, he always cheerfully snapped a *salaam* and smilingly escorted me to or from the gate. I never knew his real name. *Chowkidar* was his job. *"Chowkidar,"* we called him. The gang-style protection racket was foolproof. We never had a break-in, but I felt little less secure after discovering our *chowkidar* was a *dacoit* on the police wanted list.

At Sandhurst my batman "did" for me without being ordered, or when I asked him. "Would you mind…Please…When it's convenient…One might like…" But in India my polite requests were met with puzzlement, forcing me to unlearn my British manners. I trained myself to call imperiously, "Bring… Fetch…" "They expected it," someone informed me acidly. It was true. I observed how Indians themselves treated their servants. Seated in a "hotel," in the shade of a coconut grove soon after I arrived, I asked the waiter, "Do you have coconut?"

"Oh no, Sir," he replied blankly. As I was speaking, a group of seven or eight Indians sat down at the adjacent table.

"Coconuts all round, *jaldhi karo*—hurry."

To my astonishment, the waiter clapped, a youth shinned up a tree, and in a flash, a coconut appeared before each guest.

Enlisted and non-commissioned men were also pampered. Mugs of *chai* and gunfire biscuits appeared at daybreak, uniforms were laid out, baths filled, and night-soil boxes emptied. Maybe it's a tall story, but rumor was the barrack Barber shaved some men while they slept. Like us, they had only to keep their rifles clean and polished, and appear smartly turned out on parade.

As well as our 5th Fusiliers, a Field Battery, Royal Artillery, the 1st Royal Battalion, and the Jat Regiment manned the cantonment.

Why Britain maintained such a large presence in Fyzabad was a mystery. With the fierce battles and the bloody massacre of British troops in the late 1850s long since over, and no uprisings, no revolts to put down, we had little to do. Training, parading or occasionally strutting our strength on flag-showing exercises were the only requirements. I concluded our role was as an Occupying Force to ensure Britain was never again caught out. Breaking the no-weapons-in-church rule, we marched to services in the cavernous red brick church with loaded rifles. Battle-ready, we placed them in purpose-built racks in the pews. Just in case.

With long afternoons, evenings, and three-day weekends to fill, I soon became proficient in the art of gentleman's sports, "huntin', shootin', fishin' and ridin'."

I discovered and became addicted to polo despite my aversion to horses. Nothing like the torture of Sandhurst's training ring, in Fyzabad nobody yelled, "I can see the bloomin' world between your knees and saddle, Rose, Sir."

Remaining seated, and hitting the puck true, were all that mattered in the wild game of flailing hooves, flying divots, and the crash and slams and encouraging shouts. I quickly became a sought-after team member for the Fyzabad Tent Club. Colonel Sandiland, a friend of my father's, suggested it was time I owned my own ponies, but with Army pay my only money, I had to borrow from the regimental polo fund. Jade and Marble became mine.

"Dual purpose—summer, polo, winter, pigsticking—not really an extravagance," I convinced myself. I wanted to excel.

In the late afternoons after the sun lost its bite, I went pigsticking with a couple of friends. *Topee* on my head, chinstrap firmly buckled, a long lance in my hand, I rode into the bleached beauty of a landscape so unlike England, so expansive, reality merged to a dream.

An excited commotion told we had flushed our prey, and the chase began. The ponies pricked up their ears and galloped into action, egged on by wild cries. Scrambling across and along dry-river *nullahs*, kicking clouds of dirt, flattening high grasses, we tracked and backtracked the boar's frantic twists as it tried to shake us off. Though Jade and Marble were sure-footed, they did occasionally unseat me, I was never thrown face to face with an infuriated pig rearing to charge and gore both my, and my pony's guts—*tuskers* luckily for us preferred escape to attack. I wasn't proud, but adrenaline coursing, we cheered when the cornered *tusker* was "stuck," pinned down by a hunter's spear in a cruel, undignified end. For me, the sport was in the thrill of the chase and in the telling back in the Mess.

"Nearly had him, by Jove. Gave us one devil of a run." It was always the one that got away.

As an officer, I was expected to be a crack shot and keep my eye in by joining weekend shoots of six or seven guns in nearby *jheels*. The first time I crawled belly-down in those marshy swamps, I imagined the slithering of black mambas beside me. Leeches latched to my legs swelling fat with my blood. Muggers—crocodiles—waited invisible in the reeds, competing to put up game. Nervous as a toad, it took all my willpower not to scream and flee.

My eye was good and I usually made a fair contribution to the bag. Rarely less than two hundred head of duck, a brace or two of geese, snipe and partridge, and an occasional peacock, gruesomely displayed in rows, the day's bag was photographed and carefully recorded. The gurkhali beaters especially loved peacocks' forbidden meat and accidently-on-purpose often bagged one. One time, a screaming mob of villagers, believing peacocks sacred, chased and caught the culprit demanding vengeance, even death. Money talked. The man was saved.

Junior and senior ranks traditionally never mixed socially, but a distant cousin of Father's, Colonel Sandiland, broke the rule and invited me on the occasional crocodile hunt when his nieces were visiting from England. Floating down one of the main tributaries of the Ganges, the Gogra River, in a hired boat, eating a grand picnic lunch served by liveried servants, we waited for the beaters to spot one. Mooring a few hundred yards above the "mugger" sunning on the riverbank, we wriggled on our bellies towards the unsuspecting reptile—the best part of the hunt for me, a sex-starved bachelor. Lecherous, I "purved," eyes fixed on his nieces' bottoms, taut in their jodhpurs, rolling enticingly inches from my face. At a signal from the beater, our guns fired a volley at the crocodile's neck. I only once saw the bullet find its mark. The paralyzed beast reared ghoulishly onto its tail. The girls squealed. I slid my arm soothingly around the soft pudge of their waists.

With the "fishing fleet" of unmarried girls so woefully small, Geoffrey and I stood no chance of hooking a catch. Our social life was dismally restricted to obligatory formal regimental dinners and cocktail receptions where the only guests were married women, aging spinsters, and men, men, and more men. Whenever we could, we sneaked to the forbidden, less hidebound Eurasian Railway Institute to waltz and two-step their less chaperoned daughters in our arms as closely as we dared. We flirted. They seduced, hoping to attract us as suitors and husbands.

I still smile thinking of a subaltern friend's adventure. Peter fell for a beautiful green-eyed Eurasian girl, and was asked round to tea by her family. Formal, making polite conversation, she invited my startled friend, "You like, please, come to the compound. I show my beautiful white buttocks."

Buttocks, ducks, the words sounded the same in Roman Urdu. We teased him unmercifully, lewdly gesturing, dropping our trousers.

In class-conscious British India, Fyzabad's layout carefully divided "Us" from "Them." One railway station for the British Army and their families, another station to serve civilians, Eurasians and the rest. Three polo grounds and a disused racecourse acted as a barrier between our military cantonment, Fyzabad's small township, and the Civil Lines where *box-wallahs* lived. The Deputy Commissioner, Superintendent of Police, Forest Officer, Officer of the Public Works Department and the Civil Surgeon, etc., disparagingly labeled *box-wallahs,* were generally looked down on—until their highly skilled services were needed.

Though I crossed the great divide every time I visited the Railway Institute, I carefully avoided Fyzabad's sprawling shanty native city south of the cantonments, having heard it was home to *dacoits* and the *thugee* stranglers. Palls of smoke, firecrackers and the frequent rat-a-tat of gunfire rose from beyond the rubbish-tip-cum-latrine on the far side of a no-man's land. Only military police and the army's servants dared enter its ramshackle alleys.

One night, my platoon officer encouraged Geoffrey and me to go on a bandit raid with Freddy Young, the Police Superintendent and locally famous "*dacoit* catcher." According to Freddy's informer, a notorious gang of *dacoits* was to meet at a ruined bungalow in the jungle about fifteen miles from Fyzabad that night. With our faces blackened, we set off in single file along a narrow track as the light faded. The cry of nightjars, the sudden call of a startled jackal, and the crackle of dry grass underfoot were the only sounds to mark our passage.

Treading as stealthily as prowling panthers, we arrived in the wee hours after midnight. Freddy concealed us so every possible approach was covered. Armed with my service revolver and crouched behind a deodar bush, I bit my lip, feeling as giggly as I had in childhood games of game of cops and robbers.

Brilliant moonlight deepened the black shadows edging the clearing and the ground along one side of the crumbling mud walls. The bungalow's glassless windows stared hollow. I wondered who had lived in such isolation, and what caused it to be abandoned. The silence was absolute. I opened my mouth to slow and quiet my inhalations, and quell any urge to sneeze or cough. I crouched uncomfortably for what seemed hours. No movement, not a person in sight. I was utterly alone.

Suddenly from a nearby tree, a roosting peacock uttered a shrill call. I tensed, coiled ready to spring as the grass rustled a few yards off left. Dappled in a patch of moonlight, naked except for a loincloth, a man materialized, as still as the tree trunks around him. He slowly turned, checking the surroundings, and I swore his eyes pierced the shadows of my hiding place and spotted me. I understood the expression, "stiffened with fear." I stiffened. High-high, low-high-low whistles followed as the *dacoit* signaled others of the gang. By twos and threes, eleven *dacoits* slid soundlessly into the clearing, their bodies oiled slippery to evade capture, then muttered what I supposed was a password. Squatting on their heels in a semi-circle facing their leader, they passed a hookah to one another, dragging deep and long. Heady puffs of *ganja*–the local marijuana, wafted in my direction.

Freddy was in no hurry. Biding his time, he waited until their whisperings became relaxed murmurs as they dropped their guard, and their meeting got under way. At a pre-arranged signal from Freddy, we sprang from our hiding places.

"In the name of the law.... Drop your weapons...."

But Freddy's voice was drowned by startled cries and angry shouts as we leapt from behind our bushes.

The skirmish was short and swift, a flash of knives, swords, clubs and sticks. Although the *dacoits* fought violently, it took barely fifteen minutes to overpower them. I was completely useless. I had no idea what I was meant to be doing. Best not to get in the way I decided, so kept to the fringe of the melee and fired a couple of rounds into the air. Several constables received sword or knife wounds, and Geoffrey received a nasty gash from a rusty spear. He might have been killed but for one of the *dacoits* leaping forward and deflecting the spear with his sword with a cry.

"*Hamara Sahib.*" He flung himself at Geoffrey's feet and clasped his ankles. "*Sahib. Sahib,*" he cried, "Save me. I am innocent. I saved your life."

Chowkidar—our own watchman—a *dacoit* protecting us from *dacoits.*

Freddy checked each handcuffed *dacoit* against his posters.

"Wanted for murder."

"Wanted for robbery."

He scrutinized each face carefully.

Our *chowkidar,* although as guilty as the others, received only a short prison term. Geoffrey certainly owed him his life. The others swung from the gallows.

I saw no other action during my first year in India. I was not yet a soldier.

24

RANIKET

Summer Interlude

May arrived. Relentless, the thermometer rose by increments into the hundreds. Cooked alive, my face glowed, yet the hot weather had barely begun, and the rains were not due for months. My love for all things Indian wavered. Sodden, the toweling "sweat-rag" round my neck was useless. My sweat splattered the ink I'd so meticulously penned across my final report.

"What was the bloody point?" I swore.

The very act of breathing scorched my nostrils. I arranged my pens in a neat row on my desktop one last time, and pulled the office door closed. Resigned, the skeleton staff watched me go. Poor buggers, left to suffer it out on the sweltering plains until our Company's return. Trying not to gloat, I waved my orders to leave for a three-month tour of duty at the Fusilier's Hill Station, Raniket, in the cooler foothills of the Himalayas.

I marshaled my men in the half-light before dawn and boarded the train. The temperature was still tolerably fresh. I chose a corner seat beyond reach of the rising sun's probing fingers. Sweat pooled. Impatient, I prayed the train's speed would create some air movement. Bad idea. Worse than stultifying stillness, hot blasts battered my face. Pulling the leather strap, I notched up the window, leaving the merest sliver open. Company One, my company, wilted comatose. A rag doll, I stared glassy-eyed at the countryside, half reading the names of passing Halts.

"Nainital." Twisting I craned to catch the name as it disappeared. Nainital—where Grandfather Samuel and Grandmother Isabella Knowles were buried. The heat-dulled haze of Nainital's waters shimmered me alert. So much had happened in the ten months I'd been in India, the name had slipped my mind. I peered back at the curving tracks following the shorelines' forested slopes.

White flashes winked in the sun way above the band of cloud and tree line. Snow. With a final chuff and whistling shriek of steam, the slowing train hit the railhead's buffers and bounced backwards to a stop. Kathgodam, the end of the line, the end of the road. I swallowed a salt-pill to reenergize before tackling the 5,000-foot climb.

The sergeant yelled the mules, men and baggage into order, while I pinpointed the exact ridge on my Army survey map where, hidden below the snowline, Raniket perched twenty-five miles up.

"....and a quick march. Ahaa.... left, right, left....."

The sergeant major marched the men from the station towards the scrub grasses beyond Kathgodam's fields.

"Usual to take a break here, Rose, Sir."

"Stand down. Take ten minutes." I ordered, following his prompt.

The deeply rutted dirt road petered to a winding cart track in the lower jungle. Blinding dust kicked up from the column ahead penetrated the kerchief I'd tied over my mouth. Sweat-flavored, the stuff stuck to the back of my throat. Cursing, I hawked and spat like my men.

"Break step." The sergeant commanded, to allow us climb at our own pace.

All around were mountain rhododendron and pine. Dust turned to humus, spongy soft beneath my boots, and crackling leaves. Alternating 10-minute breaks every fifty minutes, with 5-minute ones every fifty-five minutes, I could march forever. The higher we climbed, the less grueling the heat, the less wicked the odor of sweat, men, and mules. I sucked in the resinous aroma, and damp earth, smells I'd not inhaled since England.

We camped for the night in a jungle clearing at Bhim Tal, beside a small reed- edged lake. Rubbing the grime from my arms and face in the brown-flecked shallows, a gaunt face shook his head when I shook mine and stared back at me from the water between the reeds. I held my dripping arms above the water's surface to catch the breeze, and as my skin bumped to goose flesh, remembered the feel of cool. At bedtime I dragged my cot outside my tent. With the Milky Way as my coverlet, I slept while Jupiter and Mars stood guard.

Next morning, the men had breath enough to whistle and burst into song. Lighter, almost jogging the remaining half,

"...the soldiers are coming, Tra-la-la-la. The soldiers are marching into town, Hurrah. Hurrah...."

Singing, we marched into Raniket.

The great Central Massif of the Himalaya connecting Nepal to the Simla Hills silenced any small talk. Wanting my first sight of the Himalayas for me alone, I left my *burra* peg of whisky on the cane table and walked to the verandah's railing. Four thousand feet dropped to the plains. Gripping the rails, looking down, I followed a pair of eagles' pencil spirals. Heaven lay below. Earth's needle peaks plumed white in sapphire blue. Mountains floated discarnate in sky's waterless sea.

Back at my table, I spread my Army survey map on a small table and picked out Nanda Devi's 26,000 feet, the highest peak in the British Empire, then Trisul, Kamet and Nanda, peaks I dreamed since they had peopled Mother's bedtime stories.

however hard I looked
not comprehending such height
child's eyes saw but a distant cloud
fixed in bluest blue
white above the others
I looked again—
and then it was
I saw the floating ship of Everest

For those three months in Raniket I spent every spare second exploring. If I weren't trekking, I was poring over Army survey maps. I was tracing routes along India's outer line to mysterious, forbidden Tibet. I noticed a vast, white, unmapped area devoid of detail. "Hoti." I daydreamed—Stanley in Africa, Rose in Hoti. I became obsessed. It was me Rose who'd be the first to map the region.

But Raniket's bazaar and its Tibetan traders were the closest I got that summer. Tibet and the Hoti would have to wait.

The Regiment was on stand-down with no more to do than maintain an outward display of discipline. Command busied its men with pointless drills, rifle and football training. By night, obligatory social duties filled officers' evenings, so many, my smile stiffened, thin. To the small pool of ex-pats the annual arrival of the Regiment heralded endless fun. So homesick for the life they'd forsaken, they'd built a "London Club" and a nine-hole golf course. British Raniket, like the other Hill Stations, epitomized Colonial India. But for his public affair with Mother, Father would have fitted perfectly into Raniket's "Little England." But the two of them were now pariahs to be snubbed.

My idea of hunting was not killing, but an excuse to be in nature, to hear silence while trekking in the mountains. I pretended otherwise of course. One weekend I joined a friend on a camping trip, ostensibly to hunt small game. Climbing the rough grass goat trails of the lower slopes, I relived my wild scrambles in the Black Mountains above Hereford as a child. I saw myself again, a lone observer, a hawk, a swallow, claiming all I saw as mine. So, dreaming, I walked beside a trickling stream stuffing wild strawberries into my mouth. Giant magenta-red rhododendrons, sparse aspens and meadows of wild flowers reminded me I walked in the Himalayas.

"Ahh... I froze, startled.

Ambling towards me, foraging for berries, a V-necked Himalayan bear. As surprised to see me as I him, he reared onto his hind legs, roaring. Instinctively, I raised my gun. Instinctively, I fired both barrels.

"Maro. Shoot. Maro." My *shikari*-guide shouted excitedly.

"I say, Rose. Jolly good shot." My companion was impressed.

Studying the crumpled sagging fur which only moments before had been a living creature, my pride evaporated. "Self-protection." I absolved myself, unconvinced.

Wanting rid of my kill, I gave the skin to the Mess, who mounted it gruesomely spread-eagled, stuffed head hanging downwards, with its twenty-three-inch claws grappling uselessly into the scalloped-edged blue baize cloth. Wherever I chose to sit, I couldn't escape his reproachful staring glass eyes. Though bear maul and kill many hill men each year, I couldn't shake off my guilt. Big game hunting was not for me.

Himalayas from Raniket.

25

GONDA

I Find My Origins

Early September, towards the end of the hot weather, I returned with my Company from the cooler Hill Station to the steamy plains of Fyzabad with five days to spare before reporting for duty. It was the opportunity I needed, my chance to glean every scrappy detail of Mother's Indian childhood.

Beyond Lucknow, hidden in the Terai Jungle, forty miles East of Fyzabad where I stood, lay Gonda—Mother's birthplace, Grandmother Isabella and Samuel Knowles' Mission, the Taroo Indians. I caught the next train. A cross-breeze blew through the carriage and I closed my eyes. Questions. Answers.

"I was born in the ruins of a Hindu Temple." I replayed Mother's familiar story in my head.

With my connection not leaving till the following day, I treated myself to a night in Lucknow at the Royal Hotel, a hotel with plumbing. Stretched full-length in an enamel bath, wiggling my toes to avoid scalding drips, I lingered till my fingers wrinkled and my whisky glass was drained.

I was the only passenger to alight at the Gonda Halt. The quarter mile to the village lay across a grid-work of cultivated fields cut from the Terai jungle.

Wondering what I had got myself into, I started slowly towards the village along the raised single footpath topping an earth-bank dividing the fields.

Halfway across, I came to a young man diverting brown rivulets of water into the furrows of an alfalfa field by damming the main irrigation channel with great clods of mud. Seeing me approach, he stopped what he was doing and stared at me suspiciously.

"I am the grandson of Padre Knowles *Sahib*." I introduced myself.

To my astonishment he burst into tears, ran over, and jumping onto the path, fell to his knees and kissed my feet.

"Oh. *Sahib*. Oh. *Sahib*. Long time no come." Then, "Where you live?" Then, "How many sons? Daughters?" Then, "You also Padre?"

Bombarded with so many questions, I had no time to reply. Finally he pulled himself together and made sense of what I asked, "Take me to Knowles *Ghar*."

"Follow, *Sahib*. I show you." Almost running, he led the way gesticulating excitedly, and calling, "Knowis *Sahib* here. Knowis come." And like the Pied Piper, we soon headed an ever-lengthening procession.

We stopped in the village center at a crumbling, and probably cobra-ridden, temple shaded by an enormous banyan tree ringed by a low stonewall. Fine white prayer threads wound about its trunk, and, to denote the tree's sacredness, scarlet Kum-Kum powder smeared the bark. Beside a small shrine between the roots, contorted into an impossible yogic pose on a makeshift wooden platform, sat a naked Sadhu smeared with grey ash, unmoved by the commotion. Was this temple Mother's, Emma Knowles', birthplace? I asked but no one knew.

I had just settled on the wall, when the crowd momentarily stilled, then parted to materialize the *thulsidar*, the village headman, flourishing his black umbrella threateningly to investigate the disturbance.

"Knowis *Sahib* come. Knowis come." They explained, pointing.

Sweating profusely and increasingly uncomfortable under the gaze of so many pairs of eyes, I wiped my forehead. The headman tapped the ground, and my crowd of escorts squatted obediently around us, but noisily competing to better one another's stories. They spoke of my grandparents in the present tense as though they were alive.

"Under this tree Knowis *Sahib* give good medicine. Make many people well."

"Under this tree, Knowis *Sahib* make outside Church. Make many prayer here. Long time later, we build *Jadughar,* God Magic House. Look, name."

Sure enough there it was, "The Reverend Samuel Knowles. Padre to the Taroo." The church still bore his name.

"Magic House bell ring every Sunday."

"After Magic House, build *Sahib*'s bungalow."

"*Memsahiba* have many sons, many daughters."

"*Memsahiba's* Misty-dog buried here. Stone keep whitewash white."

"Emma, missy-*sahiba*, married here. Judge *Pukka Sahib.*"

I was startled. Mother married here? They must have remembered wrong. Perhaps they muddled mother with another sister, I asked. But no they were adamant.

"Missy Emma married."

The uneasy puff of truth escaped, contracting my belly. That explained certain hints and change of subject in the Regiment whenever I asked about Father, the frowns and the silences at home. Unable to deal with my thoughts, I changed the subject.

Anecdote by anecdote, my grandparents' lives unfolded. They built a dispensary. They built a school. They taught the villagers English and to read and write in exchange for converting to their Christian God. My only disappointment, Mother's birthplace—the Hindu Temple ruin of Mother's birth story was no longer. Dissolved into the earth, I got no sense of its crumbling walls and dust.

So much information. Overwhelmed, I was tiring. Noticing, the *thulsidar* graciously invited me to his house, and sat me on a stool in his courtyard under a mango tree. Under the scrutiny of the village population peering over and through his fence, his wife shyly offered me sweetmeats and black tea made with thick buffalo milk. I stood to leave. The *thulsidar* bowed low, his hands in prayer mode moving from heart to forehead. He placed a marigold and jasmine garland about my neck. I bowed in response to his touching display, my hands like his, held in prayer. As our eyes met, I saw a place beyond his physical form. Equals, we honored who we really were. My throat tightened and I couldn't speak. Recovering, I straightened, and made an impromptu speech thanking the *thulsidar* and villagers for their hospitality, their loyalty and of the great honor they did me and my family by keeping the memory of "*Sahibs* Knowis," as they called my grandparents, alive.

"Yes. Yes," I promised in reply to his invitation to hunt in the nearby Zamindari jungle.

I remember nothing of my walk back to the Railway Halt. Caught up in my grandparents' lives, undigested thoughts ricocheted round my skull. I relived their bravery, their fears as they first arrived at the tiny Taroo Kingdom in the close, pressed jungle. Had the Taroo allowed them shelter because Grandmother Isabella carried a baby, my mother, in her belly? How had they coaxed the Taroo from the jungle, gained their trust, and persuaded them to build a "Magic" church to a white God? How fearful their first wakeful night, lying stiffly alert, shadows playing tricks in the moonlight, the sudden alarm calls of peacocks, the *sambhar* and monkeys' warnings of tiger stalking towards the village from the open "Sal" forest. A black elephant materialized from the jungle, trumpeting and startling me from my reverie—the steam engine, black, hooting. I mounted the train, my ghosts laid to rest.

I never returned.

It was as well I'd made the trip then, for on arriving back to Fyzabad the following day, I learned my years attachment was over and I would take up my posting to Father's old regiment, the First Battalion of the Third Queen Alexandra's Own Gurkha Rifles stationed in nearby Almora.

I was ceremonially "dined out" as a guest of the Regiment. A card, heavily embossed with the Fifth Fusiliers crest read,

"Lieutenant Colonel R. Sandilands and the Officers of the Second Battalion the Fifth Northumberland Fusiliers request the pleasure of your company...."

The port completed its circuit, sliding around the mahogany table right to left. We raised our glasses to our King, the Emperor of India.

Hill Station

26

ALMORA HILL STATION

Third Queen Alexandra's Own Gurkha Rifles

"Watch yourself. Panther and black bear territory."

"I'd take an armed orderly with you after dark, if I were you."

With this warning ringing in my ears, I walked the lonely paths connecting my quarters to the scattered married quarters, conscious of hungry eyes watching from the encroaching trees. I never was attacked, but the panthers' sawing and tigers' roars reminded me I was an intruder.

My regiment, the First Battalion of the Third Queen Alexandra's Own Gurkha Rifles, ceremoniously dined me into their Mess, and welcomed me as one of them. Really no more than a five-roomed log cabin, its plain walls overflowed with historical memorabilia commemorating the regiment's victorious campaigns. Portraits of every Commanding Officer since the time of Sir Robert Colquhoun Bt., in 1815, covered its dark panels. Though I searched, Father's name was not amongst them.

Again, active deployment was not on the regiment's agenda. Another year yawned. Thanks to my year with the Fusiliers, I knew the form. Yes, yes, officers were gentleman. Officers played. Officers strutted. Officers never carried parcels.

Officers never, but never, wore white *topees*. Fact was the Army was turning out not to be the exciting career I'd expected from Father's tales of heroic skirmishes. There was no *badmash*, rebel tribesmen and no Rani Jhansi, Warrior Queen, for me to capture.

I wondered what I was there for—in charge of musketry training and the time-wasting art of football, a game I could never abide, my only regimental duty. I was expected to impart some knowledge I didn't possess to men whose skills put mine to shame. Wrestling for the ball and breaking every rule in the book, they trampled the umpire and completely ignored me. Surrendering, I retired to the sidelines pretending I was in charge and cheered.

On weekends, aimless, I organized lines of Gurkha beaters to wade the undergrowth above me and drive birds downhill in my direction. I edged sideways along Almora's perilous slopes, shotgun cocked in readiness, poised to blast off at the first thing within my sights. The poor *chakor*, I let them have it. Bang. Bang. My boredom, decompressed by the ancient cure of letting blood, dinner of *chakor*, a pheasant-like bird never tasted so good.

One weekend, I wandered the civilian lines searching for Father's bungalow, Kanda Koti,

"You'll know it by its apple orchard," Father told me. Sure enough, there it was, nestled in a grove of deodar trees.

I tried to visualize Father rocking on the verandah, imagine the "what-ifs," but—nothing, and I saw no point going inside. For an instant I mentally scanned their illicit love affair. Had Father built it before he met Mother, or after he met her, as their love-nest? Did he carry her over its threshold? I squirmed. Taboo. My thoughts had no business there. I turned away and walked briskly back towards the bazaar.

Approaching the village, I skirted the many flocks huddled on the hillside meadow, keeping out of snapping reach of the snarling Bhutia watchdogs—their teeth almost as vicious as the spiked, steel collars around their necks worn to keep marauding panther and tiger at bay.

A rambling jumble of shanty buildings and narrow streets, Almora's bazaar sprawled down the steep *khud* north of the Army cantonment. Though no more than a village, several important trade routes crossed there. Tibetans arrived on foot in ones and twos, herding sheep and goats along the narrow paths over the high passes from as faraway as Gartok, the capital of Western Tibet. Strapped on its back, each animal portered leather bags of salt and borax to trade in the thriving bazaar.

On market days Almora's narrow streets overflowed. Baas, bleats, and the dull clunk of wooden neck-bells resounded in the alleys—sights and sounds I never tired of—smells included.

Walking beyond the famous Indian Dance and Yoga School, past the row of teashops, the market sellers squatting on the ground behind baskets piled high with vegetables and fruit, and Tibetan tribesmen proffering sheepskin, a handful of turquoise, garnet and amber beads, I kept going until I reached the blackened ghee-lit shrines. There, Tibetans twirled hand-held prayer-wheels and focused on their prayers, rendering me invisible. I stood beside them, moved by their devotion and, transfixed by a force I had no knowledge of, I, the mountains, sky, village, sheep, and man merged as one. I dropped all my small coins into a naked fakir's begging bowl.

Perhaps the hypnotic flute, sita, drum beat, and the harmonium's *ragas* hanging in the pine-laden air persuaded me to listen to and swallow the strange tale told by a Tibetan traveler I met one Hindu holy day soon after.

ghee lamps' steady flames
illumine beyond vermillion,
indigo and saffron fluttering flags
beyond rattling wheels' endless prayers
to a compassionate God still hidden

Tibetan Nomads. Lansdowne Bazaar.

27

THE HOTI

A Tibetan's Strange Tale

I met him—the lone Tibetan—swinging down the bridle path from the isolated village of Binsar fifteen miles above Almora, on my way to stay with a Scots couple for the weekend.

"Bring your gun and a few lethal bullets, we may sit up for panther," the husband suggested.

Shotgun in hand, rucksack on my back, I trudged slowly up the steep forested slopes above the village with no thought but the visit ahead. 1,500-foot of climbing still facing me. I paused to catch my breath in an aspen meadow, panting in the rarified air, when a snarling Bhutia dog burst into the clearing, warning me not to move while his obedient flock passed. I became as a tree caught in a bobbing surf of bleating sheep, as they swirled about my feet and brushed against my legs. An anchor-man, their herder, nodded in greeting and disappeared as rapidly as he had appeared—his tidal wave with him.

An hour later, the ridgeline path broke through the trees into a small grassy meadow. A scene too perfect to pass by without stopping lay before me—an orchard of flowering almond trees, and two musicians playing a type of zither seated on one of two makeshift benches outside a rickety shack that served as an Indian teashop.

I ordered *Masala chai,* spiced milky tea.

Sitting on the unoccupied bench, I leaned my back against the hut's sun-warmed wood wall and willed the idyllic scene to last forever. No past, no future, the present was all there was. I drifted with the quavering notes, rested.

Then I saw him—the solitary Tibetan striding down from Binsar by way of the high meadows encircling Mansarowar Lake. Curious… he was unaccompanied by sheep or dog. Giving me a cursory *salaam*, he squatted on his haunches opposite me and ordered buckwheat tea.

While he noisily slurped, I started chatting to him in fairly fluent Urdu, a language most Tibetans spoke.

"Where have you come from?" I asked.

He pointed north.

"Gartok, *Sahib*," he replied.

"Gartok? Tibet?"

"Ha. Gartok."

"Which way did you come?"

"Hoti." He pointed towards Trisul, the 25,000-foot peak, and the paler virgin snows of Nandi Devi beyond.

"Hoti?" I gasped. "Hoti?" —the mysterious uncharted blank territory marked on the Indian survey map I had studied a year before in Raniket and had sworn to explore?

The Hoti lay along the frontier of British India and Western Tibet. Bordered by the impassable avalanche-swept Rishi Ganga gorge, an unexplored tributary of the Ganges on the north, and the remote, untrodden mountain of Nanda Devi to the east, it had never yet been crossed.

Suddenly attentive, I cross-examined him further. "By which pass did you cross the Hoti from Tibet? Where are your flock of sheep and dogs?"

"Nai, sahib."

"How many days? How high? By what way did you say you crossed?" I struggled to make sense of what he was telling me. I'd never heard of Tibetan traders using that route.

"Naksha men nai hai, Sahib," he replied in his poor Urdu. He did not know the name. "Hoti haunted," he stated firmly.

I strained to catch his words.

"Big blizzard come. All goats, all sheep dead. Much rocks. Much snow and ice. Cold. Wind. Me only, alive."

"Monks save me," he continued, "from die too."

"Monks? What monks?" I asked, his tale turned suspiciously fanciful.

According to him, a party of monks found his semi-conscious body in the snow and carried him on a litter for how far, for how long he didn't know. When he regained consciousness, he was in a very old *jadu-ghar* built into caves on the other side of Nandi Devi where many Llamas lived in a religious community.

"On the slopes where the sun rises..." he described poetically.

He told of an earthly paradise below the caves, of grassy meadows on a sheltered plateau, of sheep and yaks grazing unmolested by the yeti.

"Yeti?"

I was about to probe his Yeti reference when I clearly heard, "Preserjon Jadu-Ghar." He named the monastery. "Much magic, Presserjon Ghar," he reiterated.

"What magic?"

I stiffened, intrigued. Could "Presserjon" be a Roman Urdu corruption of the name "Prester John," the legendary mystic priest reputed to have founded a Neslorian Empire in Persia reaching from Kashgar to Tibet beyond the Himalayas? Myth related his kingdom housed the fabled biblical treasures of the Three Wise Men. "Hang on. Hugh," I checked myself. Although Preeserjon sounded remarkably like "Prester John," so might other Tibetan words. It was something to research.

I got him to repeat the name and story several times. Consistent, his answers were the same. Then he proffered, "Monks different, not same like Buddhist monks. *Jadu-Ghar,* much yoga."

"Different? How long you stay? How you get here alone?" I kept at him. Excited, I pried more details out of him.

The monks nursed him back to health for a week, then carried him on a "floating litter" to a shepherd's hut at the foot of Nanda Kot glacier, where they left him with a sack of food after pointing out a route over the Pindari Pass.

He suddenly clammed up. Though I plied him with rice wine, I got no more information out of him.

My head spun. Pindari Pass was unconquered. Survey maps dead-ended at Pindari, the head of Trail's Pass. Twenty thousand feet of ice cliffs between Nanda Kot and the Nanda Devi's 21,000 feet blocked access to the massif some ten miles distant.

Studying the map, I searched for a possible Eastern Sanctuary as described by my Tibetan raconteur. I looked for any possible route over the sheer ice-cliffs of Pindari's inaccessible northern face. I began to pick holes in his story. Crossed the glacial pass? Impossible. Carried in a litter by monks? Ridiculous. But something intrigued me about his story and his unwavering conviction. Could it be Prester John's lost kingdom, his monastery? He's made up the whole story hoping for *baksheesh*, I reasoned. But something nagged. I couldn't shake the questions. I needed answers. I needed the truth.

Climbing the last five miles to 8,000 feet to Binsar my boots pounded

"Hoti, Hoti, Hoti," with each breathless step. I renewed my promise to explore the Hoti for myself when I'd accumulated enough local leave.

My Scot hosts had no answers and little interest. They knew nothing of the Prester John myth and the unknown Hoti. Why should they care? They lived in utter contentment above the clouds, focused on their own flower-filled and orchard paradise with 200 miles of snowy peaks as their horizon.

they dwelled in every breath inhaled
no regret for what might have been
no need to seek for joy but in the present

28
TRAIN TO PESHAWAR

My posting to the North West Frontier arrived before I'd fully unpacked. I was to join one of our regiment's battalions for a two-year stint at Landi Khana Fort on the Kyber Pass. All a man could stand on the Afghan border, I was told. Finally—action, other than sticking pigs.

"You won't be needing these, *Sahib.*" My bearer held up my dress uniform, spurs and waistcoat and packed them in my tin trunk with a liberal sprinkling mothballs. "Fatigues for the frontier, *Sahib.*"

Dragged through a wall of heat for two long days, the train still had two to go. Almora to Peshawar; Peshawar to Jamrud; Jamrud to Landi Khana. The first leg of the journey nearly over, Peshawar lay less than an hour away.

The Peshawar Club… I pictured the hot bath and the proper bed awaiting me. Had we arrived? I poked my head out of the carriage window as the train slowed. Two blockhouses crowded either side of the rails with no city in sight. A platoon of armed Sikhs bore towards us at the double, faced the train and presented arms. My skin prickled alarm…a raid?…an attack? I withdrew my head smartly.

"Tradition, old chap," the officer sharing my carriage reassured. "Always present arms to the Royal Mail as she passes."

Iron against iron, the train squealed to walking pace and inched onto the Attock Bridge to cross the dizzying divide. I hung suspended between the Punjab and the wild North West Frontier, my past and future, security and adventure, as had the many who'd journeyed before me, some never to return. Would I join them—become a treasured picture clutched to a bereaved mother's breast?

I looked down at the thin blue thread of the Indus River sparkling in the sun two hundred feet below. The mighty river did not look so mighty that day. My companion must have read my thoughts...

"You should see it in spring spate, old chap. Snowmelt from K2 so swells the river, the water rises almost to the rails. Tragic. Sweeps thousands to their death."

Peshawar, the very name romantic, its sienna mud walls, alleys, minarets, caravanserais, and groves of mulberry shade trees beckoned, mysterious as my dreams, with tales of blood feuds, bazaar quarrels and swift, thrusting daggers. I imagined myself in Richard Burton's footsteps—a young Lieutenant in the East India Company, a spy dressed as a Peshawari, eavesdropping in the Hammams as he watched their dancing boys.

"Not a good idea, old chap. Verboten, wandering about without escort or a police pass." The officer sent to meet me was adamant. "Killings and fights are two-a-penny. Our Frontier Police patrol in pairs." Then he added, "Every day is hanging day at the jail."

The double-wire perimeter fence surrounding the Peshawar Club convinced me. There'd be no sightseeing outside the club. I wandered the club's protected English garden before dinner. Only darkness lay beyond the patrolled wire perimeter.

I didn't talk much that evening; I listened. I absorbed every snippet of chatter— "Peshawar, a hub of intrigue and illegal arms trading....stolen British Lee Enfield Rifles.... muzzle-loading *jezils* manufactured...a factory in tribal territory... a place called Dehra Ishmael Khan." I heard talk of Peshawari tribesmen armed to the hilt with curved daggers, antique rifles and strung about with bandoliers, the disregard for boundary lines, and of tribesmen pouring back and forth along traditional trade routes by foot and camel from Afghanistan, Persia, Turkistan and China laden with carpets, silks, spices, salt and precious stones. And of migrating nomadic farmer-traders herding sheep to winter to summer pastures as they had for generations before straight lines dissected their land.

"The tribesmen have a valid point," argued an officer further down the table, but he was on his own.

The general opinion was Britannia ruled the region to the Durand line, the line demarcating India's administrative boundary. Beyond, blood feuds between local tribal populations raged unchecked, Afridi against Afridi, Orkzais against Orkzais, one tribe against another, but every last one of them united against us British, the occupying foreigners.

The men spoke of Alexander the Great as though he was still based in Abbotabad in command of his string of frontier forts built to control the major mountainous passes onto the Karikoram Plateaus. Only now it was we, the British Fifth and Sixth Gurkha Regiments who manned the strategic forts above Abbotabad—our problem, the same as his of two thousand years ago—to secure the borders from Chinese-Turkistan and Afghanistan invasion. Trade, defense, invasion, power, nothing had changed. Though the British could not put a toe over the border, the Government of India acted covertly on our behalf from their Consul in far off Kashgar, the capital of Chinese Turkestan.

My head buzzed. So much information I feared I wouldn't sleep. Wrong. Dreamless, I slept.

Jamrud Fort

29

JAMRUD FORT

Live Fire And A Train Through The Kyber Pass

The Peshawar train pulled up opposite a painted sign. "Jamrud Fort," it read. Late afternoon sun drilled my bare arms and legs. I shifted the chinstrap of my *topee*, tilting it to shade my face.

"Good journey, Rose?" Captain Jackman stepped from the narrow stripe of shade beneath a corrugated tin roof and greeted me.

Border trains ran only three days a week. With no "up" trains running until the following day I had no choice but to stay overnight in the fort, guest of the Royal Jat Regiment. A mud fort, squat in the stony plain, menaced from inside a nest of barbed-wire coils and armed perimeter posts, with not another structure in sight.

I was stinking hot, red in the face, with my shirt plastered uncomfortably to my back. Braving the full sun, I followed Jackman. Rifles, barbed wire, hostile stares. The perimeter guard allowed us to pass.

"Care for a swim?" Jackman startled me.

"Where?" I wondered. The arid land held no water I saw.

"There's an ancient underground artesian reservoir below the mud floor.

No idea how old. Probably dating earlier than the first Afghan War."

Hygiene forgotten, I lay motionless in the fort's drinking water until my puce skin cooled pink.

A burst of distant rifle fire interrupted my pre-dinner chat with Jackman. My words hung unfinished in mid-air. Jackman chattered on, unconcerned.

"An attack?" I queried, peering through a slit window.

"Just another blood feud. Nothing to do with us," he reassured. "Let the buggers kill themselves and good riddance, I say. Save us the trouble."

"The perimeter posts aren't going to return their fire?" I was puzzled.

"Strictly verboten unless actually under attack, Government property is endangered, or tribesmen fire across a Government road. Waste of ammunition."

He explained the *maliks*—the warlords and head tribesmen of the villages— were in British pay, and were bribed generously to keep control of their tribesmen. One incident and their purses were docked. One shot at a convoy, or a sniper bullet passing within a hundred feet of Government property cost the *malik* a fine of a hundred, two hundred, even five hundred rifles.

"Sometimes," Jackman added, "the British Political Agent—P.A.— orders the Battalion to burn their villages and crops."

"Bit stiff, isn't it? Burn them out?" I interjected, horrified by his callous talk of killing and burning homes over dinner. Did the North West Frontier so change a man? Would it to me? I kept my revulsion to myself.

"Keep them in their place. Can't have a bunch of tribals running amok taking pot shots at the convoys just for the fun of it. It's the *malik's* job to keep his gang of *diwans* in order if he wants his bag of silver coins." Jackman's expression never changed.

I kept silent, thankful the Battalion Colonel called us in to dinner. He wore battle-ready patrols, not mess kit. Acceptable protocol in the North West Frontier, I noted.

Glued to my side, Jackman introduced me to the enigmas of frontier politics.

Twoc-dong. A bullet ricocheted off the heavily tiled roof of the fort. A distant bang followed. I jerked. My spoon lurched, spattering tomato soup across the white tablecloth. Nobody looked up. Nobody appeared to notice. I took a sip of sherry, hoping it wasn't obvious this was my first time under live fire.

"Local Afridis having fun," Jackman announced casually, inclining his head towards the source. "Last month, Afridis shot out the floodlight on one of the posts, crawled under the wire, slit the sentry's throat and buggered off with a Lewis gun, two rifles and some ammunition."

"And then?" I gasped.

"Most awful stink. The Brigadier was apoplectic. Demanded we send a Punitive Column to burn the raiders' villages. Didn't happen. The P.A. in Peshawar refused to sanction it. Denied the culprits were his local Afridis.

Swore they were Orakzais from outside his agency's domain. Compromised finally, and agreed to a jirgah, a meeting of local *maliks*, and a fine of two hundred rifles."

Jackman, enjoying his teacher role continued, "The P.A. and Brigadier dueled constantly, each insisting their way was the only way to control tribes. But as much as the Brigadier hates defeat, the Foreign Service rules out here. Can't make a blessed move without the F.O.'s—the Foreign Office's—say-so. We've even an Assistant P.A. embedded with us in camp. At least he has a handle on what's going on, unlike the P.A. who governs from afar in Peshawar."

Jackman didn't let up. I dug my fingernails into my palm to keep awake. Tribes... territories...boundaries...politics...Pathan...Afridi...Orakzais...*malik*... diwans. My brain scrambled.

Twoc. Another bullet hit the roof.

Unperturbed, the Colonel seated at the head of the table continued the delicate operation of lighting his cigar from red-hot charcoal smoldering in the silver *quaich* proffered by his bearer before glancing pointedly at one of the officers.

Without a word, Dickie, the duty officer recognizable by his cross belt, red sash and slung sword, rose, drained his glass of port, and left the table with a scowl.

"Poor old Dickie," remarked Jackman, "It's the third run this week the Afridis have acted up on his watch."

I did not sleep well that night. Pathans and Aridis creeping through the wire, knives in their teeth, materialized and dematerialized into the shadows at the foot of my cot.

Captain Jackman saw me onto the Landi Khana train at daybreak.

"Keep your head inside the carriage if you want to keep it." Jackman saluted, smiling.

After the previous evening's education, it was comforting to see the glint of rifle butts poking through the slits of two cement Picket Posts overlooking the Halt. Jamrud Fort's protective walls stood distanced too far for my liking. I glanced around the hellish place. I couldn't imagine worse. An uneasy thought flitted through my head—the camp at Landi Khana, the fort where I was headed, might be as desolate.

"A fortified township on the highest point of the Kyber Pass guarding two major routes from Kabul and Jalalabad to Peshawar over the Afghan border..." I reread the description. It didn't sound too bad.

"Tough place, the Frontier," my friends had nodded on hearing of my posting.

Two iron engines drew alongside the platform pulling four "rakes" behind them, more like relics from the 1850s than a modern carriage. Though Jackman assured me the line was cleared of tribesmen and every picket along the route manned, I took no chances. Wedging my back to the corner, I settled as far from the carriage window as I could.

Laboring into motion, the train picked up speed. "Moving target: Less danger." I relaxed, dozing. "Au Masjid," the receding sign read. We slowed to almost walking pace. I sat up alert. Zigzagging up the steep gradient of the Kyber Gorge, whistle shrieking on rounding every bend, and whoo-whooing on entering every tunnel, I counted sixty before giving up.

"Blasted and dug by Welsh coal miners," my carriage companion shouted.

The train reversed frequently into run-outs where it sat, a sitting target, till the overworked engines cooled sufficiently to continue. Jumpy, I scanned the hillsides, wondering if I were a bull's-eye in a tribesman's rifle sights.

Whitewash calling cards splashed homesick and victorious graffiti across the rock faces. One read, "Scotland forever." Another, "Jay Suffolk Hill," commemorated the bloody battle fought by the Suffolk regiment during the Third Afghan War. Every hillock, every major ridge sported a lonely blockhouse or a picket sited within rifle fire range of another and the railway. Hated *ferengi* footprints of an occupying force in a country which did not recognize us or want us there. As if in proof, rifle shots pinged against the train's metal body as it gathered speed for the final spurt downhill into Landi Khana where the Pass widened into a narrow plain. Snatching up my gun, I craned my neck out of the window.

After two years of playing at being a soldier, I was ready to act as one.

Khyber Pass. North West Frontier.

30

LANDI KHANA

North West Frontier

Dropped off alone in no man's land, momentarily abandoned on Landi Khana's wooden platform, I stood for a moment straining for the train's last chuff to fade and disappear on the up line through and over the Kyber Pass and into Afghanistan. Conscious of being observed, I stared back at the glint of metal protruding from the blockhouses and watchtowers spaced along the camp's wire fence. Not one tree, not a blade of grass—the North West Frontier.

"Good to see you, Rose," a voice made me turn. I exchanged salutes with the smiling Adjutant, the Senior Subaltern, sent to greet me. "Charles Boucher." He introduced himself.

"Just our Gurkhas cooling off. Better get used to guards. Armed escorts are obligatory beyond the perimeter fence." Charles inclined his head, noticing my eyes dart toward two Gurkha soldiers aiming their rifles at a large water tank standing beside the rails beyond the platform.

An orderly picked up my kit and we followed him along the dirt track between double apron coils of barbed wire. Under the scrutiny of heavily armed guards, I entered the fort—it would be my home for two years.

Bare, treeless, open ground, a scattering of a dozen wooden huts isolated in the middle of a fenced half-mile section, rows of about fifty pitched-roofed tents ranged along the fence—Landi Khana. I made to swallow. My parched mouth was dry of spittle.

"Built by Alexander the Great, by all accounts. Bargh Fort." Charles nodded towards a low fortified tower crouched inside the perimeter fencing with a bulldog on guard, its squat mud walls barring access to the Khyber Pass. Again I made to swallow. But my tongue had turned to wood.

"Your roommate, Desmond Whyte, arrives on the next up train in a couple of days."

Blazing hot, the temperature inside my wooden billet barely less so, I fell into a heat-drugged sleep only to be shocked awake and thrown from my bed to the floor. Disorientated and greatly alarmed, I stumbled to Charles' adjoining hut.

"Go back to bed, Hugh, it's only an earthquake," he grunted sleepily.

It was the beginning of a lifelong friendship. "It's only an earthquake" became our private joke, our way to defuse tight situations, and skirmishes such as the time we got trapped inside an abandoned hut, bullets thundering against the walls.

"Welcome to Landi Khana. Glad to have you with us," my Commanding Officer smiled pleasantly at my introductory interview. "Here, take a pew." He indicated I should sit.

I hadn't expected Colonel Tuck to be so short. Perhaps stocky is a more accurate description. Coffee-brown from the sun, he was no taller, no more white-skinned than the Gurkhali men under his command. After asking after my "old man" and running through the obligatory wheres-and-whats of my schooling, my military background and my aspirations, he stood and proffered his hand,

"I am sure you'll do well here. Tough place, the Frontier, Rose. But damnably good for your career. Couple of things to get under your belt." He spoke in phrases.

"Requirements of the Indian Army. Retention Exam. You've six months to pass. Urdu language exam. Two years. Gurkhali optional extra."

"No problem, Sir." I had plenty of time.

I liked Desmond, and he me. We became inseparable friends. He was a splendid roommate and study companion despite his gorilla appearance. The hairiest man I ever came across, tufts of black hair protruded from his collar, tufts grew on the backs of his hands, his toes, Desmond Whyte was so hairy, he could walk naked without fear of indecent exposure. He brushed off bear and Yeti jokes with a smile, and I never heard him lose his temper during his two years of goading. If the Army had treated me they way they did him, I'd have exploded.

New boys together, we drilled the Company, brushed up on frontier warfare tactics, surveying, map reading and other mandatory subjects for the Retention exam. I passed. Desmond failed and re-sat and re-sat it till he passed. The exam under our belt, we tackled Urdu.

Our *munshi*, Yusuf, a gentle Pathan tribesman from Peshawar, patiently force-fed us sentence structure and vocabulary till we acquired enough basic conversational skills to sit the exam. Yusuf clambered the Khargali Ridge many miles and many times a day to reach his scattered classrooms in fortified block-houses, stone pickets, in Landi Khana itself and, lastly, our hut. Arriving at the day's end, like us, he'd usually lost motivational steam. Throwing him the occasional Urdu word to satisfy our consciences, Desmond and I sidetracked him into entertaining us with stories. He described the village where he grew up. He told wild tales of his *"pagal's"*—his uncle's—Khan *Sahib*'s brave deeds during his service in the Raj and Civil Service; we pleaded to meet him.

"Next time you go Peshawar, I arrange," Yusuf Khan agreed.

Oral tests in Urdu were held in Peshawar a train ride's world away. Both Desmond and I made sure we didn't pass, not the first time, nor the second, nor the third. Four times we were issued passes, four times we fled camp and caught the train to Peshawar. Four glorious visits we luxuriated in the green and tented oasis of the Officers' Club. Unable to postpone passing the test any longer, the fourth time we passed. Three hundred rupees was my reward for passing the exam. With nowhere to spend it, I stashed it into my growing furlough fund. I toyed with learning some obscure Indian and Burmese dialect to earn the five-thousand-rupee compensation, but the idea of more studying… no. My Urdu, Gurkhali and smattering of Hindi were enough for the present.

Yusuf met us when we got off the Peshawar train and led us through a maze of twisting, high-walled dusty back streets to stop before a heavy wooden gate deep-set in a mud wall.

"Khan *Sahib*'s house," he announced, pushing the open the gate.

We stepped into a Persian garden paradise where soothing fountains splashed and a heady perfume filled the air from flowering jasmine, gardenias, and roses. Shade trees of mulberry, sweet and bitter orange, apricot and almond edged the formal beds and geometric pools, the very sight and sound of which induced cool. A handsome man with a white flowing beard and wearing an embroidered skullcap rose from a swing bench hanging from a bough in the shadows, his hands pressed together in welcome.

"I am honored to meet you. Yusuf's friends are my friends." Khan *Sahib* escorted us into his large two-storey house.

Respectfully we removed our boots, touched the floor and the lintel briefly with our fingers before stepping over the carved wooden threshold into the formal *Majlis* he used to receive guests. The outside barely intruded. Geometric light and shadow patterned the floor through fretwork panels set into the wall, and it was a moment before I could make out the room's detail. A framed gold and crimson quotation in praise of Allah on one wall was the only decor. A mud platform opulent with Persian rugs and silk cushions ringed the room. Khan *Sahib* folded his legs beneath him, pulled down his knee-length grey silk over-shirt, and settled onto a swing bed hanging from the ceiling across from where we sat. Then he reached for a chased-silver and maroon-tasseled Hubble-Bubble Pipe. I sucked in my breath. My stocking feet had left a trail of sweaty footprints across the marble floor.

"A little refreshment?" Khan *Sahib*'s fingers snapped. A servant bowed before us, offering a tray with two glasses of warm champagne. I couldn't refuse. I sipped politely though I'd have much preferred fresh *limu-pani,* the lime water he and Yusuf were drinking.

"To remind you of home." Khan *Sahib* laughed, drumming his fingers on his knees as a servant cranked the handle of an ancient music box for our benefit, blasting us with an incongruous British Music Hall rendition of *"Knees up, Mother Brown."* Thankfully he had just one English record. He changed it for a haunting Indian Devotional *raga*. Conversation ceased. Lifted by its tumbling, cascading note, the past, the future and the present disappeared. Was I in Mughal Shalimar with *"a jug of wine, a loaf of bread… missing only Thou…?"* Seeing my rapture, Khan *Sahib* smiled.

Once the music faded, he called a servant to for his collection of medals and certificates. Nostalgically praising the Raj, he raised the lid of a glass-topped case and handing us his treasures one by one, described how each was earned. Charming, so gentle a man, he lived in paradise. We, with such different lives, returned to our sweltering hell.

My appointment as Junior Company Officer was to an encampment of marquees seven hundred feet above Landi Kotal. Fort Tent, so jokingly named, was laid out in precise grids marked by whitewashed stones within range of the main camp's artillery. A stinking furnace when it was hot, ball-freezing when it was cold. With the flaps tied open, the canvas heated the interior into a sweat-drenching steam bath. With the flaps secure in winter, the seeping cold had us shivering around a charcoal brazier. Not exactly bulletproof, I noted when I arrived. The constant twoc-twoc and pinging ricochet of sniper fire just beyond the thin layer of canvas kept me tensely alert those first nights, but soon the sounds became no more than blasted interruptions to my sleep.

Night fire landing too close spooked the mules. White-eyed, they'd stampede from their enclosure, ripping guy ropes and collapsing tents in their terror.

"Don't let it happen on my watch," I prayed when I was Duty Officer. I dreading the hellish task of restoring order.

As in Alexander's time, our responsibility was to man the string of pickets along Khargali Ridge that separated British India from Afghanistan's tribal territories. Three Afghan Wars later, the Russians, the British, and Alexander the Great himself had all failed. Still the Afghanis remained defiantly independent. It was our turn again, but this time round we better understood the play of war. Afghanis would never be conquered. Our presence was mere political posturing.

Held down by sniper fire, crouched behind the string of pickets and protective low-walled *sangars* along the Khargali Ridge above Fort Tent, our men were frequently outnumbered and needed artillery backup from seven hundred feet below. With spectacular precision, the gunners' cannon avoided our positions and landed their shells exactly on the snipers.

"Bull's eye." How our troops cheered.

My company of men and I spent our days being goaded up and down the Khargali Ridge's steep seven hundred feet towering above Fort Tent, on patrols and picket inspections by our Company Commander, Charles Boucher. I climbed, I ran, I jogged till at last I toughened lean and fit.

"Look more like a soldier, now." Charles acknowledged, not that he let up on his regime.

Like "The Grand Old Duke of York," he marched Company A *"to the top of the hill, and when we were up at the very, very top, he marched us down again…"*

I began to look forward to our first ascent before breakfast.

"…when the ridge loomed stark against the pale eggshell sky, when the air tinged cool, and dawn's brief breeze announced heat closely on its tail …"

But penning poetry would have to wait.

Once we had left the barbed-wire perimeter and crossed the plain, "Company. Break step." Charles gave the order, and we jogged in our own rhythm up the rocky slope to the top.

"…and when we were only half way up, we were neither up nor down…"

Annoyingly, the rhyme buzzed in time with my footsteps.

Charles lived for sport and enlivened our daily routine with what he called a *khud* race back to camp. With whoops and yells, their arms spread wide for balance, digging the heels of their hobnailed boots against the rocky surface, the men bounded, slid and leapt in the air, setting off mini-landslides without ever missing their footing. Gurkhas, born mountain men, unfailingly beat us to the bottom, then lolled, waiting mockingly to cheer their slowcoach-*Sahibs* to the finish.

"Come on, Sir. You can beat him."

Charles in van trailed in second last, then me, "Tail-end-Charlie." The ability to race down the precipitous rocky slopes without falling was an essential life-or-death skill in Frontier Territory. "Once more, Hugh. Race me again." Faster." Charles made certain I developed that skill, and became as sure-footed and as fit as my men.

In the mounting heat after breakfast, Charles and I ascended the seven hundred feet for the second time to inspect the outlying pickets. Traversing the stony ridge, we checked the permanent breast-high *sangars* were in good repair, were sited within range of Landi Khana's guns, and covered the railway track in the Khyber Pass below. We set the troops massing piles of loose stones ready for building emergency shelters on the off chance of being caught in the open by a Pathan ambush or sharp shooter.

"Again. Again," we ordered, stopwatch in hand, each time shaving off seconds. Lives depended on a *sangar's* speedy building.

Sangars were used in a deadly sort of "I'm-the-king-of-the castle, so-you're-the-dirty-rascal" game of leap-frog. First our own sharpshooters hurriedly built and sheltered behind a *sangar* from where they covered slow-moving brigades until they'd passed safely out of danger. Signaling evacuation, the picket troops rapidly leapt from the *sangar*, ran to the next position, built and leapt into and out of another, then another and another and so on while at the same time fending off the Pathan tribesmen snapping at their heels. Springing from hiding, the Pathans scrambled for the vacant shelters as they were vacated, and fire at our retreating backs.

"Are you sure I'm ready, Sir?" I asked when both commanding officers, Charles and Guy from Company B, left me in sole charge of Fort Tent during a quiet spell.

"Jolly good practice for you, Rose."

They waved cheerily, disappearing on the down train to Peshawar for some well earned R and R; Charles to follow the hounds with the Peshawar Hunt, and blue-eyed Guy to "poodle-fake," the strange expression we used for chasing women.

And so it was, good practice. I carried a loaded pistol with me at all times.

Accompanying Charles on his rounds and the occasional maneuvers "Showing the Flag" were the few times I escaped the perimeter wire. Camp fever was endemic. I missed Yusuf's lessons. In Fort Tent we resorted to desperate measures for amusement. Shameful measures.

Cat-hunts became our after-dinner sport. Feral cats seeking refuge from the cold invariably sneaked into the space between the double fly and canvas wall of the Officers Mess. Egged on by flailing pig-sticks and wild, "Go get 'ems and tally-hos." we would flush out the poor moggies into the waiting jaws of the camp's two resident pit-bull terriers. Culls were necessary, we may have been bored, but our callous laughter and the method, inexcusable.

Less brutish than their British *Sahibs*, Gurkha troops kicked footballs around the wide, stony ledge inside the fort's mud walls, and played cricket with makeshift cricket bats and wickets with shouts of "How'z zat" in true British fashion.

Signalers. 3rd Gurkha Rifles.

Standing Down. North West Frontier.

31
MY FIRST COMMAND

The Afghan Border

Major McSwiney, our Company Commander-to-be. His reputation ran before him and we looked forward to his arrival with curiosity. He had received awards for bravery—Distinguished Service Order, Military Cross. He was said to be brave, conscientious...efficient ...austere.... He had survived being gassed and months on the Somme during The Great War...slept with mobilization equipment under his bed...was obsessed with health ...religion.... The list grew longer with each telling. Stories of his eccentricities ricocheted around the Mess.

When a grey-faced officer with a pencil moustache stepped off the Peshawar train and returned our welcome salute, I was taken by surprise. Tougher and more brilliant than his reputation, it was only his looks that lied. He turned out to be a "spiffing" choice, we all agreed. Though, from the startling list of rules he read at our first meeting, all of us briefly wondered. Clearly, he was different, peculiar even when it came to health.

"Any officer contracting malaria or sand-fly fever will be held culpable. Sick time will be docked from your leave. Since mosquito and sand-fly are rife in the Kyber, mosquito nets are to be used and properly secured."

"Each officer is to keep his own supply of Bamber Oil. Apply nightly, covering the entire body."

He forced a smile before elaborating,

"I, myself, get up twice nightly to renew the oil. I expect you to follow my example."

He stood immaculate, crisp, in the sweltering Mess hut. We dripped.

"I look forward to meeting each one of you privately later today. At ease."

Saluting, he left us open-mouthed and silent till he was out of earshot, then erupting incredulously.

"Damned if I'm oiling twice a night."

"Penalized for falling sick."

"I say, whatever next?"

At my personal interview his rattle of rapid questions so flustered me, I was often caught in mid-answer as he fired the next.

"How's your father? Still serving? Met him in Bareilly. Give him my regards. What of you? Planning to get married? I hope not. Too young. Ruin your career and...Describe your time at Sandhurst, your military ambitions..." Stopping abruptly, he fixed me with a penetrating stare and barked, "Are you saved?" While I struggled how to answer, he explained, "Do you believe in Jesus Christ?"

As I got to know him, both off and in the field, McSwiney became an example of everything I liked and respected in a man. He mixed efficiency and firm discipline with fairness, and took a friendly interest in my, and every man's personal welfare.

Meanwhile, his radar was fixed on me, a lazy devil who sloped off at every opportunity I could get away with. Not on his watch though, I soon learned to my cost. There was no hiding from that man.

During my first command, my remote blockhouse clung to the Khargali Ridge perched out of sight of Fort Tent and the main camp below in the plain. With only myself to obey, I habitually slept till the unsoldierly hour of eight.

I was peacefully dreaming, safe under my mosquito net, when Major McSwiney's voice shot me from my cot. I sprung to attention, attempted a salute, tripped on my bootlaces and fell tangled in a heap. His pencil moustache thinned grim. His only comment, "Report to my office, Rose. Thirteen hundred hours sharp." He never put his officers down in front of the men.

Standing before him in his office, ears blazing, ego withered, I shrunk, crushed by his hail of angry words. Not to say I never lazed in bed again, but he never caught me out. I primed the Fort's Platoon Commander seven hundred feet below to crank alert on the field telephone the minute McSwiney set off from Landi Khana on a spot check.

"Red Wolf on the prowl."

I kept a starched pair of shorts standing upright beside my cot, scramble into them, pull on an ironed shirt, stockings and mirror-polished boots, buckle on my web, and ankle puttees, and slap my *topee* on my head. With a loaded Webley pistol in my holster, I marched about, purposefully poking stones with my cane, and feign surprise as he approached the blockhouse. Immaculate, inspection-ready, I snapped a salute at attention.

"Company, present and correct, Sir." If McSwiney had his suspicions, he never let on.

He enjoyed testing me on his inspection rounds to the outlying pickets.

"Hugh," he sprang on me. "Stand your men to."

At his command, I'd blow my whistle three times, racing at the double to my "alarm position" while he clocked my time with a stopwatch.

"Good show, Rose," were words of praise I worked for.

When inspecting the blockhouse itself, McSwiney routinely checked if the Lewis guns were fully loaded and their sights aligned accurately to the white blobs marking "dead ground." At one spot inspection, he checked my pistol and found no bullet up the spout.

"Hugh," he rebuked with an austere smile, "Such a forgetful mistake could cost your life. I should be upset if that happened."

Little by little, he coaxed me into shape and taught me to take my responsibilities seriously.

"Kaffir Kot," White Man's Post, the Afridi Tribesmen called it. We did as well. Five hundred feet above and a mile west of my own blockhouse, it was my nearest neighbor; I visited it often.

I assumed the picket was named after us pale *Angreezes*. But no, its name, its very site had survived two thousand years, since 300 B.C. when Alexander the Great built the fortification. Perfectly sited on the Khargli Ridge, Kaffir Kot dominated the Afghan border. My imagination fired, I repeated its romantic name, "Kaffir Kot," picturing Alexander's men swarming the ridge armed with primitive weaponry.

Though poetry escaped me, I dreamed. Isolated in my lonely perch, I followed Alexander's surefooted elephants, the columns of kilted men and laden mules relentlessly marching foot by foot up the precipitous ridge separating Afghanistan from his conquered kingdom. Dust stung my face. The wind. Snow. I suffered heat and bitter cold, the very conditions I experienced were the very same Alexander's troops endured all those years ago.

Nothing happened. The first day. The next. Nor the next. Alone. Bored. Long days turned to weeks. Endless weeks to months. To relieve the tedium, I used my helio lamp to flash, to "helio," unimportant "all's-well-anything-to-report?" messages to my nearest neighbor, Lester Forster, in Kaffir Kot above me. Pretending urgent business, we visited one another for no greater reason than to chat to a fellow Brit.

"Take over, Subedar Khan. Going on inspection." And I scampered the five hundred feet from my picket to Lester's with a couple of men.

As we were nearing Kaffir Kot on just such a fabricated business, a bullet whistled past, narrowly missing my head. A hail of gunfire followed. Bending low to the ground, my men and I raced for the nearest *sangar* and jumped behind its stone walls. Bullets ping-thocted into the dirt. The gunfire didn't let up, keeping us pinned down for an interminable couple of hours. Evacuation was impossible without risk to my men.

"Take a small detachment. Check the number of snipers, their positions, and deal with the problem," I ordered my N.C.O.

Moving cautiously under cover of the dry *nullahs*, he and a couple of Gurkhas moved stealthily out of sight, while we drew the heavy sniper fire away from them. Half an hour passed. Suddenly, silence. Shortly, I saw my detachment scrambling safely down the ridge towards the *sangar* where we crouched.

"All quiet, Sir. Sniper dealt with, Sir." The N.C.O., Kul Bahadur Gurung, snapped to attention, saluted crisply.

In proof, he emptied his rucksack, rolling out a glazed-eyed, blood-besmirched head of a red-bearded Afridi at my feet. My stomach hit my throat. I just made it outside before spilling my horror on the ground. My orders were worded very precisely ever after. "Deal with…" took on another meaning.

Shortly after that episode, it was Company B's turn to relieve us at Fort Tent. Leaping and whooping down the precipitous *khud*, abandoning my picket, we fled to Landi Khana's comparative civilization. Oh, the luxury of sleeping in a wooden hut, eating a proper meal in a Mess surrounded by chums after so many solitary weeks. I showered the dust from my hair and grimy skin, and dropped back into a world where humans played and talked the way I did.

Polo on the Frontier was nothing like the game of a gentleman's Country Club. Three-aside, our sticks wildly swinging at the puck, dodging sniper fire, our feet skimmed the ground raising clouds of dust. The stocky tribal ponies, understanding the play, wheeled to better place us for a shot without any command. Charles Boucher gave me his two polo ponies when he left for England. "Have ponies, will play," and how I played. After months of being cooped up on the ridge, for a few hours I forgot I was an unwelcome *ferengi* in a foreign land. I whooped and laughed, cursing, and wildly swung my stick to let off steam. A fairly level strip of dirt outside the camp's perimeter fence did for a makeshift polo ground, but kicked up so much dust the puck frequently disappeared, never to be seen again. Despite our being watched over by armed guard, bullets frequently rained on us from the surrounding hills and made the ponies bolt for the higher ground. Sniper fire certainly spiced up our game, but we dodged the bullets, undeterred, without breaking step.

To stop us from going stir-crazy, a couple of weekends during the cold weather, the C.O. packed us off to shoot partridge on two rock peaks we named Big Ben and Little Ben beyond the plain. I ignored my ever-present armed escort and the incessant sniper fire, and each footstep beyond the wire took me a step further from hell. Sniping was mostly just for show, a reminder of their presence. I never saw a man hit. Not many partridge either, though if we did bag one for the pot, it made a welcome change to tinned Bully Beef.

Fit and lean from Charles Boucher's daily madcap races up and down the *khud*, I never lost breath running on the steep hillsides, or scampering along the dry *nullahs* pursuing our quarry, French Red partridge, birds as dun colored as the earth. The ping-thoc volleys from our guns echoing in the valley doubled as a warning to any lurking snipers in the hills. Officers fired at the game, the snipers fired at us and the Gurkhas fired at the snipers.

We grumbled among ourselves of course about the heat, cold, flies, food, no women, but I look back at my time on the North West Frontier with nostalgia. There, I was an important cog in a mighty wheel. I was not like the desert frog waiting for rain; it was the very ruggedness, the isolation of that arid place that gave me life.

Subedar-Majors. Rajaputana Rifles.

32

MARCHING ON COLUMN

My First Engagement

The operation "Going on Column" was as stylized as Kabuki Theater. The motive was to show the flag; flaunt the might of Britain's face to the Pathans. The performers—officers and troops—headed the Column, brandishing props, flags and weapons. Stagehands followed—bearers for officers' personal care—*bhisties,* the water carriers—sweepers to remove the night soil—cooks from Goa—*dhobi-wallahs* for laundry. Backstage trailed a horde of camp followers to erect tents and unload furniture, bathtubs, even wood-burning stoves, each sundown at ceasefire. Pre-dinner sherry appeared on a camp silver salver, dinner on regimental china. Tin mugs and enamel plates would have done just as well, but *sahibs* roughing it? Unconscionable to those who served us. Though not in the Army per se, camp followers still earned Frontier medals the same as the troops if caught in enemy fire. No surprise the Column avoided overnight stops. Snipers' potshots apart, setting camp was a business I feared. Unless the site had been previously used, the troops had to hack through bedrock to gather stones enough to build *sangars.* Men, mules, cannon, ammunition, tents, food, all to be unloaded, secured, and readied, without mechanical transport of any kind.

Often the night sky was brightening by the time camp was squared away.

The Brigade Commander heading the column raised his baton. Poised. Three...two... one...ACTION. The show began.

The Brigade Commander indicated sites he wanted secured: a hill, a promontory, a *nullah*, that he wanted secured. He waved his pointer, sent a group of Picket troops scurrying up the rocky terrain. Quickly gathering loose rocks, in minutes they constructed protective *sangars* Crouched safely inside, they covered the advancing Column. A man popped up briefly, waved a red flag, signaled "Abandon Picket." At which, Picket troops sprang from cover, raced to build and occupy another low *sangar*, simultaneously firing potshots to deter Pathan snipers from firing at the Column's retreating back. Leapfrogging in and out, as the rearguard pickets abandoned one *sangar*, the advancing Pathan tribesmen commandeered it. Jump. Thud. Occupy. Vacate. In, out, in, from one to the next, Pathans and our Gurkha troops hopped to each in turn. Once safely beyond Pathan range, our signaler semaphored the Artillery Battery in Landi Khana below for cannon backup. Part game, part in earnest, Going on Column was a performance we looked forward to playing.

"Punitive Column," I dreaded. Soon after my arrival on the Frontier, I was ordered on such. On it, I first saw the brutal way we British dealt with defiance. I knew then, why they wanted us out.

Our Company was ordered on Punitive Column by the Chief Political Agent in Peshawar to deal with what he called those "damn, confounded troublemakers," tribesmen who had refused to cough up the five hundred rifles, fined for having fired at an up train traveling towards the Kyber Pass. Our orders: "Fine, confiscate all rifles. If they persist, burn the *malik's* village."

Under the watchful eye of the P.A., Political Agent, a mandatory observer representing the Foreign Political Service, we surrounded and stormed the village at dawn, and confiscated every weapon. Ignoring their sobbing pleas, we herded women and screaming children from their homes. Done, the Sappers advanced. Their orders: blow up the buildings, the village watchtower included.

Their only means of defense destroyed, the villagers had no place to barricade themselves from marauding tribesmen bent on rape and pillage. Sickened, my lip quivered. I had taken part. "Bastards." my mind screamed. "Unnecessary cruelty...and in the name of justice."

The *malik*, the headman, put up no resistance. His glowering face, however, plainly displayed his hatred and resentment. Villagers hurled stones along with curses. That was the limit of their opposition. Then. I should have guessed.

"Splendid Job, men." Our Commander beamed. Smug. It was time to head back to camp.

The Column withdrew, wending slowly back to Base, every hill and hillock en route having been cleared by the advance guard of Picket troops. Brigade Commander, and his P.A. watchdog led the way, the main Brigade of Royal Artillery and Sappers followed. Behind them, under Colonel Tuck, our Company in rearguard, then last of all came "Tail Arse Charlie" bearing a large red flag.

Showers of sniper fire slowed our progress. I saw a bullet rip through a man's leg. I saw a man fall. Though we suffered minor casualties, the long, snaking Column pushed forward thinning to single file along a narrow, tortuous path between two hills. A heavy hailstorm of bullets rained down onto our left flank from the stony hills, drawing our counter-fire. My attention was momentarily diverted. As I aimed my rifle left, a group of Lashkars, righteous, sword-flourishing Pathans, leapt from a side *nullah* on the right, charging directly at us in the rearguard screaming.

"Kill, Kill, Allah Akbar. Kill the infidel *ferengis.* God is Great."

Hand-to-hand, life and death combat, was nothing I'd ever trained for.

"Fire." Colonel Tuck ordered counterattack.

But the Lashkars were too close upon us. Rifles were useless. *Kukris* and pistols in hand, we swiped at our attackers. Curved blades flashing, pistols brandishing, we parried and charged. I have little recollection of the wildly disordered skirmish beyond the splash and smell of blood. Colonel Tuck's tactics had our attackers fleeing with their dead and casualties as suddenly as they'd stormed us. Over and again on the long march back to camp, I replayed what I remembered: zing thoc, a bullet hitting a rock... brown faces, contorted... discolored teeth bared... the surprising green of a Laskar's eyes...clouds of stinging dust.

My Company Subedar-Major assured me I led the charge like a "Boy's Own" hero. I had fired my Webley pistol three times. "Performed very well, Sir." He couldn't be sure if I had actually scored a hit. But I had survived my first engagement.

It was a race to reach our fallen, both dead and wounded, before the Pathans, before the poor buggers were castrated, and their genitals stuffed dangling from their mouths. Tribeswomen, as well as knife-wielding tribesmen, vied for these gruesome trophies. Policy was, never leave one of our own behind.

The return to Landi Khana blurs, no memory left of whether we fell under further fire. Some casualties were sustained, I know, and one fatality. It was dark when we marched into camp. We sat for dinner in the starlight. So late. Laughter jerked me awake, my head inches from hitting my soup bowl. I flopped onto my bunk unwashed and awoke fully clothed.

Nothing remained static in the Army. Change and separation were the norm and only the strongest friendships survived.

My Colonel Tuck left for England on long furlough. Company "B" took over Bagh Fort and the Khargali Ridge. "C" Company, under John Morris, moved to Landi Khana to replace Company "A." At Christmas, Charles went home to the Staff College in Camberley. Guy applied for and was posted to the Khurran Militia at Parachinar, and the game of box-'n-cox did not stop there. Both I, and the Regiment, were in for a change. New blood in the guise of Jack Colenso temporarily filled Colonel Tuck's boots as Commanding Officer.

Marching on Column. North West Frontier.

ARCOT

33
HAIRY DESMOND VERSUS THE JOCK

Colonel Tuck's replacement was unpopular before he even arrived, and when he did, we disliked him on sight. Definitely "not one of us," Major Jock Colenso, the Seventh Gurkha Rifles, came from a five-year secondment with the Burma Military Police. If being a "bloody *box-wallah*" wasn't damning enough, his unappetizing looks, gross physique, bullying, and laziness sealed it. Jock Colenso favored his favorites and unmercifully hounded the men he disliked, my roommate Desmond, for example.

For some reason Desmond never discovered, his posting to the Regiment was unwelcome, even before Jock's arrival. The Army had it in for him and employed the meanest tactics to dislodge him. They shamed him, put him on "special report," took away his privileges and appointed him duty officer for the worst duties on the most unpopular shifts. Well aware of his fear of horses and poor horsemanship, the bastards assigned him the Battalion's most feisty charger. To no avail, Desmond smiled and grimly stuck it out for three full years before admitting defeat and transferring to the Indian Army Service Corps, or Rice Corps, as it was nicknamed. Though he eventually became quite popular with his peers in the Mess, he was never invited to join the Regiment.

Jock fixed his lance on Desmond and picked on him at every chance. But Desmond, "the hairy one," got his own back on one memorable occasion.

Soon after Jock's arrival, our Adjutant left on furlough, leaving Desmond as acting Adjutant. Unfortunately for him, his appointment coincided with an important ceremonial parade designed to display the "mighty" British Empire. The massed Battalion assembled in review order behind Desmond. Mounted on his charger, sword drawn to his face, he waited for the C.O. to arrive. Desmond was no horseman. His restive stallion pawed the ground, tossed its mane and gave an occasional buck. Trepidation growing, it became evident the horse would eventually take charge.

"Don't 'arse about, Mr. Whyte," hissed the Second-in-Command from the saddle of his perfectly behaved gelding.

Arsing about was the last thing poor Desmond wanted to do. His only thought was to control his mount and stay seated in the saddle.

Trumpets blared, drums rolled, and onto the parade ground rode the impressive figure of Jock Colenso with his drawn sword vertical before his nose. Crossing the ground at a controlled slow canter, he reined in his horse and halted facing the Battalion to take the salute. The Adjutant's role was to canter at attention towards the Commanding Officer, sword before his face, halt, salute and report, "Battalion, present and correct, Sir." Well, it's what should have happened.

Instead, swaying from side to side, clutching the feisty stallion's mane with his left hand, his sword horizontal aimed lance-like with the apparent intention of running its point through his hated C.O. and unseating him, Desmond galloped full tilt towards Jock as in a jousting tournament. At this alarming sight, and there was no stopping either of them, Jock's horse turned tail, and carrying Jock with him disappeared in a cloud of dust with Desmond in hot pursuit.

The Battalion collapsed cheering, jeering, and hooting with laughter. Poor Desmond. Jock never forgave him. Retribution was not far behind.

In March just as the real heat began, Desmond's and my three months' "Privilege Local Leave" fell due, our reward for serving abroad, courtesy of the Lee Commission's ruling: "Henceforth, Officers posted to the Frontier shall be entitled to three months' leave in addition to the three-times yearly ten days 'casual leave.'"

We planned to travel together as far as the Seraj railhead and then go our separate ways. Mine to explore and hunt in one of the side valleys of the Kulu, Desmond to fly-fish the upper reaches of the Beas River in the Kulu Valley. Packed and ready, armed with maps and gear, we caught the train to Peshawar one day before Desmond's birthday. Good reason to celebrate we decided. Spend a night in one of the Club's canvas palaces set permanently in the grounds, eat and drink ourselves silly, then take the next morning's train.

Staggering a little unsteadily to our "palace" after a lavish and very liquid dinner, we fell into the deepest of sleeps. Reveille from the neighboring camp beyond the wire blasted me panicked, scrambling for my clothes, thinking I'd missed Parade. Then I remembered. I was on Leave. The day was glorious. It was Desmond's birthday. We still had three hours for a leisurely shave and breakfast before our train. We were about to head to the dining room, when to our surprise our unpopular Staff Captain from Landi Kotal, Captain Beard, stuck his head through the tent flap.

"Happy birthday, Desmond." He smiled pleasantly. "Orders from Jock Colenso. As an officer on special report your leave is cancelled. Return to Landi Kotal at once." Beard sneered vengefully, adding he'd be back later that afternoon to escort Desmond back to camp on the up train.

Jock Colenso exacted his cruel revenge with perfect timing.

"The bloody bastard. The loathsome bugger." No swear words were adequate.

I left Desmond gloomily packing his bags. Such a good sport, he clapped me on the back, wished me all the best, and even saw me onto the Lahore mail train. Cursing Jock's spiteful injustice to my friend, it took me hours to simmer down before I could look forward to my leave.

Transport.

Mountain Village. Kulu Valley.

Kulu Valley.

Valley of the Flowers. Kulu.

34
LOCAL LEAVE IN THE SERAJ

My spirits rose the nearer I got to the snow line. Craning my neck from the carriage, absorbing every inch of the 17,000-foot hills folded below the Himalayas, I tried to pinpoint the valley where the mountain range divided into the Pir Panjal and Dhauladhar and swung north to merge with the Karakoram beyond Kashmir.

I was headed for the lush wooded valleys and alpine meadows of the Seraj's remote game reserve managed by the Forestry Department, where I'd rented exclusive shooting and fishing rights for the next three months. Though my permit allowed me to hunt one *thar*, one brown bear, a snow leopard, and any quantity of small game I needed for the pot, my only interest was small game and the occasional *thar*.

Dismounting at Pathankot—the railhead for Mandi State and the Kulu Valley, I was met by the Forestry Department's *shikari*, my hunter-guide for the next three months. He was charming and intelligent, and his infectious enthusiasm made it easy to be friends—as much as social custom allowed. We never knew one another's names. "*Shikari*" and "*Sahib*, Sir" sufficed.

He rallied our entourage of coolies hired to porter our supplies and gear. One coolie grabbed my small bag, another hoisted my bedding roll onto his head, and my adventure began. With infinite patience, never lording it as teacher, *Shikari* schooled me in the subtleties of tracking.

Shikari set our first base camp in a meadow at 8,000 feet where two snow-fed streams tumbled from the high valleys to form a delightful pool. Its reflective waters so clear, I swam in a cloudless sky. Crawling sleepily from my tent in my underpants, I plunged with a yell into its icy waters, gasping and rolling for as long as I could stand. Goose-bumped and blue, I leapt onto the sheep-cropped turf bordering the pool, threw on my robe to dry in the rising sun, my tingling skin smoothed to silk.

"Your *chai*, Sir." Without change of expression or comment, *Shikari* handed his crazy *sahib* a mug of scalding tea. Though from the coolies' shocked faces I clearly suffered a case of altitude sickness, or worse, had gone *Doolally Tap*.

By day *Shikari* led me along precipitous hillsides in search of the invisible *thar*, whose camouflage was so perfect even he had difficulty spotting one. I was secretly glad. Small game for the pot was thrill enough. It was rare we returned without a *kalij* pheasant, a *monal*, an exquisite peacock-like bird, a hare, a snow pigeon or a spotted *chital* deer.

Servants, master, united, content, warm around the embers of a fire, we dined together beneath the stars—kings on a carpet flying above the world.

We were never attacked, but *Shikari* ordered the fire stoked all night after hearing the sinister saw-sawing of a hungry panther or leopard only yards from our tents—man being a favorite kill.

I slowed down after the first month. I had other things to do apart from hunt.

"Take the day off, *Shikari*. I'll trek alone today." And for the sheer exhilaration of solitude, I'd climb above the tree line to the Himalayan meadows bright with violet gentian, peach columbine and yellow primula. Nestled on a bed of sweetgrass and wildflowers, I could only gaze, gaze and gaze some more. Sometimes "waxing lyrical," I let a poem burst from me like poems had from Vetter's lips in the Alps.

I love thee Himalaya
your rainbow meadows
grass fingers
your folds in which to lie
above the Valley of the Flowers
and the Kulu

I startled a shepherd one day. In rough handspun clothes, made from spinning wool and goat hair, he walked with his flock in the high pastures, his flute-like pipes sprinkling the idyllic pastoral scene with notes so sweet, tears sprung to my eyes, making real the dream I was in paradise, my paradise alone.

One early morning high above camp, accompanied by no one, I crossed a snowfield high beyond the meadows. Stepping from an aspen grove, I surprised a male snow leopard lapping at a pool barely a hundred yards from me. Lifting his head, curious, he gazed at me with his limpid yellow eyes before padding majestically into the grove. I lowered my gun. His life was more valuable than any fine rug.

dawn's purple shadows still linger in the sky
trap the leopard's un-winking stare
poised motionless to catch a shepherd's pipes
beneath the snows of Himachal

Small game apart, my total bag for the three months was one thirteen-and-a-half- inch *thar*, one *bhurrel* (a kind of wild sheep found at high altitude), and one *chital*. More in love with exploring nature than killing, and tanned, fit and rested, I returned to Landi Kotal a changed man.

There is no accounting for the vagaries of the Army. No sooner had I re-joined my regiment at Landi Kotal and completed an undemanding two-week gunnery course with Royal Artillery in Akora, than I learned I was top of the furlough roster of donated leave. I'd quite forgotten putting in for it months earlier when I discovered I could claim another officer's unwanted leave. A whole year's furlough on full pay was too tempting to turn down. Dumfounded, I packed my bags again.

On the long rumbling ride through the Indus, I turned my eyes towards Europe, hungry to see my family and friends again. With two years accumulated pay in my pocket, I had money to burn, and burn it I did. Bombay, the *S.S. Pilsna*, the Corinth Canal of the Greek Islands, Brindisi, Venice, skiing in Cortina d'Ampezzo, gambling in Cannes, and dining in Milan. In London I made a lightning visit to Mother and Kathy, and finding them happy and well, I selfishly abandoned them for the exciting bed of my latest love.

Stepping from the train in Delhi, nine months furlough in Europe blurred as in a dream. My uniform had become a straitjacket; it no longer fit. I closed my eyes to blot out the present. My battalion and Lansdowne's dreary depot lay seventeen gut-wrenching miles ahead. Hair-pin bends twisted through thick forest, skirting terraced fields and villages. Dizzied sick, I needed frequent breaks.

"This very good, clean place," my driver said as he stopped beside a road-side "hotel," an unlikely looking shack built against the hillside.

Inside, pungent spices, rice and *dhal* bubbled in charcoal-blackened pots. A banana leaf for a plate, fingers and fire-roasted chapatti for a spoon, served with a tin cup of sugared, buffalo-milk tea, the simple meal rekindled my love affair with India. A land of sweet surprises, a land where no traveler passed by unfed. To serve a stranger was to serve God.

The owner welcomed, bowed, hands clasped. "*Namaste Sahib.*"

"*Namaste,*" I replied.

I offered cigarettes all round. India welcomed me back.

Lansdowne

35

LANSDOWNE HILL STATION

Home Of The Gurkhas

Our battalion's two-year stint on the North West Frontier over, purposeless soldiering yawned once again with bugger all to do.

Named after the Viceroy, Lord Lansdowne, Lansdowne Hill Station in the foothills of the Garhwal in the United Provinces abutted so close to the 6,000-foot drop it seemed in danger of slipping over its perilous edge. A place where panther, tiger and bear waited hidden to reclaim their jungle territory, and defiant pugmarks and pungent spray proclaimed their presence.

Many men lost their balance in Lansdowne's isolated place of ghosts and death.

A friend of mine, Teddy Edwards, fell to his death during a Garhwali guest night. It was the time of brilliant falling stars. Drinks in hand, a group of us moved outside after dinner. A low stone wall protected the Mess garden from the North Khud, a precipitous dwarf oak and rhododendron covered slope falling unbroken to the North Mall path below, before tumbling a further three thousand feet to the river. Teddy was particularly tight. Egged on by our gin-soaked cheers, he teetered unsteadily along the wall waving a glass of whisky. Teddy turned, balanced his glass on his forehead and made to walk.

"Get down, Teddy. Don't be such a bloody fool," I begged. But he slipped and disappeared.

We found him a hundred feet down below in the jungle scrub, sitting propped ghoulishly against a tree, his neck broken. "Suicide." The possibility was whispered.

Three years before I arrived, charging an imaginary foe during squad training, a deranged officer had launched himself over the edge of the parade ground, sword drawn.

"Avaunt. Avaunt." His cry was heard on many a moonlit night, and men swore they'd seen the flash and parry of his ghostly sword.

A long-dead Major Gregson, a Garhwali Officer killed during the Great War, regularly turned out the Quarter Guard riding on, what else, but a white horse?

The Regiment's own Mess ghost, tame by comparison, tossed books to the floor from the library shelves. And my Subedar-Major insisted he'd seen Gurkha Riflemen stuck to the barrack room ceiling levitating while asleep.

"Load of bull," I laughed with my friends.

Harry, my good friend, caught my eye uneasily. We both remembered the clink of a sword and spurs and the sound of approaching heavy footfalls on the veranda of our shared bungalow. My skin crawled. On opening the door—nobody. I had a flashback to the mysterious sound and smell of striking matches I'd heard as a child in Belgium.

Lansdowne spooked us all.

After the Nepal War early in the last century when the Gurkha Battalions were raised, High Command got the crazy idea the Nepalese couldn't withstand the summer heat of the plains. "Best keep our Gurkha boys happy. Get the regiments to build their Stations above 6,000 feet." And so our Hill Station in Lansdowne and many others, Raniket, Mussouri, Almora to name a few, mushroomed along the scarp slopes of the Himalayan foothills. The story goes our Brigadier chose the most inaccessible site he could find to deter H.Q. in Bareilly from sudden inspections. With no road, a hard two-day march the only way up to a sprawling, terraced two-mile jungle-like ridge overgrown with Rhododendron and dwarf oak, 4,000 feet above a snow-fed tributary of the Gogra River, High Command kept their distance. Our nearest neighbors, the Royal Garhwal Rifles lines, perched three miles further to our west, could be only reached by a lonely bridle path we grandly called the North Mall.

Whenever I dined out at the Garhwal Rifle's Mess, I took along my orderly to light the way with a hurricane *butti* and carry my shotgun. Nobody but a fool walked the Mall at night alone. We traveled in raucous groups whenever possible to ward off wild beasts. They watched us, we knew. Frequently the hurricane *butti's* light caught the glint of a pair of orbs from between the trees. Too often I heard of panthers, tiger and black bear killing children, adults and domestic animals, dragging them alive into the jungle by their necks leaving nothing but a sad scrap of clothing or body part to bury.

Beautiful, but boring, Lansdowne. Overseeing endless dreary drills and individual training, I dreamed nostalgically of my year on the Frontier; Landi Kotal, Khargali Ridge, Fort Tent, Pickets, even Going on Column under sniper fire. I'd felt a soldier, battle ready, alive. I missed my pre-breakfast *khud* race from the blockhouses… its mocking Ghurkas bounding by. I missed Charles' rallying cry.

"No dilly-dallying, Hugh," he'd bellow. "Bound. Bound. Think goat."

More a woolly sheep from my yearlong furlough, I devised a fitness plan partly to regain my waistline, partly to relieve the tedium. I hiked the same route, same path, to the same spot every day, timing myself.

A massive boulder overhanging the Northern Khud would be my challenge. By pressing my back hard against the granite, and pulling on an embedded rusty iron ring, it was just possible to edge sideways around and up the overhang along a foot-wide hewn ledge. *"Keep your eyes in the heavens. Don't look down. Don't look down,"* I steadied myself past the dizzying drop until I grew as confident as a tomcat on roof-tiles.

"Hahhhhh." My breath escaped at God's magnificent display. I never got used to its spread. Scarcely a peak laddered less than 25,000 feet skyward. Not recognizing them as mountains at first, I saw only floating clouds till I realized the clouds I saw billowing in the intense blue northern horizon were snow. Snow plumes. The range of jagged peaks stretched the full horizon from the barely discernable Nepalese border to the Simla foothills just forty miles away. With the help of a brass plate screwed to the rock, engraved with positions and names, I identified Dunagiri, Trisul, Nanda Devi, Kamet, the Zaskar Range, Nanda Kot.

"One day, I would, I'd make those peaks mine and reach Tibet." Closing and opening my eyes, I imprinted every one. To fill the hours, I studied Army Survey maps plotting expeditions, and discovered my passion.

Down and south beyond the cantonment, a maze of bridle paths traced from the military buildings to the native village and untidy bazaar sloped over the edge and out of sight to the railhead in Kotdwara in the plains several thousand feet below.

Cold air down my collar and frost-edged grass told we would be leaving soon.

Both Battalions were gathered for the Regiment's Centenary. Bareilly's Camp's city of five hundred tents blazed symbolic power. Built on the old racetrack's immaculate rows of whitewashed stone, tents boasted brick floors, wooden furniture, and attached bath tents. Numbered streets and painted signs indicated Officers' Quarters; First Battalion, Second Battalion; Officers' Mess, H.Q. Command, Chapel, Mess Halls for "other ranks" and troops and servants.

Latrines clustered on the camp's outskirts. For privacy, canvas screens separated officers' from those of other ranks. Adequate for the stocky Gurkhas' on the holers "doing their business," inadequate for us British whose heads and shoulders protruded disembodied above the curtain. For pure devilment, Gurkhas scurried back and forth in front of the canvas curtains, scoring how many times they could force an undignified but mandatory salute from their bare-arsed officers. High Command finally ended the farce.

"Gurkhas of other ranks will in future use their discretion when paying compliments to British officers."

To honor our beloved Colonel Tuck's departure, Bareilly High Command combined the occasion with the Regimental Centenary celebrations. Bareilly's population lined the streets as one hundred and one caparisoned elephants and marching men took part in a *Durbar* unrivaled by anything I'd ever seen. Our two Mess marquees morphed nightly to glittering banqueting halls hosting formal dinners, cocktail parties, garden parties, receptions and balls. Displaying Britain's wealth and power, we entertained maharajas, their maharanis, and dignitaries. We sipped French champagne from gold and silver goblets. Beneath shimmering chandeliers, beside the be-jeweled guests, I dined at one of five tables each with seating for one hundred. Liveried servants hovered, epitomized the Raj, its arrogant magnificence. Scissors cut, needles stitched to create the finest costumes, wangle the finest seating. Talk was of nothing else.

1819 UNIFORMS FOR GENTLEMEN.
PERIOD DRESSES FOR WOMEN.
BAREILLY CLUB.

That Centenary Fancy Dress Ball was the most extravagant occasion I ever attended.

Bedazzled by the glamour, or whether from lust or loneliness, true to pattern I fell hopelessly in love. Sybilla, the daughter of the General, loved me back. The Army wisely forbade our marriage. We glued together the broken pieces of our hearts and quickly forgot each other.

I turned my attention to the weekends and Thursdays, "Guru's Day," a Hindu holiday in India. Regimental duties occupied the other four.

Monday: Collective Training.
Tuesday: Company Training.
Wednesday: Battalion Training.
Friday: Brigade Training.

I was a pawn. We all were. Our duties were so negligible I concluded the explanation for our being there was just that, our presence. Even in the nineteen-twenties, there were whisperings the days of the British Raj were coming to an end.

Every couple of weeks, the District Deputy Commissioner ordered us into the countryside to Show the Flag, go on Color March to proclaim our British domination. A "friendly" call involved a stilted conversation with the *thulsidar*, the headman, while sipping endless glasses of sweet, buffalo-milky *chai* for an obligatory two hours, then marching to the neighboring village and repeating the ritual. Horribly embarrassing to me, our C.O., ignoring or ignorant of Indian aversion to direct questions, barraged the *thulsidar* with inquiries demanding specific answers, forcing the poor man to politely evade commitment with vagueness and inconsequential observations about crops, God's blessings and other generalizations. We staggered away, stiff from sitting on the beaten ground, garlanded with scented blossoms.

If playing the leisure sports of the Raj demonstrated superiority, we succeeded. Most weekends my friends and I camped Indian style beside the shallow waters of the nearest *jheel*. "The men," the natives bivouacked on groundsheets beneath the stars, swapping tales of servitude to relate later to their villages; of dragging ropes over stands of sugarcane to flush partridge for the *sahibs*, of filling and heating tubs with water, of setting carpeted tents with cots, and of meals cooked and served in style.

Christmas was coming. I needed a break.

I wrote to Mother's brother, Jimmy Knowles, a magistrate in nearby Bareilly, a mystery man, an uncle to claim, to shed light on Mother's family. I wangled an invitation for his Christmas Shoot at his forest Rest House in Haldu Parao. Jimmy's reputation as a crack shot was almost on a par with that of his good friend, Corbett, the legendary hunter of man-eating tiger. I looked forward to our meeting.

"Bottoms-up"

Sikh Regiment on Parade.

Guards. Queen Alexandra's Own 3rd Gurkha Rifles.

36
TIGER HUNT

The dawn train delivered me mid-afternoon to a remote station in the Morghati area of the Terai jungle, renamed Corbett Tiger Reserve, after my Uncle Jimmy's friend. I lasted one minute riding the bone-breaking, springless bullock cart sent to transport me the twenty miles to Uncle Jimmy's Rest House.

"We'll walk ahead, *Shikari*," I said, leaping out and handing him my rifle.

We struck out along a narrow path between the Sal forest's sparse trunks into the deeper jungle. Spongy underfoot. Silence echoed. Two ten-mile Hunting Blocks lay ahead to reach Jimmy's. Shooting was forbidden except in self-defense. My trigger-finger itched each time we put up small game and spotted *sambhar* deer. About five miles in, *Shikari* froze, mid-step.

"*Bagh. Sahib. Bagh.*" He whispered urgently, handing me my rifle and jabbing his finger right of the track.

"Maro. *Sahib.* Maro. Shoot."

Staring in the direction *Shikari* indicated—nothing. So when a full-grown tiger stalked calmly across the track ten yards ahead of us, I blinked, astonished. With a low growl, he crouched and sprang high onto a rock across the path.

Lord of the jungle, yawning, he dismissed us with a show of yellowed fangs and the longest pink length of tongue, before settling stretched flat, tail dangling.

"Maro. Maro. Shoot. Shoot," implored my orderly, eager to ignore the no-shooting rule. Much to his disgust, I handed back my gun. My hands were tied. I could hardly argue self-defense.

The low, red sun tightened the forested foothills, switched out its daylight as we reached Haldu Parao Block. No longer able to see clearly, I waded a river's swift blackness, and scrambled its mud bank onto a clearing and made for the beacon of light from the Rest House. Uncle Jimmy greeted me with the customary British firm handshake and stiff upper-lipped comment, "Your mother's well, I trust."

It was the only personal reference he made during my visit.

Over tea in front of a roaring fire, we skated—formal.

"How's India treating you?...Enjoyed the trek?...My man met you all right?"

I told of the yawning *Bagh* crossing the first Hunting Block. In anticipation of my visit, he said, he already had a bullock staked out as bait and a *machan* built, where a tiger or tigress lived.

Sitting on the veranda in the moonlight after dinner, a flickering hurricane lamp on the table, the jungle vibrated, alive. Deep roars echoed off the nearby hillside, setting off a chain of alarm calls: shrills, chatterings, shrieks and coughs, warnings from frightened *chitals,* barking *kakars,* monkeys, and roosting peafowl. My eyes straining, I saw nothing move save the dappled shadows and sliding silver of the moonlit river.

Jungle music orchestrated sleep. Knots, tangled questions taunted my dreams, rolling in restless waves. Emma, my mother...tell me, Jimmy. Tell about you and her...the games you shared...my grandparents, Isabella and Samuel... What bad thing happened back then? I need to understand. Jimmy returned the ball, unraveled.

Dawn came all too soon. I couldn't broach the subject. And during the remainder of my visit, Jimmy never volunteered. His earlier statement, "Your mother's well, I trust," was just that, a statement, not a question, to prevent further discussion.

First thing on waking, Jimmy checked whether the unfortunate bullock had survived the night.

"Taken?" He enquired, hopeful. "Taken?" It was the same each day.

"Can't sit around. I'll take you *ghooming.* A local Raja loaned me an elephant."

As we clung to our seats in the rocking howdah, Jimmy hoped to spot tiger and leopard, and I hoped I wouldn't lose my breakfast. Onward plodded Tiku-the-elephant, flattening waist-high grass, clambering slopes and fallen trees. Relentless, she waded mud and river, raising nothing larger than jungle fowl, quail and sacred peafowl.

Morning three. Trumpeting wild elephants had us quickly lumbering in the opposite direction, and away from a dangerous encounter.

Morning four. *Ghooming.* Hiking again.

Day seven. *Shikari* beamed. "Kill. Bullock all dead, *Sahib* Knowles. Half, only gone. *Bagh* come back."

The tiger or tigress had dined during the night. The prospect of spending a night perched alone in a *machan* excited Jimmy more than it did me.

"*Machan* ready. *Mahout* waiting, *Sahib.*"

It was time for me to kill a *Bagh.*

After dinner, armed with a double-barreled express rifle borrowed from my Regiment, I stepped from Tiku's back onto the *machan's* rough, wooden perch fifteen feet up in the treesabove the kill.

A little too much in range of a tiger's leap, I mused. Feeling as vulnerable as the poor bullock below, I settled uneasily, back pressed to a trunk.

Tiku's plod and snap of crushed vegetation receded. The jungle closed about me.

Silent. Menacing. Expectant. A three-quarter moon illuminated the kill below. Cool night air seeped into every bone. Pulling my blanket tighter, I shivered. A mouthful of hot coffee from my thermos flask perked me up. On high alert, I checked and re-checked. "Yes. Both barrels loaded. Safety catches on."

My buttocks numbed. The *machan's* boards hardened. Cold became colder. Still it was impossible to stay awake. Eyelids fluttered. I dozed off. A peacock's high-pitched shriek shocked me alert. A tiger roared somewhere left. I urgently need a leak. Straining to pinpoint the sound, an answering roar blasted right. Two tigers. Both headed for the kill. I raised my rifle to my shoulder. A minute passed. Two. Into the moonlit glade, stalked the crowned King—a male tiger. Magnificent.

It was an easy shot. I aligned my sights immediately behind his right shoulder and pulled the trigger. With a furious roar he recoiled, springing back into the trees as the bullet hit the ground grazing his nose. I reeled, almost knocked from the *machan* by the rifle's mighty recoil. Both barrels had fired simultaneously.

"You arrant arse," I cursed myself. "You blithering, arrant fool." A borrowed gun, one I had never used before. "You dolt." I had neglected testing its sights.

Hurricane lamplight between the trees and the crash of Tiku's heavy steps announced Uncle Jimmy's arrival an hour later. Jimmy's sour face said it all. Disgust. Utter disbelief. No dead tiger, no dead tigress lay at my feet. Shame-faced, I confessed.

Our relationship ended. Two days remained. On the 31st of December I rejoined the Battalion.

37
DISCONTENT

Colonel Tuck gone, the hated Jock Colenso took his place. We had a history, he and I. Since the day he sprung his miserable birthday surprise on my friend Desmond Whyte, finally forcing him from the Regiment, I had despised the man, and he knew it.

"A military policeman from Burma, not one of us," we taunted behind his back. Ignorant of our regimental traditions, Jock Colenso relied on his acolyte, Captain Beard, and his Adjutant, Captain Hubert Skone, to keep his blunders hidden from his senior officers. His blustering and posturing didn't fool the rest of us. He knew we saw through him, but it was he, Jock Colenso, who wielded the power.

One dawn, when Jock was still asleep in his bivouac, the large shape of His Excellency the Commander-in-Chief of India, General, Lord Rawlinson, levered himself from his red Bentley on a surprise visit to observe our Battalion's pre-dawn maneuvers. Quickly thinking, Jock's Adjutant bellowed, "Welcome, Your Excellency." Loudly pointing out the different companies' positions, he successfully alerted the sleeping Colenso. Jock slunk from his bivouac, pulling on his uniform and strapping on his weapons while snaking low to the ground. After a hundred yards he popped into view saluting smartly.

"Apologies, Sir. Just inspecting one of my companies," He lied, completely ignorant of its position.

To Jock's consternation, the General demanded a visit. I almost admired the canny bastard's smooth cover-up as he briskly ordered, "Lead on, will you, Skone. The General and I will follow."

Jock's ingratiating manner and imposing physique fooled his superiors. He plied inspecting officers with good food and wine and built an impressive reputation, thanks to his efficient Adjutants. Smiling pleasantly to our faces, he'd hand one report for us to initial sprinkled with compliments such as, "Good Horsemanship. Works Hard. Well respected by the men," then replace it with a second derogatory report to the higher authorities. Jock ruined many a career.

When he played his cowardly trick on me, I confronted him. Jock's version falsely stated I'd failed the machine gun course I'd just completed with a "good pass." Luckily a friend saw the fake and suggested I refuse to sign it. I demanded to see the Brigadier, exposed the two-faced bully's double standard, and Jock was forced to redress his lie. Forever after we circled one another like two fighting cocks caught in the same ring.

Jock banished me for the remainder of the cold weather by sidelining me as Company Commander to an inglorious cantonment of a dozen thatched bungalows and an Army clothing factory in Shahjahanpur, near New Delhi. At least Jock was out of my hair. Life improved, but it was no career. Our military detachment apart, Shahjahanpur boasted a Rosa Rum factory employing a few civilians, and a Club. I was king. The factory manager took me on partridge shoots. The ladies invited me to dance and dine with them, and a beautiful Eurasian redhead fell into my bed. But I was trapped, my career drowning in a monotonous sea of leisure and pointless routine. What to do? I dreaded returning to the plains for annual collective training. I dreaded the sequestered months ahead in Lansdowne. I had to change something; get a promotion, transfer, or resign. I settled on promotion.

In March, back in the Hills, I used the time studying for the Promotional exams. Once again my bungalow-mate was my long-time friend from Landi Kotal, Harry Garland. Like me, bored and fed up, he was considering transfer to an Extra-Regimental branch. Option. Options, we explored them all. The only relief that summer was being sent on a week's reconnoiter to the hillsides around Thanda Pani above Lansdowne to find suitable company training grounds.

Crossing the rickety rope bridge into Chitoli's village bazaar ahead of our cook and porters, Harry and I were caught up in a wild mob of drunks. A lone pair of local policemen flailed their *lathies* uselessly, attempting to control the red-eyed Tibetans, the dirtiest of whom wielded a knife. Jumping into the fray, we went to the policemen's aid and between us restored order. Infuriated, screaming obscenities, a Tibetan lunged at me with his knife. Instinctively, I knocked the blade from his hand with my hiking stick, then thwacked him soundly across his back and legs. The police dragged him to the lock-up. Still yelling threats, the hatred from his eyes burned into mine. His rancid butter odor coated my nostrils. I couldn't shake it, or his image.

The minute we set camp, I astonished our modest porters by stripping off every stitch of clothing and plunging into the icy pool beside our tent to scrub the smell of him from me.

"I'll join you." Harry jumped in after me.

The campsite was perfect, the view exquisite. Later, comfortable in our camp chairs sipping a *burra* peg of whisky, the Army faded. I was on holiday again. We traced the silver thread of a Ganges tributary along the valley 4,000 feet below us. It was clear from the start the plateau was too small for the Army's needs, but we spun out our task by collecting meticulous measurements and sketches. Only a sudden November snowstorm chased us back.

That night of silent snowfall, a nightmare woke me, shouting. The Tibetan I had beaten crouched over the foot of my cot, his knife poised to strike. His rancid butter body odor pervaded the tent. Harry jumped from the cot beside me brandishing his pistol, but there were no trace of footprints in the snow. I felt less foolish when Harry agreed he smelled rancid butter lingering in the tent.

whirling smoke of yak-dung fire
a crazed hermit with matted hair
disturbs my rest
his rancid blizzard breath
his gnarled fingers weaving death

Reluctantly, we trudged down the snowbound trail towards Lansdowne. As we crossed Chitoli Bazaar, the Police Constable signaled us he wanted to talk. The knife-wielding Tibetan whom I had beaten had escaped the lock-up, intent on revenge. The police and a posse of villagers had tracked his footprints for five miles up the path towards our camp, then stumbled on his blood-soaked body lying in the snow mutilated by a bear. My skin crawled. Had his vengeful spirit continued on its intent to do me harm, or had Lansdowne spooked me yet again?

38
CAREER HICCUP

In July 1928, to escape Lansdowne's boring routine, I signed up for a three-month signal course in Poona, a town near Bombay. Plunged suddenly into its steamy climate from the Himalayan cool, I contracted a bad bout of malaria. During my convalescence in the "the Dog's Home" in the Nilgiri Hills, the Simon Commission arrived at Lord Tata's two-storied European-style house to haggle the contentious issue of Partition. A Captain Atlee, a member of the Commission, stretched languidly in an adjacent lounger on the verandah after lunch one day, and started chatting. Boldly direct, I asked him about the possibility of Partition.

"Over my dead body," he shouted.

"Over my dead body." His vehemence stayed with me.

Malaria worsened. I was repatriated to England's cooler clime for a year's sick leave. With the Officer's Convalescent Hospital on the Isle of Wight, Osbourne House, a favorite summer Palace of Queen Victoria, as my home, another idyllic year passed unfettered, un-uniformed: golf, squash, croquet, picnics on the lawn, tennis, and nightly sneakings down the fire escape to Saturday night dances at the Sandown Hotel. I played the field and loved. Though run on military lines, Osbourne House was more a country club than a hospital

I fell in love, promised undying love and proposed to Winifred, who I'd accidentally met meandering one day behind the bushes. Winifred and I found many ways to be alone.

I often glimpsed Princess Beatrice hobbling around the Rose Garden she'd so loved as a child: her garden.

I made a particular friend of a fellow a patient, Colonel Ogilvie, newly retired. I found him stark naked, without embarrassment, in the sun pavilion darning his socks, for no reason other than he liked the feel of sun on his body. Unlike me, he spoke his mind and did only what pleased him even if it dented his career.

"If it was good enough for Caesar, Sir, it is good enough for me." He once retorted to a Brigadier critical of his maneuvers on an exercise.

I laughed, envious of his forthrightness.

"Conformity kills. Compromise castrates. Your own beliefs are what counts."

His dictums stuck and I adopted them as my own.

Pronounced fit, I returned to Poona to complete my interrupted signal course. Irksome timetables once again curtailed my day. Thankfully, much of the course was spent in the field, waving flags, tapping codes, and coaxing unwilling mules burdened by our heavy field equipment. "Carrots, lovely carrots." We enticed our mulish beasts back to school HQ with barely time to change and get to the elite Poona Turf Club in time for the for the opening parade. Built in 1883, the Poona Turf Club was famed throughout the horsy world.

Brandishing my "Good Pass," I was appointed Signal Officer, no thanks to Jock Colenso. To evade him, I had taken as many courses in as many locations as I could; musketry at Pachmari, the Vickers machine gunnery course at Ahmednagar, a camouflage course at Ambala and a transport course in Bareilly.

I had hardly unpacked before my regular two-month leave fell due, and I was off again.

"Really?" I checked in disbelief.

The Hoti called. I'd use those months to explore it.

Rose, Caldicott, Plunkett, Gurkha Shikaris.

Gonsali Village.

Unta Dura Pass.

Camp. Foot of Jainti La.

Camp. Charchin.

39

THE HOTI

Another Strange Tale

Dedicated career officers accept tedious drills as part of their job. I wasn't one. I did what was expected of me while my mind climbed high into the Himalayas. It was trekking I lived for. A rucksack on my back, a stout stick in my hand, I fell as easily into place on a mountainside as a missing piece completes a jigsaw puzzle. I belonged.

Bursting into a flower-filled meadow from the tree line, taking that final step onto a summit, or discovering a lone stand of birch trees quivering in the stillness of a blue snowfield, I was reborn. I scooped a cupped hand of ice water to my lips. I drank the Ganges, the Brahmaputra, the Indus and other holy rivers. With every step, I walked naked, raw as when I entered this world and everything was new. How could I not love the mountains after such experiences?

1931. I counted the days till my two months local leave fell due. I had a plan. I didn't know it then, but it would shape my career.

Without revealing my personal ambition, I volunteered my services to the Indian Survey Office to map the unmapped Hoti. They not only agreed to my plan, they also offered to fund my expedition. I had dreamed of exploring the

Hoti ever since my encounter with the lone Tibetan above Almora my first year in India. I'd never forgotten his mysterious tales, his rescue by monks, the mythical Abbott Prester John's monastery beyond Nanda Devi, or his convincing description of a religions community hidden somewhere in an absurdly fanciful lush valley hidden in the snows. Though my research had only uncovered the existence of myth, I wanted to prove or disprove his stories for myself.

As the expedition's official leader and surveyor I chose my companions carefully. Success and our very lives depended on each member playing his part. Captain Plunkett, a doctor and a keen hunter, and Caldicott, a young skilled artist-gunner I'd met in Bareilly, both jumped at the chance. All three of us experienced trekkers, my team was perfectly balanced.

The first five days, we trekked in incrementally longer distances to prepare for the strenuous ten-day, 10,000-foot climb to Dung in the foothills of the Himalayas. After a couple of days surveying, we were fit enough to climb to 14,000 feet, reacclimatize to that altitude, and only then attempt the Milam glacier and the higher passes into Tibet.

The first evening, camped beside a tumbling stream in a high meadow circled by mountains, relaxed around the embers of the campfire after dinner under the stars, how enthusiastically we jabbered, planning and defining our roles and exchanging trekking and hunting experiences. We had much in common.

At dawn Caldicott and I set up our plane tables for the first time to sketch the terrain, while Plunkett disappeared down a deep *nullah* stalking a herd of *bhurrel*, a Himalayan sheep, grazing on a distant grassy slope. We dined that night and most nights on succulent meat. My dream was becoming reality.

After four days' hard climbing via Sancha and Lapthal, we reached Shaishal at 14,570 feet and set up a base camp near a clump of *burtza* bushes to use for fuel. Day long, Plunkett disappeared with his *shikari* stalking bhurral, and kept us well supplied. Caldicott and I, armed with our sketchpads, trekked to the surrounding peaks ostensibly to plot and measure, but with every direction providing a stunning gasper of a view, my pen poised uselessly above the paper. Sitting below a summit five miles east of camp, we traced a stream draining the Hoti all the way to Girthi Gorge where it exploded into a mist-cloud as it plummeted over the edge, on its way to the distant Ganges. And I was being paid for this, for living my passion?

One day while Plunkett was hunting, Caldicott and I, intending to map the area, followed a faint rocky path upwards through old snow patches still lying in the north- facing *nullahs* towards two overlapping peaks. The narrowing path flattened, exposing an unknown gap below the 17,000-foot craggy rock-face. We clapped one another's backs whooping with joy.

"Fame. We've done it, old chap." We discovered a pass not marked on the map.

Our exuberance clearly mystified our Gurkha *shikari*. Perhaps the pass or territory wasn't new to him. Hunting was his interest.

Beyond the pass, the Tibetan plain exploded thousands of feet below us, dominated by the magnificent Mount Kailas protecting all she surveyed. The abode of Shiva, some saw his *Lingam* in her snow-capped form. But I saw snow-milk flowing from her rounded breast, sustenance offered to her devotees. I understood why she was revered, why pilgrims of so many faiths venerated her holy peak. Directly below, an intricate pattern of sun-silvered rivulets marked the source of both the Indus and Brahmaputra. Though their deltas on the Indian Ocean lay three thousand miles apart, one step closer and I could have planted one foot in the spring of both mighty rivers at once. We sat in reverent silence until the creeping cold told us it was time to return to camp.

Much to our *shikari's* disappointment, the herd of Ammon sheep had long gone. Our near-empty larder would remain empty unless Plunkett had been successful. He had. Babbling, "Plunkett…unknown pass…discovery…stroke of luck," we huddled close to the blazing *burtza,* spooning curried *bhurrel* from the pot.

"To the new pass. A toast." We raised *burra* pegs of whisky.

To reach the Hoti area safely, it was imperative to cross three daunting passes in a single day. A sudden blizzard mid-trek could mean death. But we were weak, doubled over from stomach cramps and headaches as if we had been meat-cleavered. We glanced balefully at the magnificent Milam Glacier we so longed to see, then crawled back inside our sleeping bags. Five days adjustment later, we were ready to face the difficult 5,000-foot climb from Dung to the Unta Dhura La towering enticingly above us. One look at Nanda Kot and the north-east face of Nanda Devi, India's second-highest mountain of over 24,500 feet, made up for the effort. For sheer exuberance, I took a side trip up a minor ice and snow-encrusted 20,000-foot peak humming, "…to see what I could see…" My loyal Gurkha orderly followed close on my heels.

"Where *Sahib* go, I go," he insisted, simply.

Sitting, backs pushed hard against a rock protecting ourselves from the wind's biting, twenty-degrees-below-zero lance, I swept my Zeiss binoculars across the slope, hoping to glimpse "Presser Jon's" mysterious monastery or some trace of life. The icy-clear air pierced every bronchial tube of my lungs. Frozen, and teeth chattering, we scurried down the side of the mountain avoiding the crevasses, and rejoined our party at the foot of the Jainti La. Doggedly plodding upwards, we crossed the Kungri Bingri La early afternoon. One left to go. Though the high paths were clear of snow, frozen rocks and ice patches slowed us down. Our coolies and ponies trailed far behind. Pausing, we watched them, small specks, moving incrementally below us on the trail. Too cold, too late to dawdle, with one final spurt of energy we made the last pass in shadow, early evening.

Exhausted, we stood exultant beside the fluttering prayer flags of a Buddhist cairn. Obeying custom, we added a stone each to the cairn, took a tooth-chattering second to marvel at the still, blue waters of Mansarovar Lake far across the plateau as the last rays of sun flared Mount Kailas gold, then slithered down the fast-vanishing path. We settled on a campsite 3,000 feet below at Chitichun, unaware we had illegally crossed the outer line between British India and Tibet.

Bone-chilled and hungry, our *shikaris* quickly built a fire with yak dung. As we huddled round its flames in the open, the already icy night air chilled even colder with freezing vapor blowing off the nearby 14,000-foot glacier. It was 1:00 a.m. by the time our coolies, leading our ponies, had straggled in with our gear, set camp, and hobbled the ponies, and we could finally fall into our tents. Not one of us slept well in that unearthly, desolate place. Over *chai* we discovered we had all shared the same disturbing dream: a swarthy Tibetan creeping into our tent with a knife in his teeth. At first light we packed up and fled that haunted spot.

We made it over the difficult 18,000-foot Charchin La Pass and to the Hoti plateau in a day. Last, came a two-day march to Kio Gad, another inhospitable, stony, goat-and-yak site littered with droppings. Plunkett bagged a yak with horns so massive it made up one pack pony's entire load. Moving on between the ranges, we at last reached the pleasant plateau of Shal Shal. Perfect for our mission, we set up our long-term camp to complete our survey. We could relax at last.

I turn the prayer wheel on the pass the pass called Unta Dhura La
for the ghosts of men who died alone on the icy path of Jainti La
seeking the sacred waters of Lake Manasarovar
filled with Brahma's infant tears
shed for Shiva in his snowy dome
the far white peak of Kailas

Routinely, Caldicott and I left camp after breakfast to sketch and map, and returned mid-afternoon. He enjoyed the sound of silence as much as I, and we trod gently on the earth, intruding as little as we could. We followed snow-hare, bear and leopard tracks, saw their scat, but never spotted the animals that left the markers. One morning I sent Caldicott and both *shikaris* to take sightings and measurements from the far side of the plain. I watched them plod—three figures bent beneath the weight of theodolite, tripod, triangle, compass, altimeter, plumb line. Good. They'd be gone for hours. I busied myself with my tape and triangle.

Perhaps due to the lack of oxygen, or perhaps to the notion of such miniscule humans as Caldicott and his men, of me, reducing those massive peaks and glacial fissures into measurements captured in a ledger, the sheer ridiculousness of man hit me. I could no more catch milk from the Milky Way with a net. Bubbling silently at first, an avalanche of laughter gurgled from inside, the explosion of which only made me laugh the more. I made to wipe away the tears but they had set, frozen on my cheeks. I laughed again.

Resisting the urge to hurl my instruments, I lay back against the slope. The sky spun off the distant summit, scattering any cloud daring to sully its pristine blue. I sat up, hugged my knees and stilled. The mountains stared at me, and I them. Undemanding, uncomplicated, they were what they were, rooted in their very being. I didn't turn my head. I didn't look around. I became a mountain, my mind empty. As the clouds evaporated off the peaks, so too my thoughts. I existed in some profound place of which I had no understanding.

I told no one of my experience, but something changed, no, solidified in me that day. I "became," as a Buddhist might put it. Compromise was no longer an option. I had mountains to climb.

enveloped in the magnificence
I melt invisible as my breath
still as the mountain I rest upon
the only movement
scudding clouds a slow circling eagle
the only sound
the beat of his wings
the beat of my heart

Biting wind and ultraviolet rays darkened our faces to the same leather-brown of our Ghurkas' till only our clothing and size told us apart. Off duty, sitting cross-legged around the *burtza* bush and yak-dung fire together, we spoke each other's languages and sang each other's songs as only brotherhoods who have shared great hardships can. Come daylight, we reverted to our roles—*sahib, shikari, coolie*—it was understood.

Feasting beneath the moon one evening, after rejecting a long list of unsuitable suggestions, we decided the new pass be named after our campsite, "Shal Shal La."

Plunkett had seriously infected his knee by kneeling on a poisonous *burtza* thorn while taking aim at a *bhurrel* two days earlier. The swollen knee joint was by then a pus-oozing football. The offending thorn had to be removed, and quickly, proper sterilization or no, thanks to low boiling point at high altitude.

Plunkett laid out his surgical instruments.

"I need to cut down to the joint. The blasted thorn has worked deep into the joint. In case I pass out, you'll have to take over..."

Grimacing with pain, he made us memorize the procedure, and more horrifying still, when and how to amputate his leg. I blanched, unsure if I could.

I'd nearly fainted watching Caldicott squeeze out a cup of pus. Then came my turn to clean and dress his foul-smelling wound. I looked away. Plunkett sliced into his own flesh. The thorn floated out. I retched but remained by his side.

No choice but to wait for the knee joint to heal sufficiently for us to pack up and head for home. Our sketch maps and measurements long completed, I was anxious to reach Gonsali, a tiny village the other side of the Bali Hoti pass, and there, replenish our dwindling supplies. Just making it to Rimkin at the foot of the pass would take several days. The intense cold helped, but it took a week before Plunkett, still unable to walk, could ride one of the pack ponies.

Three days crept. Crossing and recrossing the spider web of what felt like a hundred deep ravines, we finally struggled into Rimkin too exhausted and too late in the day to attempt the pass to Gonsali. Fresh food would have to wait.

Hemmed in by mountain ranges and towering peaks, the barren landscape was littered with bones, and not even a *burtza* bush broke the monotony. Rimkin's desolation was worse than our campsite beside Charchin's glacier.

Worrying dark clouds loomed over the western horizon. We watched, uneasy. We were right to worry. A heavy snowstorm buried us during the night. It was still falling when we woke. Next day, the day after, and the day after, thick snow whitewashed anything beyond two feet from sight. Our valiant coolies channeled paths between the tents, to the latrine area, to the ponies huddled head to tail, and most importantly to the fire.

Four days later when the sun at last came out, it was obvious we were marooned. Deep snow blocked the route out over the Chor Pass, making it impassable. Our situation was serious. The coolies huddled together in a single tent for warmth, and we three did the same. I divided the little food remaining, grimly aware it would run out in a few days. Time and time again we attempted to leave. Each time the animals floundered, hooves flailing, sunk to their withers in snow.

Rising to the south, Nanda Devi's 25,000 feet dominated the snowy Himalayan range; East, the Himalayan spur we had just crossed; West, another 20,000-foot spur dividing the Hoti from the Upper Kumaon. Among so many massive mountains, the snowless Tun Jun La pass over the lower 17,000-foot Zaskar Mountains to our north looked positively inviting, but we had no way to reach it.

Each man, lost in his private thoughts, huddled miserably around the communal fire for the fifth night eking out the last of his rations, the firelight reflecting the resignation in his eyes. Death. Plunkett didn't lift our gloom by rending the air with mournful notes from the bagpipes he'd insisted on dragging with us. The moonrise revealed what should have been the most sublime vision of silvered snow softly gleaming in the valley and on the peaks, but now only emphasized our isolation. Perhaps in response to the bagpipes' wail, a snow leopard passed no more than a hundred yards away, his luminous yellow eyes curiously inspecting the strange invaders sitting beneath the stars. In the clear moon and starlight, Nandi Devi's stark pinnacle stood polished to a mirror shine. I thought back to the time I'd first seen her from Almora, the time I'd met the Tibetan on the trail to Binsar and heard his story, and wondered if this would be my last night on earth.

The power of suggestion maybe, but that night as I slept, I had a dream so vivid it was real. Though the tent flap was closed, I clearly saw two figures approach. Walking on the snowfield, they left no footprints.They stood outside my tent. I noticed they wore monks' habits and only sandals on their feet. All at once I stood beside them in the snow, extricated somehow from my blanket roll between the sleeping Caldicott and Plunkett. I don't know in what language they spoke, but I understood every word.

"We've come from beyond Nanda Devi, from Abbot Prester John's Monastery. We've seen your plight. To reach Gonsali, travel after dark. Yonder." They pointed to a black line crinkling the northern ridge I hadn't noticed before.

"Keep the rock outcrop you can see there on your left, and you'll safely reach the pass. Go alone, at night. The frozen snow will bear your weight."

"Take, eat this to give you strength." They proffered a lump of lard.

A warm sensation and a surge of vitality flooded my body as the melting grease slid down my throat. I didn't see them leave, but suddenly they were gone and I was back cocooned in bed, not knowing how I got there. Reality and the numinous blurred.

Next morning, both Caldicott and Plunkett sniffed, and said hunger was making them hallucinate because they could smell ghee. I kept my dream—or was it a visitation?—to myself. I didn't want to hear the taunts. All morning I relived what I had seen and heard. It made perfect sense to travel when the snow was frozen. My messengers had shown me the way. By mid-morning I made up my mind.

"Tonight, I am going to cross the pass to Gonsali and go for help. It's our only shot. If we stay here, we'll surely die."

They did their best to dissuade me. But they recognized my plan made sense.

After supper, a mug of *chai* and one chapatti per person, the men grouped around me silently. I tested the frozen surface. It held. With my ski poles over my shoulder, a thermos of coffee and a cold chapatti in my pack, I turned to leave. They waved farewell as they watched my shadow fade in the moonlight.

An hour later I reached the base of the ascent leading to the pass, paused and strapped my skins to the bottom of my skis. Testing every step, I plodded up and up, careful to keep the rocky outcrop on my left. Countless times the crust broke, plunging me up to my waist and forcing me to shovel myself out.

The laborious digging had me both drenched in sweat and shivering in the freezing cold. Up. Up.

Odd. Near the outcrop large tracks stamped across my path. Man's? But the length of stride, and size of the footprints were too big to be human. Yeti? Could Yetis really roam the Himalayas? I had other concerns.

Counting each toehold kicked into the crust, out loud I panted, "One step. Two step. Three step."

Counting from one, two, three to one-thousand-and-one…three thousand… four thousand–depressing, too discouraging. Three hours it took to reach the top. So tired...rest...sleep...

"Just a little while," I agreed to myself, collapsing in the shelter of a rock on the far side of the pass.

Warm...deliciously drowsy....dreamily peaceful. I could have slept forever. Suddenly alarm bells rang, refired my brain. *"Danger. Danger. Hypothermia, you fool."* I jumped up, shouting at myself, and shook my limbs. Sleep means death. Plunkett had warned me, "However sleepy you feel, on no account allow yourself to fall asleep."

Packed, hard snow made the going easier, and appearing like an apparition from the frozen hinterland, I staggered into Gonsali village at 6:00 a.m. A group of startled men escorted me to the headsman's house.

Sitting as close to his small brazier as I could sit without scorching myself, Teeth chattering, I related my tale while his wife plied me with hard-boiled eggs, curried partridge, and most welcome of all, hot sweet *chai*. Too tired to dream, I slept on his *charpoy* under a pile of padded cotton covers until midday while the headman rounded up two experienced porters who had recently portered for the Kamet expedition. I woke scratching. My skin crawled with bloated bedbugs feasting on my flesh. The family shared their midday meal with me and I dozed fitfully until it was time to leave

With the sun just past its highest, the two porters, Lewa and Kesar Singh, and I made the top of the pass by 5:00 p.m., before the snow froze completely hard and the descent iced too dangerous to attempt. Before leaving the sunlight for the blue shadows of the far side, the porters and I added our stones to the cairn to appease the gods. I closed my eyes and bowed my head "to the monks, my dream, their message, my salvation, to God" before following Lewa and Kesar down the 2,500-foot slope.

The waist-high softer layer over the frozen snow base made a perfect brake and we made it safely to the valley floor. We pinpointed the tents from the upper slope, so skied towards them as rapidly as we were able. The camp was ominously silent. No sign of life. No one waved to greet us. Fearful of what we would discover, we pulled open the tent flaps. Semi-comatose, barely alive, the men lay huddled in their sleeping bags and under blankets, too drowsy from hunger and cold to understand their rescue. Lewa and Kesar quickly got an enormous bonfire of *burtza* blazing. Then hot, sweet tea laced with brandy did its work and soon every one was talking and laughing, showering us with questions and thanks.

Lewa and Kesar re-heated the curry and rice they had carried from Gonsali. A meal never tasted so good, nor life glow so precious. We rested two days, eating and sleeping, gradually regaining our strength.

Miraculously the ponies had survived. Men and pack ponies sticking together, Lewa and Kesar led us to an easier crossing over the Zaskar range via the Jainti La to Gonsali. The whole village streamed from their houses in welcome, chanting prayers of thanks for our safety. Before we left, we threw a feast with our newly purchased rations. Lewa and Keshar, as guests of honor, were a little overcome at being the center of so much attention. In turn each Gurkha touched their saviors' feet in obeisance, then hands together bowed. Though Plunkett, Caldicott and I didn't touch their feet, we bowed low, humble, hands pressed in *Namaskar*, thanking them for our lives.

On the long march back to Almora via the Jowan pass, my mind wrestled with the uncanny resemblance between the story I had heard all those years ago on the path to Binsar and my own bizarre encounter. Whether a supernatural experience or just a vivid dream, I still cannot decide. Partly for fear of ridicule, and partly for fear my story might incite a madcap mountaineer to climb the glacial northeast face himself to check the story, I have kept it to myself. Today as I write these memoirs, in my quiet moments I humbly acknowledge those monks and thank them, for it was they who saved me, and my expedition, from certain death.

Because we were late back to our regiment by several days, our respective C.O.'s greeted us grimfaced.

"Not only are you A.W.O.L., but you also crossed into Tibet without a pass. Had you been detained or even killed, it would have caused endless trouble to the Government of India," my C.O. stormed. "Every Tibetan is under an obligation to report the presence of strangers to the provincial Governor of Gartok, the capital of Western Tibet. You can think yourselves fortunate you weren't spotted."

To the Survey of India however, I was a hero. Excitedly they studied my sketches of the Hoti area and route over the Shal Shal La pass. A dot still marks their survey sheet, "No. 53N. Survey sketched by Captain Rose."

I donated them the ammonite fossils from the Zaskars, offering, "Any time you want an area mapped, I'm at your service."

My career pointer swiveled. Mapping…?

40

CHOICES. TRANSITION

Elated from my adventures in the Hoti, at the thought of another round of quick-march-and-a-one-two-three about the parade ground, I groaned. Unbearable. I had had enough. My mind was clear, peacetime soldiering was not for me. Spoiled, seduced—too much leisure, too long absent. I was stuck.

"Bit of an oddball, that Rose." I once overheard my peers remark. I wasn't offended. Quite pleased, really. I took it as a compliment. Perhaps I was different as a result of my impoverished upbringing, the tainted legacy of my parents' affair, my paranormal experiences, my long absence, coupled with my disrespect for rules and for the Army's constraints. Then there was my relationship with my Commanding Officer…

Marooned in Lansdowne for the hot weather summer months, I had time to think. Beneath the stars after dinner, feet propped on the lawn's low wall, whisky in hand, my good friend Harry and I concluded we wanted out. He, to become a priest, I to…? I wasn't sure. But it wasn't this.

"Rules are made to be broken. Conformity kills."

Now mine, I quoted the eccentric Colonel Ogilvie's dictums. I described the vision of him sitting naked in the conservatory darning his socks. How Harry laughed.

With Harry, I considered and dismissed my choices; Somaliland Camel Corps, British Trade Agent in Tibet, Burma Military Police, Assam Rifles; Aide-de-Camp to His Excellency the Viceroy of India…

"To be an Aide-de-Camp you need private means, Hugh." Harry scotched my choice.

I could veer completely off the career rails by seconding to one of the so-called irregular Frontier Militia. Romantic for a year, oh yes. But a career based in some fort more isolated than Landi Kotal, its covert raids, constant sniper fire, attacking, tracking tribal insurgents in waterless mountains? No, Sir. Though I wouldn't have forgone time spent on the North West Frontier, my lonely sojourn in the Picket, in the tented and Bharg forts, nor bounding races down the *khud* with my Ghurka men. Not for anything.

Abbotababad, Bannu, Razmak, Wana, and Quetta. As with the French Foreign Legion, mystique hovered around their names. Zhob Militia, Chitral Scouts, South Waziristan Scouts, Khurram Militia—the "irregular" forces who taught their skills to Britain's frontier brigades. Two-thirds of the entire British Army was stationed on the Afghan/Indian border, present-day Pakistan. "To give soft peacetime troops an experience of live gunfire."

I settled for the Foreign and Political Department, otherwise known as "Fazul and Pomp Department." Fazul equaled foolishness in Persian. Fazul? Was I a fool? Time would tell. Pomp? The *Durbar* Parade in Bareilly's streets with its caparisoned elephants, massed marching bands, swinging kilts, bagpipes, and the glitter of the Maharajas' and the Maharanis' emeralds and sapphires…. Yes, though I was bedazzled by such theatrical pomp, it was not the reason for my choice, I chose the Foreign Service to better understand our role in India, experience India without a gun, to work alongside differing ethnic and religious groups: Hindus, Muslims, "Tribals," Eurasian and British civilians. Foreign Service handled Indian Penal Code, Revenue and Civil Law, Opium Regulations, and the workings of internal security. So much to learn.

With more applicants than positions, to be selected, I needed a spectacular report from my C.O., Jock Colenso. He couldn't wait to get rid of me, and wrote a glowing recommendation. Like many bullies forced to back down, Jock turned into a woolly lamb. He even asked me to dinner. A wolf disguised is still a wolf. I trod warily.

Two interviews lay between me, and my appointment. I traveled to the newly established capital, New Delhi. The Foreign Secretary saw me first, then Lord Irwin, the Viceroy himself. I was as charming as I knew how, for social skills were as important as intellect for the post.

"Hugh could charm the monkeys from the trees," friends teased, encouragingly.

Pleasantries over, Lord Irwin sprung a question, "What did I think of Gandhi?"

To my shame, for I learned later to greatly admire the man and his philosophy, I made him laugh at Ghandi's expense by retorting, "What? That half-naked fakir?"

My interview involved an elaborate luncheon at Viceroy House. My dress, table manners and every smile fell under scrutiny. Two hundred guests and I stood waiting, arranged behind gilt chairs before the longest, most heavily laden table I'd ever seen. Preceded by two aides-de-camp, the Viceroy and Vicereine swept into a hushed banqueting hall. They took their places. The first bar struck. *"God Save Our Gracious King."* Ladies curtsied. Men bowed. Scarlet and royal blue uniforms, silk gowns and *sarees* rustled as Maharajahs, Governors and High Officials took their seats to the flash of precious stones and military medals caught in the light. I took mine at the far end of the tablr. The Viceroy's bodyguards, immobile along both walls, stood at attention, chests thrust out, a lance in each man's hand and scarlet *puggries* on their heads. One pleated end of a *puggri* fanned proud in a cockscomb; the other end dangled pigtail-like. Impassive, eyes unblinking, the guards stood still as the frozen figures in the oil paintings hanging behind them.

After such a banquet during his Official Tour of India, Edward, Prince of Wales was overheard laughing and remarking to his Equerry, "Now I know how Royalty should really live." Truly, the Viceroy lived like a King.

Back at the Regiment, word came I was through. I had passed my exam. My five year secondment to the Political and Foreign Service was approved. My appointment—Assistant Deputy Commissioner, Bareilly.

Last days with the Regiment telescoped alarmingly to one. Suddenly it was time. Time to abandon my regiment, brother officers, and my Gurkha men. No longer one of them, standing on the Mess lawn with my friends after being formally dined out, I half-regretted the step I'd taken. The full moon rose, silvering distant Himalayan snows. The Regimental Band closed the evening with the haunting hymn, *"Abide With Me, Fast Falls the Eventide."* My chest and throat constricted. Each star smudged blurry one by one as the buglers' Last Post evaporated skywards. Ramrod straight as the National Anthem played, I could only mouth the words, *"Long Live Our Noble King."* Shadows on the moonlit lawn blackened our faces, hid my emotion. Harry Garland clapped his hand hard across my back, walked with me in silence to our bungalow.

Bareilly Tent Club. Pig Sticking.

41
A YEAR'S PROBATION

Foreign znd Political Department

I awoke with a start my first morning in Mickey Nethersole's bungalow. No Reveille. No bugle shock. A civilian household. A full year's probation. Mickey kept me tethered to his side every waking moment.

"Up at cock's crow and late to bed. We start before breakfast, siesta after luncheon, then work some more, and often don't finish 'til dinner."

Paperwork, completing reports, planning. Mickey was a stickler and checked what I'd written up the previous evening. Every minute detail had to be recorded, reports written, and solutions outlined. Tap. Tap. Tap. My Remington and I became wedded. One day after a few weeks, Mickey remarked, "Hugh. You write very good judgments and have a pretty turn of phrase."

To pass the local Departmental examinations and understand the workings of a P.A., I studied the Indian Penal Code, Revenue Law, Opium Regulations and Civil Law. Riding horseback beside him, I inspected village crops, irrigation systems, and cattle, shared *chai* and sweetmeats with village *thulsidars,* and listened to Mickey's interaction.

"See and be seen," was the motto he lived by. It worked. Tough, fair, he was a great teacher. He defused trouble before there was a problem. He was responsible for preventing famine and failed crops, looking out for the health of the bony cattle, and preventing outbreaks of disease, then as a Magistrate, for settling land and marital disputes and dispensing law. I had no idea a P.A.'s net spread so wide.

When Mickey donned his wig attending Court, I sat beside him on the bench observing, listening to the plaintiffs. Through their stories I caught glimpses of their families, their neighbors, their homes, villages, and damaged crops. I heard their disputes, the cries of the wronged, the anger, the pleas for justice and for their *laghan* to be reduced. I learned to understand and feel their pain. I saw how people struggled. I saw their pride. Distrust, I saw that too.

It was a shock when, a little too soon, I thought, Mickey appointed me a Third Class Magistrate. I didn't feel qualified to take on such responsibility.

"Don't worry, Hugh," Mickey assured me, "I'll be reviewing every case and advising you on sentencing."

But the job came with the terrible duty of reading death warrants to condemned prisoners before they were hanged. Quite rightly, Mickey believed, "When you become a full Magistrate, your turn will come to sentence a man '....to be hanged by the neck until you are dead.' Feel it. See it. Fully understand the consequence, the finality of killing a fellow human being."

The day came. The Civil Surgeon, Colonel Nash, and I were escorted across the prison yard to a secluded walled enclosure where the condemned men waited, hands tied behind their backs. A steel plate inside my head guillotined thought. My voice wavered for an instant as I asked each man his name and read the warrants. Two warders led the condemned up the wooden steps. He positioned them over the platform's traps. The hangman adjusted the noose. I fixed on a distant point, sweating. The Civil Surgeon signaled. The hangman pulled a lever. The traps swung open simultaneously. Under my breath I repeated, "Lord, forgive me. Receive their souls," imagining kites soaring free. Then drop. My stomach heaved. Stiff, at Attention, I couldn't stop my ears. Dangling, limp. Living beings no more. The Civil Surgeon checked their pulse. A black flag hoisted over the main gateway announced their deaths. I never valued freedom more. I stumbled home for breakfast. Boiled eggs, cold partridge, curried chicken, toast and marmalade remained untouched on hanging days.

Unlike the Gurkha regiments, there was no cooling off in the hills for the Foreign Service. Apart from a couple of long weekends in Naini Tal, I spent the hot weather sweating on the plains. I worked hard and did my Court work. Though Mickey never took a weekend for himself, he did allow me an occasional break. One exception: the annual Tent Club's two-day camp to hunt what he called warrantable hogs. A "warrantable hog must measure thirty inches across the withers." Mickey insisted. I never saw him so excited. Beaters, elephants, guns and all the paraphernalia needed for a camp. He planned and organized for weeks. He closed the office and it was he who organized. Sweeping through high grass, the beater line, which included a couple of loaned elephants, stretched perhaps fifty coolies long. We, the hunters, followed, poised on horseback. Pigsticking in such heat was pure madness, but Mickey, wildly enthusiastic, charged and "Tally-ho'd," determined to bag a warrantable hog. By eleven we were puce in the face, finished. Armed with buckets of well water, giggling coolies repeatedly doused us until we revived. Dripping, steaming, we sat for lunch at long trestles in the shade of some enormous tree drinking *shandy.*

Bareilly. May. My blood boiled. My brain coagulated. I yearned for solitude, mountains, to breathe pine-scented air.

My place of escape was Naini Tal, a lakeside resort created by an immense landslide blocked one end of the valley eons earlier. Damned, the river swelled with snowmelt to form a pristine lake in the forested foothills. From my rented bungalow I watched its sparkling waters though the pine trees. Mornings I trekked, afternoons I spent on the water. Lacing up my well-worn mountain boots, I grabbed my stout walking stick and tramp the trails alone, free from civilization. If I was not trekking, I lazed swimming the lake's deep waters away from shore, or rowed a skiff to the far lakeside to down a beer at the Royal Hotel with friends. In mid-lake, I often shipped oars, and lay in the bottom of the hull. Soothed by the lap-slap ripple of the water overhead, drifting lost in the blue expanse I imagined my friends marching, drilling and parading above in Lansdowne. I didn't envy them. Snows and clouds buffeting along the skyline set me dreaming another pilgrimage to paradise.

Calm, cool and collected, I returned to Bareilly ready to work.

Like his predecessors, Mickey closed his office to spend a month "Going on Circuit," touring his district by horseback. He took me with him when the cold weather came. I rode beside him, unaware I rode the same path my mother had ridden as a young bride when she had accompanied her first husband, Judge Harrison, on the Bareilly Circuit, perhaps to the very same villages and courts beneath their banyan trees. Discovering the coincidence so many years after her death, I shivered. Had she trotted on Chestnut unseen beside me, then?

"See and be seen," Mickey reiterated his motto. "Great way to settle disputes before they escalate to violence or even murder." It worked. Outbreaks of violence just didn't happen in his district. One sight of Mickey and his cavalcade was enough.

Mickey traveled with two camps. One leapfrogged ahead to ready the marquee in the new location, while he stopped to hear and judge cases in the villages along the way from beneath the shade of some village banyan tree. Ten miles often took all day. Brick floor, solid furniture, and bathroom tents, he traveled in style. I watched. I listened. I saw the results of Mickey's fair dealings in settling disputes. Irrigation, land squabbles, cattle thieving, wife abuse, crop levies, opium control or revenue, his concern was genuine. He was a great example of how the Raj should, could behave.

Away from our desks, the two of us trotting side-by-side, Mickey's chattering, the slow pace of our horses, the sunlight, browns and greens of the fields, it was glorious to be alive. Glorious to be in India.

"Tricky business, passing judgment in a different culture," he announced. "I had a case once–had me stumped." Mickey confided. "A man knifed his hated neighbor. Caught in the act, he was clearly guilty. However, two sets of reliable witnesses swore they had both seen him in two places fifty miles apart at the same time. The proof was irrefutable. He was indeed in both. Many adept yogis are capable of bilocation. Locals believed in bilocation. They knew he was guilty. With only British Law to guide my judgment, I was forced to let him free."

Mickey started on another tale. "Before my time...."

He told me of a magistrate, Mr. Percy Marsh, the "mad Judge" of Moradabad, who, far from mad, was a very clever member of the Indian Civil Service despite his uncontrollable temper. Once, a lying witness so enraged him he sentenced the man to climb a large banyan tree in the compound and stay there in the hot sun until thirst and heat drove him to tell the truth. Another time, another lying witness, Mr. Marsh flung his judge's wig to the floor, seized his polo stick, leapt from the dais and struck the unfortunate liar. "...unpardonable of me," he apologized later, "but you lied and lied and lied," and worked himself up again into such a rage, gave the poor man another whack.

"Not my way of doing things," Mickey concluded. "But somehow he got away with it."

My probation year was over. Time to sit the three days of Departmental examinations in Lucknow. And what a farce they turned out to be. The invigilator, watching the exams to make sure there was no cheating, sat nonplussed, waving his hands. When he banged his fist, we banged ours. When he called for order, we did the same. We shouted answers across the room and cribbed shamelessly from our neighbor's paper. Everybody passed.

A fortnight after I returned to Bareilly, Mickey handed me a telegraph.

"Congratulations, Hugh. You've been appointed Personal Assistant to the British Resident and Chief Commissioner in Aden."

"Aden? That's a surprise,"

I spoke no Arabic, knew nothing of the people, their culture or the purpose of our British presence. Mickey, my mentor, my friend...my mind tumbled.

Through Mickey's eye's I had learned to see India, to breathe her very breath and make her mine.

I turned my back. Faced another continent.

Haile Selassie. Aden. 1931.

Aden Harbour.

Haile Selassie 1931, Aden. Official Portrait.
Colonel Reilly (Pop) center front. Hugh center back.

Tiffin with Haile Selassie and Prince Alfonso.

British Residency Aden. Hugh Rose right.

Steamer Point. Aden.

42

ADEN

Political Assistant

I arrived in Aden in 1931 after five gin-sodden days sequestered in the aft bar of the promenade deck with a Colonel Pug Ismay expounding on how Britian should rule the world, particularly the North West Frontier.

"The North West Frontier could be controlled entirely by the R.A.F. without need for ground troops," he argued.

I disagreed. "Ground troops are vital. How else to occupy rebellious villages or to show the flag?"

We shook hands, parting still friends.

With a civil war in the interior, a war brewing in Abyssinia, and Yemenis claiming territory we claimed was ours, Britain's plate was full.

"Call me Pop when we are alone. We don't stand on ceremony here in the Foreign Service," Colonel Reilly, the British Resident, instructed at our first meeting to explain my duties. An Arabist scholar, intelligent, direct and charming, there was nothing devious about him. From day one we got along famously.

Explaining the role of the British Protectorates they governed, Pop realized no British Resident had actually made an official visit to the territories under their jurisdiction. "Better put that right and bloody soon," he added.

"Keep them on our side. Make sure the b****s stay pink." He smiled at his own humor.

"Aden is a valuable springboard into the Hadrumaut and the Protectorates of Lahej Oasis, the Sheikhdom of Socotra and Qishn, the disputed territories in the Yemen, and the remote Sheikhdoms of Seiyun, and Shiban in the Interior. Whether the Sheikhs and Sultans like it or not, Britain intends to stay," Pop explained. "We have the Aden Levies, the Sudan Camel Corps, and a Squadron of the R.A.F., as well as the Indian Army to enforce the point."

Under Pop I wore many hats. Personal Assistant, Harbor Magistrate, Governor of the Jail and Superintendent of the Gardens of Sheikh Othman. What a strange mix. I tried out each in turn and took advantage of each one.

My job description included greeting infinitely forgettable officials off the stream of liners docking in Aden. Dressed in white, a spiked helmet on my head, I escorted them ashore in the official launch. A few stand out: Evelyn Waugh on his way to Addis Ababa as *Times* Correspondent, Haile Selassie, King Alfonso, and the explorer, Boscawen. It was my job to fuss over and entertain them.

I'd been in Aden about a year, when His Imperial Majesty, Emperor Haile Selassie, Emperor of Abyssinia, steamed into harbor accompanied by his two sons and uncle. "Collateral against a *coup d'etat*," it was rumored. The Emperor had hardly anchored when the luxury liner of King Alfonso of Spain also pulled into port. Dilemma: Should an ex-king married to a British Princess, or a ruling Emperor, sit in the place of honor on the Resident's right? A ruling Emperor took precedence over an ex-king, I decided after furious consultation. My choice did not go unnoticed. Haile Selassie, the Lion King, invested me "Chevalier of the Order of Menelik the Second," so named after an ancestral Ethiopian Emperor.

A photo dated 1931 shows me posed buttons straining, in a too-tight white suit, standing in the back row behind the Lion King's two boy princes.

I turned my attention to King Alfonso. Easy. Wanting to see the landscape, the emptiness, the nothing of the Empty Quarter, where no one or thing but the nomadic Bedu camels and gazelle roamed, I drove him to the 48th Squadron's date-palmed outpost on the fringe of the desert. Overcome, he sat silent lost in thought till sweat and heat chased us to the Mess. To the sound of the lunch bugle, a tame gazelle followed him into the Officers Mess, and tapped its small hoof imperiously on the polished table demanding a tid-bit of crisp toast. Formality broken, the King of Spain and everyone collapsed laughing. Spotting a corral of Arab ponies, His Highness mentioned he represented many Italian Polo Clubs and how he loved playing.

"It'll be nothing like you are used to, Sir, but I can arrange a game," I said.

Next day, his long legs scraping the stony ground and hollering with the rest of us, King Alfonso scored two goals.

"Splendid fun," he beamed.

Before he sailed, Pop Reilly and I joined him on his royal liner for cocktails, and as we left, he presented us both with black Moroccan wallets embossed with the Spanish Royal Cipher and our initials in gold. Mine, reading "H.V.R. from A.," has long since disappeared.

One weekly duty was to deliver the diplomatic bag to the lone British Administrator of Kamaran Island. He had the peculiar job of disinfecting Indian and Moslem pilgrims on their way to Jeddah. Being the only Englishmen he saw all week, we usually stayed overnight just to cheer him up. Nobody would have blamed him if he'd let standards slip, but perhaps to stop from going mad, he stuck rigidly to protocol and kept a ludicrously grand lifestyle. An ancient Rolls Royce with furled Union Jack fluttering always waited ready for us on the dirt airstrip, a smartly dressed chauffeur at the wheel. He and the Administrator's dozen Indian and Arab servants were bedecked in elaborate scarlet uniforms. Formally dressed for dinner, a servant stood behind each chair.

Flying over his Residence in the Wapiti the next day, I pictured him alone at the head of his too grand table, the heavy silence, his obsequious servants, the scrape of silver cutlery on his porcelain plate the only sound.

Strapped into the rear seat of the open cockpit with the hot wind blasting my face, the pilot lifted the plane into the blue, then cutting the engine, swooped silently seaward with the gulls skimming the Red Sea and startling fisherman on the dhows.

One time, returning to Aden from one such mail-run, I shouted down the intercom, "How about a decco at the Dhala war?"

Grinning broadly, the pilot turned round, thumbs up.

"Don't blame me if we ditch the mail, though," he yelled, banking sharply to port towards the mud fort occupied by the British Levies.

We flew low over the steeply terraced hills of the Yemen. White fortified villages clung dizzily to their arid precipices and, in shadowy ravines streams flashed silver in the sun. The burnt sienna mountains dwindled to pale foothills, then melted into the vast yellow sand dunes of the desert sea.

"There. Lahej Oasis." Following the pilot's pointing finger, I just made out a blemish in the haze.

I thought back to the time I first visited Lahej during the *S.S. Assaye's* stopover from England, to the nineteen-year-old, the me, so excited by the word "oasis" he'd taken the narrow-gauge train with his friends just to see one.

Dhala's mud fort swooped into view. The Wapiti's nose dipped sharply earthwards, setting the plane bumping and bucketing in the hot-air pockets, and would have tossed me out but for two straps securing me to the open seat. Intermittent puffs of cotton wool smoked from the hillside.

"Two-inch mortar fire." The pilot pointed above the mud village 500 feet below us.

At first I couldn't make the rebels out. Ant-sized Yemeni tribesman swarmed the far slope of a hill.

"Tally-Hooooooh," the pilot hollered, the plane's nose tipped downward in a steep dive.

Fifty feet shy of hitting the crest of the hill, he pulled out just in time while I hung by my straps over the side of the fuselage firing harmless emergency flares from a Verey pistol, the nearest thing resembling a weapon on board. The bluff worked. Panicked groups scattered, ducking behind rocks and hurling flat to the ground.

Minutes later, the Wapati put down beside Dhala's mud fort on a narrow strip of dirt running the length of the valley's cleft. Manned by just two members of a newly formed Militia, the Aden Protectorate Levies, the C.O. and the other officer scrambled to greet their unexpected visitors. Wildly embellishing details of our escapade, we swapped stories over iced lager and pinpointed the Yemeni positions for them on the detailed survey map hanging on their Mess wall. Their rugged life and intimate connection to the Arab tribesman might have been exciting, but just the two of them cast into the desert, no thank you. I was thankful I had not made the Levies my career choice.

Back in Aden, my boss, Pop Reilly, was not so amused.

"If you had been shot down, you would have caused a lot of trouble to all concerned," he grumbled. "And what about His Majesty's mail?"

But the glint in his eye showed he'd have done the same.

We got on very well. Pop, a bachelor, loved to party. On our rare evenings spent at home, after a meal of wonderful food and wine, he'd often suggest, "Lets go up to the roof for a coffee and a snifter, Hugh." Sprawled on low divans spread with Persian carpets, listeningto Mozart, Bach and Haydn on his gramophone, eyes half-closed, I was conscious of the Arab city lying white and silent in the moonlight, and of the shadowy desert beyond.

My two-storey bungalow in Aden's Tarshyne district overlooked the water near the Residency. Despite its slatted wooden walls, the trapped heat inside was brutal. My first night, I was blasted out of bed by *"God Save Our Gracious King"* playing full volume right below my window. Befuddled with sleep with no idea of what was going on, I jumped, saluting to attention. Pushing open the shutters, I saw a full ceremonial band assembled on the deck of a newly anchored ship playing to the moon. It was tradition, I discovered, for the Union Castle

Liners to play the National Anthem when they dropped anchor in a British Port regardless of the hour, which in Aden coincided with middle of the night. I ignored its call after learning that, and burrowed beneath my sheet.

Many Europeans had lived in Aden for years. Unlike in India, there was none of the snobbery about who could and who could not mix with whom. I found friends in every nationality. Love, too. Part Jewish, part Arab, I met Natasha at a Russian Consulate party. With aquiline features and an alabaster complexion, she was as wild as her looks. Together we chased gazelle into the desert on horseback, raced each other along the golden sands and bathed nude in the dazzling blue Indian Ocean.

Aden was madly social. Bathing, tennis, golf, dancing at the Union Club, outdoor, out-of-date cinema shows to snore through after dinner, and my favorite pastime, polo. At four *annas* per *chukka,* it was probably the cheapest in the world. Away matches against the Somaliland Camel Corps were held across the straits in Hargeisa, Somalia. Its cool high plateaus were a favorite place to hunt lion and striped, deer-like kudu. I never bagged either. Ironically, the one time I came face to face with a black-maned lion and his mate, I had no gun. They crouched to pounce. Miraculously a village marriage procession emerged from the bush beating drums and shouting and saved my life.

As superintendent of the Gardens of Sheikh Othman, where only scrubby trees had grown before, I created the Residency garden. Pop Reilly's birthday loomed.

"Perhaps," I suggested to the Sultan of Lahej "You'll consider giving a hundred camel loads of sweet earth from your oasis."

To Sheikh Othman, I suggested six-foot saplings, shrubs and flowers.

As Superintendent of the Jail, I gave myself permission to commandeer prisoners' labor for my project.

The prisoners hacked through salt earth and rock to a depth of four feet, filled the hole with concrete, loose rubble, and the sweet Lahej soil. I ordered. They built. A high three-sided wall soon protected the enclosure from the Red Sea's salt-laden wind. I, myself, patted-in the Sheikh's trees, shrubs and flowers in readied holes, and seeded the grass lawn. The fourth side opened to the broad verandah of the Residency. In front, Government House looked as bare and windswept as ever. But push open the wicket gate, and be transported to a magical English flower garden set in a green lawn beneath shade trees and sunken rose-garden encircling a sundial.

High water charges and two extra gardeners needed for its upkeep made it an expensive but wondrous gift. The Aden community admired its peaceful beauty as much as Pop. Much admired by visitors, including Haile Selaisse, King Alfonso of Spain and Evelyn Waugh, seeds and roots arrived from every homeland. When I passed through Aden in 1958, it was still there, the trees mature, the flowers blooming, and the sundial pointing the time of day.

That mini-Eden in a barren land is my mark on earth that makes me proud. If I was standing at the Pearly Gates and asked what I had achieved on Earth, I would say, "A garden in the desert. I created that."

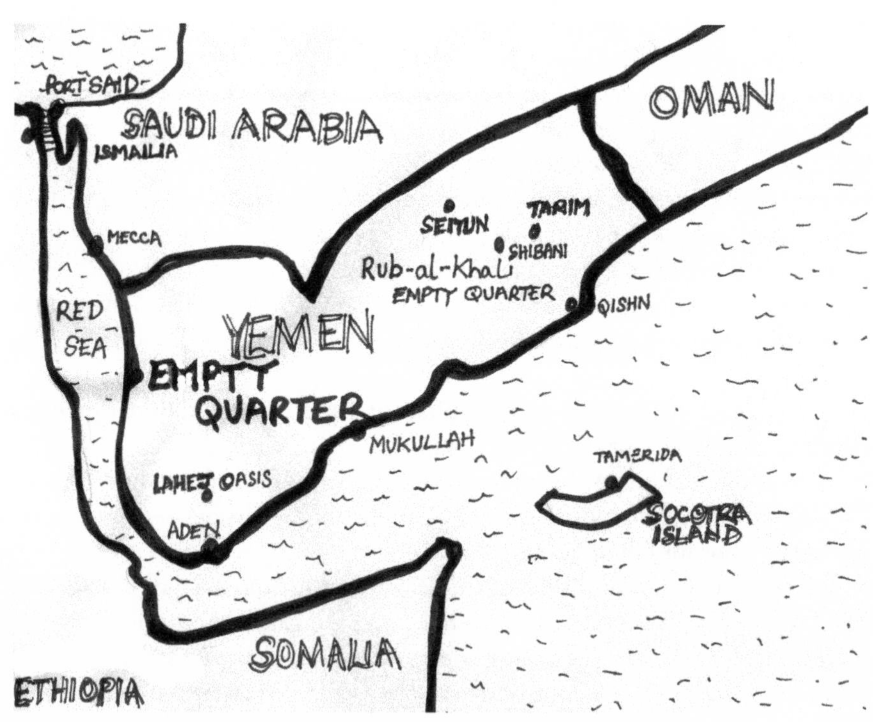

Lahej Oasis Picnic.

Dragon's Blood Tree. Socotra Island.

Qishn Landing.

Port similar to Mukullah.

Qishn Fort.

43
SOCOTRA ISLAND

"Goddam and blast it. The Sultan of Socotra has permitted one of Mussolini's Italian survey ships anchorage in his harbor. Confound the man. Hugh, make arrangements with the Navy toute suite. We sail for Socotra Island tonight." Pop's eyes blazed.

With a civil war in the Interior, a war brewing in Abyssinia, and Yemenis encroaching onto territory we claimed was ours, "It was time," he continued, "time for an Official Visit. Remind the Sultan where his loyalty lies. 'Persuade' the two-timing bastard to let us build an airstrip on his mainland territory at Qishn."

Britain had long coveted a foothold on the Hadrumaut's South Arabian Peninsula. Pop cursed again. I'd never seen him so enraged, so determined.

The *S.S. Penzance* anchored in the waters off Socotra's island capital city of Tamerida. We hoisted our pennant and looked for movement on shore. Protocol required the Sultan first call on us. Nothing. Again and again we "requested" the Sultan to call. We swung the cannon turret, threateningly to shore. Only then did the Sultan and his retinue sweep hurriedly toward his barge.

While we stood sweltering on the quarterdeck in full-dress uniform, our naval gunners fired a royal fifteen-gun salute in an insincere show of friendship. His State Barge pulled alongside. Onto the deck stepped a man of barely five foot. His dress, however, made up for his insignificant stature: a gold-edged cloak shimmering in the sun, a flowing headdress ringed with bands of golden ropes each as thick as thumbs, a curved silver *Kunji*-knife studded with precious jewels pushed in his sash. His retinue surrounded him with a forest of antiquated rifles, among them the Sultan's falconers. Deprived of sight, the birds perched immobile on leather gauntlets. I reached for my camera.

"This way, Sir." We pried the alarmed Sultan from his protesting bodyguards and frog marched him to the Captain's cabin. Surrounded by our armed naval escorts, his retinue had no option but to follow us below decks to the wardroom in the opposite direction.

"Praise be to Allah. May he grant you many healthy sons. May you have abundant camels…" a stern Pop intoned the traditional flowery greeting. After drinking the obligatory three cups of coffee, Pop announced to the Sultan he was to be granted the honor of entertaining twenty of us at his palace over the following three days. "And then," Pop continued, "we wish to visit the Interior and will require forty camels and a suitable escort."

"Impossible." the Sultan protested. "Not even my own officials travel there. The indigenous aborigines in that part of the island are unpredictable and practice cannibalism. And," he concluded, "the trails are impassible."

Pop persisted. "As your duty to the British Crown… May I remind your Majesty…"

Gesturing reluctance, the Sultan's resistance folded. Grim-faced, he swept to shore to arrange to official reception at his palace the following day.

What I had expected to find in a palace, I don't quite know, but never cuckoo clocks and cheap divans from London's Tottenham Court Road, albeit covered with priceless Persian rugs and silk cushions. Shaded cloisters ringed the sun-bleached courtyards and gardens protecting those who ventured out. A waterless fountain stood redundant in a blue mosaic pool. I pitied the Sultan's concubines and wives imprisoned in that place. Strict purdah kept them hidden in the Harem's wing. Did they spy on us from behind the carved alabaster screens along the upper floor? Did they walk the garden when we Infidels were not around?

After removing our boots, we were escorted to a dark reception room. As we entered, Negro slaves sprinkled our hands with refreshing rosewater. The Sultan, regal, posed on a dais at one end of the adjoining hall.

Sweat had plastered my shirt to my sides. For the few moments before we were seated, I edged towards a shaft below one of four wind-towers, and wallowed in its delicious downdraft. Slightly lifting my arms, my shirt steffened, beginning to dry.

"Please be seated." Silent, we sat.

I folded my legs uncomfortably, careful to keep the soles of my feet from pointing at the Sultan, and thereby insulting him. I took my place on a woven mat at one of a half-a-dozen silvered copper tables. Picking from bowls of pistachio nuts and roasted hemp seed, half listening to the drone of formal greetings. I took stock. Stained glass in muted colors arched over each of six wooden doors opening off three walls, keeping out the sun. Fretted light-pools from lattice windows illuminated a room so ornate, so overly decorated with gold leaf and garish colors, I had to check I wasn;t dreaming.

Trays of savory pilaf appeared, so heavy each took two men to carry the pyramid of food. A roasted lamb crouched gruesomely on a rice bed, its head attached. The lamb bore two headless chickens perched on a nest of boiled eggs, and on each chicken rode a quail. No plates. No cutlery. We ate directly off the copper tables pulling, grabbing meat from carcasses and scooping rice using only the fingers of our right hands. Fearful of touching anything with my "unclean" left, I sat on mine. The Sultan proffered the sheep's eyeball to his honored guest, Pop Reilly. Admiringly, I watched him down the prized tid-bit with apparent relish.

Later, back on ship, reliving the etiquette of the feast, one innocent member of the ship's crew chipped in, "I had hard time with the morsel of liver, but out of politeness, I forced myself."

"You didn't. You ate it?" We laughed. "Raw liver is set before each place to attract bluebottles and keep flies off your food." The man blenched.

Pop versus the Sultan, a verbal wrestling match ensued. Three days, it lasted, before the Sultan caved in. As direct questioning, and commitment to anything as specific as yes, no, time or date, went against Middle Eastern culture, it took poor Pop three interminable days of rambling negotiations to extract the Sultan's signature.

While they wrangled, I made for the harbor where Socotra's ocean-going dhows lay at anchor, readying to carry the next cargo to Bombay and Zanzibar in exchange for manufactured goods: ebony, spices and Socotra's prized "dragon's blood" wood. I studied their sturdy hulls, their massive prows and masts. I heard the creak of ropes, the straining wood. I smelled the creosote.

"*Baksheesh. Baksheesh.*" Small bare-foot boys tugged at my arm. I couldn't shake them.

"*Imshi.*" The "Amir-al-Bahr," Master of the Harbor—"master of the sea"—appeared from nowhere and sent them fleeing. Him, however, I couldn't get rid of.

"My harbor," he said. "Come, I want to show you." We stood before a piece of circular barnacle-encrusted brass. "Can you guess what?" His eyes darted, checking my reaction.

I traced the faint inscription, "P & O. The *S.S. Aden.*" Could it be part of her binnacle, part of the lost ship I had read about? The one that had mysteriously run aground off the northeast tip of Socotra in the 1900s with no survivors? Rumors were all on board had been eaten by the indigenous cannibals, after luring her to her doom with lights.

The Harbor Master smiled and refused to elaborate when I asked. It was then I noticed—his tarnished gold-braided peaked cap looked eerily like those worn by P. &. O. Captains.

Negotiations concluded, we readied to explore Socotra's unmapped interior. Camel-bags bulging with enough provisions for a year were slung on the camels' backs. Our official "escorts," looking like a band of armed pirates from *Treasure Island*, watched our every move. Compass set, we headed for the cloud-covered mountainous spine running the length of the island.

A few miles inland, we stepped into a landscape sprouting bottle green, mushroom-shaped trees oozing blood-red resin.

"Dragon's Blood trees. Find only Socotra," our escorts informed us.

Between the trees, massive boulders lay like carelessly kicked giants' footballs in a playground. One fantasyland behind us, we squeezed through a narrow cleft into another—a valley with tumbling waterfalls such as I never imagined existed in the deserts of Arabia.

"Twenty-minute break," Pop ordered. As one we jumped, wading, splashing, tumbling beneath the cascades like seal-puppies. Impassive, squatting on their haunches, our escorts and camel handlers watched the crazed Infidels at play.

Clouds hid the summit. No point in struggling further. We set camp just shy of the crest, yet high enough to catch the breeze. Our task was to map the area over the following five days. Using my survey skills, I plotted, measured and sketched springs, wadis and strategic sites.

For the return, Pop chose a circuitous path down steep, rocky terrain. Clambering from a ravine, we halted. People—the Sultan's cannibalistic cave-dwellers? A village of tiered caves burrowed in the rock-face connected by a series of terraces faced the coast, their inhabitants clearly never expecting to be invaded from the rear. Apparitions from the mountain, we strode through their midst. Caught off-guard, too many of us to attack, they stared—sullen, suspicious, unfriendly, muttering. There was no interaction. The cave dwellers stood about four and a half feet high, as repulsively ugly as it was possible for humans to look. The women wore high, conical black hats and tattered cloaks. Warlocks and witches, lacking only broomsticks, no wonder they had acquired their evil reputation. No doubt to them, we "tall white-skins" looked equally ugly.

Mission accomplished, it was "anchors aweigh." We caught the evening tide and were gone. Next stop was Qishn on the mainland, to tackle the Sultan's uncooperative governor.

We steamed into Qishn at dawn and anchored off shore since there was no harbor. Flouting protocol, our flotilla of surfboats roared ashore uninvited. Grouped in formation, armed, we strode purposefully toward the mud fort. There we confronted a shamefaced Governor in the rubbish-littered compound.

"What is the meaning of this?" Pop pointed his swagger stick to the solitary ruler's Colors atop the flagpole. "Where's the Union Jack? This insult to His Majesty, I refuse to condone." A lead actor, Pop ranted his displeasure.

The Governor, hands clasped, eyes averted, sheepishly excused his oversight and ordered the Union Jack hoisted, and the requisite twenty-one-gun salute. Once the smoke cleared from the ancient pair of cannon. Pop nodded, sniffed, and followed the Governor over the threshold of the bug-ridden residence, haughtily accepting his hospitality.

Pop presented the Sultan of Socotra's fiat commanding the Governor to provide labor and land for Britain's airstrip. Ignoring courtesy, we set sail the same evening.

Another quarrel, with another Sultan, in another state, waited.

Sultan's Bodyguards.

Sultan's Visit. SS Penance. Tamerida.

Sultan's Bodyguard. Mukulla.

Peace Treaty. Mukullah. Hugh Rose left. Pop Reilly back right.

Mukullah.

Re-assembled Rolls Royce. Shibani.

Wapiti.

Shibani.

44
MUKULLA

Overnight, the *S.S. Penzance* hugged the two hundred miles of coastline to the Qu'aiti Sultanate of Shihr and Mukulla to arrive at dawn. The sun's rays fingered Mukalla's jumble of stacked minarets and squat buildings on the rocky hillside above the waterfront. I breathed the last of the cool, watching the oil-grey sea slide to green. Smoke belching from her blackened stacks, wolf-like among a flock of sheep our steamer nosed between graceful ocean-going dhows and smaller craft anchored in the bay.

Relentless, the sun's heat struck the deck. Sweat poured. Wearing full tropical dress uniform, a spiked helmet on my head, My mouth dried to sand-paper. Led by Pop, a group of us stepped ashore and walked the sweltering hundred yards to the Sultan's palace. One hundred Negro slaves paraded in welcome. Inside the banqueting hall, a personal slave waited at every place—one slave per guest for the entire stay. My barefoot shadow padded behind me ready to anticipate my every need. I could hear his breathing from my cot. I felt his waiting, bowl of water and towel in hand.

"I have a slave problem," the Sultan complained to Pop. "Too many. Too many married. Make many children. Eating, eating cost much money. Too little work in palace."

He'd offered freedom, but according to the Sultan, freedom was the last thing his slaves wanted. In bondage they received food and housing in exchange for minimal work. They preferred bondage.

Perhaps he spoke the truth, because years later in 1948, I heard the Sultan set every slave free. Outraged, they rose up, seized the town, and imprisoned the Sultan in his own palace.

"How can we live as free men?" they had remonstrated.

It took two British battalions and a squadron of the RAF to quash the uprising and force them to accept their liberty, the true right of man.

The official purpose of our visit was to end the ongoing civil war between two warring Sultanates, Shihr and Mukalla, and their enemy, the Kathiris in the bordering Sultanate. Pop's primary mission was to extract a peace treaty. Pop's secondary mission was to investigate the rumored murder of a missing British explorer, the Hon. John Boscawen. For me the trip was a chance to glimpse the romantic Hadramaut and its culture.

Putting to shore, we called in to various Sultanates. I saw villages and palaces, nomads traveling with their camels, and goatherds with their long-eared goats. I ate their food. Though we didn't travel deeply into the Empty Quarter, we traveled on and over its fringes to the Sheikhdoms. The area was isolated, fortified, at the mercy of the drifting sands and rains. Fleetingly, I became one with its emptiness.

Pop chivvied. The Sultan prevaricated. The peace treaty remained unsigned. Day after day they tussled. Delay was the Sultan's means of saving face. He understood the situation perfectly but would not sign. Pop finally threatened, "Tomorrow, treaty or no, we fly to the border and negotiate the truce with your Kathiri enemy." Match over. The Sultan about-faced, revealing he had already arranged for a truce to cover the period of our visit.

The six Wapitis I had pre-arranged for, flew us to the border town of Shiban, from there it was an easy drive across the border to Tarim, the capital of the neighboring Kathiri Sultanate.

Strapped into the open cockpits of our two-man Wapatis, we took off along a narrow stone-strewn strip, banked steeply over Mukulla's picture-postcard terraced buildings and harbor, then circled over the pristine emerald sea before heading inland. Flying low at seven thousand feet and almost touching wings, we thumbs-upped and hand-signaled one another. The wind against my face, the bird's-eye views, I couldn't imagine a more glorious way to travel. Mud forts, villages, a camel train, a herd of ibex, a burial mound, an oasis, I devoured them all.

Nearing the valley ringing Shibani, the landscape below me changed.

Craggy bare rock pinnacles pushed upward from a high desert plateau. Gorges and ravines slashed its surface, revealing patches of green and water where they caught the light. Far beyond the distant plateau, the sun rose below me spreading an arc so vast it spanned the earth's rim. A vision, or was it real? The Rub-al-Khali, it was the great Empty Quarter of South Arabia never up to then crossed by man. Overcome, I closed my eyes to imprint forever what I saw.

light and shadow have no boundaries
civilization—but one aspect
of angled light
reflected in men's minds

The plane tilted suddenly sideways to avoid scraping Shibani's precipitous sandstone cliffs, then skimmed close over a huddle of mud sky-scrapers. Like a handful of sharpened pencils standing upright in a mug. they stood twenty or thirty stories high, ringed by a wall, so compacted no light reached their canyon-like streets.

Forbidden to explore, we infidels were whisked away to a whitewashed, two-storied villa far outside the city's walls built to keep us from contaminating their people. Politely, we were "invited" to remain firmly closeted. The following morning a fleet of high-powered cars swept up the drive. "Your transport to the Holy city of Tarim over the border," we were informed. No mirage.The Sultan proudly explained each Rolls had been disassembled on the coast, transported in pieces by camel, and then reassembled. I clambered in after Pop. Cocooned in the soft leather, my eyelids fluttered shut.

As we approached the Kathiri border, a loud boom-thud of cannon fire brought us up short. Another desultory shot sailed over our heads. Creeping slowly forward round the bend, an ancient Spanish muzzle-loader poked from a crumbling mud emplacement manned by a couple of men. Seeing us, the officer hoisted a white flag, beckoned us forward, and greeted us politely. He'd been waiting for our arrival before inaugurating the cease-fire, he informed us. An answering flutter of white from Seiyun's mud tower confirmed it.

Seiyun's shady villas outside the walled town looked like transplants from Surbiton in Surrey, England. Only the palms reminded me I was in Arabia. But the town itself was as curious as if had been conjured by a genie. Ethereal white in the afternoon sun, its tall, narrow buildings, flying buttresses, balconies and slender colonnades soared above the lower stories and flowered into domes and turrets that pierced the sky.

Our brief courtesy call on the Sultan, true to Arab custom, morphed into a lavish welcome. He offered his hospitality, and we as travelers were obliged to accept, though we were in a hurry to reach Tarim. Even oil-rich Saudi Arabia could scarcely have surpassed the magnificence of the Sultan's audience hall, his Mejelis, where he waited to receive us. As in Socotra, slaves sprinkled refreshing rosewater on our hands, and served glasses of lime sherbet in a Moorish room overlooking the main courtyard. His Palace Gardens were as I imagined a Garden of Eden. Water spouted from mouths of carved stone lions into a marble pool to flow in soothing rivulets along either side of green lawns ringed by graceful pillared cloisters and lattice stonework. One of the Sultan's Princes interrupted my reverie.

"Come," he beckoned, "let me show you the view from one of our wind-towers."

Expecting a hot sweaty climb up a tortuous turret staircase, I was surprised when at the click of a button an electric lift shot us to the turret.

"The only one in Arabia," he beamed. "I comissioned an Italian engineer."

Lunch and ceremony over, on no road I could see, we motored across the desert to the Capital, Tarim, to clinch the truce. Tarim, although the main seat of the Seyyids, had none of Seiyun's beauty or wealth. Our accommodation was comfortable but I was so bitten by bugs, so disturbed by the rumblings and smell of camels from a caravanserai across the narrow street, I hardly slept. Two nights were decidedly two too many.

The Sultan summoned us to attend a full *Durbar* the next day. We joined the robed nobles seated on low divans round the perimeter of the Mejlis's reception hall. Even Pop, Britain's official representative, sat below the raised platform in deference to the Sultan's throne. My mind roamed. I studied the Seyyid men who claimed an unbroken line descending from the Prophet Mohammed. I listened admiringly to Pop battle. After Pop presented a mixture of friendly persuasion and veiled threats of military intervention, the Sultan and his nobles finally settled the terms of the treaty, each without loss of face.

With the signing, the Sultan's retinue erupted into the courtyard brandishing fearsome silver scimitars and wildly firing celebratory volleys into the air from weapons so antique I was amazed fingers weren't flying through the air. Flocks of birds wheeled in fright unaware it was peace, not war, we were celebrating. Three cannon volleys announced the end of civil war. A wave of the town's citizens funneled through the palace gates. All were welcome—Prince to mendicant, *Imams*, wealthy merchant to the poorest camel driver—even we infidels. I lifted the small gold-rimmed glass of sweet mint tea to my lips and ignored the fly-blown sugar cakes offered to the honored guests seated at low tables. A sudden silence descended. The hubbub of conversation ceased. The crowd fell to their knees. The haunting cry of the *muezzins* rent the air. The sun sank in a great fiery ball, turning the sand hills to the east blood red. I thought somberly of the explorer Boscawen, dead somewhere beyond the shifting sand dunes.

At the very moment I had that thought, there was a commotion at the gate, and in stalked a lean, bearded man in tattered shorts. Behind him minced a large goat on a short lead. It was Boscawen himself with a South Arabian oryx for the London Zoo.

With both of Pop's missions accomplished, the treaty signed and Boscawen safe, we left for Aden the following morning. No amount of persuasion would sway Boscawen to leave the oryx.

"It's me with the oryx, or I stay."

The struggling beast was hobbled and strapped beside my already snug seat. By some miracle, neither of us fell out.

The Sultan and his armed courtiers fired ceremonial rounds into the air from their antiquated rifles. Pop Reilly bowed low. The Sultan presented him a jewel-encrusted Hadramauti knife. Then, in turn we each stepped forward to receive a curved Kahnjar in a chaste silver sheath. I still have mine. I keep it hanging in the hall above a silver salver.

That "Showing the Flag" expedition with Pop in the Yemen was the most dramatic and exciting experience of my year's posting. I saw how powerful our flag could be. I experienced how hospitably generous the Arab people were. I saw a fiercely proud and strong population flourish in inhospitable geography that defied most human will and learned an unforgettable lesson about human endeavor and man's survival. The land's harsh beauty seared lasting images into my soul.

The poor desert frog I'd been most of life began to hydrate. I had stood my ground, defied Father's outraged disappointment at my breaking with family tradition and abandoning his precious regiment for the Foreign Service. I had come alive.

It was the most dramatic and exciting experience of my year's posting in Aden.

Six months after we arrived back in Aden, Pop and I left on furlough. 1934. He traveled first class P. & O. I followed a fortnight later, traveling steerage in an Italian cargo ship carrying raw hides. I never returned.

Sir Hugh Boscawen with South Arabian Oryx for London Zoo.

45
NINE MONTHS FURLOUGH

My adventure began before I ever docked in Europe

The only other passenger on the cargo ship was a very unusual man. Hugh Boustead had been seconded from his regiment to command the Sudan Camel Corps and was on his way back from the failed German Everest expedition.

"The silly buggers insisted on wearing excessively heavy and inappropriate boots," he explained.

We took an immediate liking to each other. He, like my naked sock-darning colonel, believed in doing just what pleased him even if it got him into trouble. I felt a similar pull. "Conformity kills," we both agreed. Then adding "Compromise castrates," we laughed.

Boustead told me of his extraordinary life. He'd run away from school, sailed round the Horn on a Tall Ship, jumped ship to escape a sadistic ship's mate, received a pardon for desertion, signed on as an ensign in a Highland regiment, then studied to become the brilliant Arabist scholar he was when I met him. Arabia was his passion. When he heard I'd worked for Pop, he nagged me into promising I'd recommend him as the perfect man for the post of

Political Officer in the Aden Protectorate. I did, and Pop Reilly gave him the appointment.

"Pass right by Asmara. What say you to breaking the journey and staying a couple of days with my Italian friend, the Governor General of Eritrea?"

I jumped at Boustead's idea. After a couple of days in Asmara, we borrowed a jeep and headed for Kassala. The pot-holed dirt road dropped dramatically through jungle from 7,000 feet to sea level in fifty miles. I remember a wild ride clinging to the roll bars of the open car with both hands. Rounding one hairpin, we jolted to a sudden halt. Before us in the middle of the road, stood a snorting, head-tossing rhinoceros. He stood his ground. We froze. He turned and vanished up a sidetrack. If he had charged, he would likely have bulldozed the car over the precipice, or crumpled it and us like tissue paper.

We arrived early evening and caught the night mail train to Khartoum. From there Hugh Boustead flew back to El Obeid with the R.A.F. and I flew to Cairo with Imperial Vickers Victoria Airlines. With the plane lumbering at low altitude at a mere seventy miles an hour, I could almost count the goats and bushes. By chance I had Winston Churchill's *The River War* with me, so I amused myself by pinpointing Kitchener's battle sites during his relief of Khartoum.

Comfort was premium, timetables flexible. The pilot asked us, his twenty passengers, what time we would like to leave next day for Brindisi. The Imperial flying boat had two decks, one with a promenade and bar, and the other with nicely made up bunks with crisp white sheets. We flew from the Nile to Corfu in one hop, where we deplaned for the night to stay in the luxurious yacht the Airways used as their hotel. After a leisurely breakfast, the pilot rounded us up for the final leg. Over the Corinth Canal, water sprayed as we touched down on the water and skied into the terminus at Brindisi. Comfortable Pullman sleeping cars awaited and carried us to Calais. Long but totally pleasurable, my leave was already under way.

Under thirty, a bachelor, two years' pay to burn, and nine months to spend it: perfect ingredients. I was ready. Fun, family, friends, and more fun, describe my furlough. Though I will mention two adventures, risking my life in Ober Gurgl, and the brothel in Buda Pest.

I had been in Ober Gurgl three months skiing, when six of us decided to go on a five-day hut tour. We hired Jenerwein, a guide we met over glasses of warm *gluhwein* in a bar. Next day he put the bulk of our provisions on his back, we put on our skis and set off. We were an ill-assorted group, a police officer from Kenya, a Naval grass widow and three others beside myself.

I should have turned back that first night when our guide couldn't find the hut where we were to spend the night. After climbing six grueling hours on skins, standing shivering in the bitter wind at dusk, watching Jenerwein frantically dig for the hut was the last thing we needed. It was completely buried, a mere hump in the snow. At last he found it. It took nearly an hour of strenuous hacking with an ice axe before we pried open the door. Once inside, Jenerwein struck a match and had the pot-bellied stove devouring wood as fast as he fed it. Mugs of hot chocolate laced with brandy brought our limbs back to life. We watched, hungry, while he rustled up a thick sausage soup and black bread. The seven of us wrapped ourselves in one enormous cocoon, sharing body heat. How we grumbled unraveling it whenever any of us needed a trip to the thunder-box.

The next morning the wind was still bitter.

"You soon too hot," Jenerwein encouraged.

It was true. Ten-miles over a 10,000-foot pass onto the high slopes of the Wilde Spitze and I was sweating.

Jenerwein pointed out a minor mountain and raved about the view from the top.

"See all Italy. Easy climb," he assured. Trusting, we trailed along behind him.

We, I, should have known better. We should have become suspicious and refused when he stopped and tied us together with a rope then veered towards Hoch Spitze, a high, jagged peak about a quarter of a mile to our left instead of the mountain he had pointed out. None of us were climbers or had any desire to climb. We were there to ski. While we bleated like sheep, Jenerwein shepherded us with encouraging cries in German. After we had traversed a short glacier, Jenerwein leapt ahead like a goat. Cajoling, he hauled us up after him. Too late to go back, we could only creep ahead in a climb that had turned into a nightmare. Not one of us had a head for heights; I certainly didn't. Our lives now depended on an irresponsible fool. To survive we had to continue. The next horror came when the ridge petered out and we had to cross a gap over the 2,000-foot drop with only one foothold and one handhold to keep us from tumbling to our deaths. To our dismay, we were confronted with a knife-edge ridge a foot wide, with an appalling precipice on either side. At first we all refused, but as Jenerwein had already crossed the ridge and was tugging at the rope, there was no option but to follow. The first to lose his composure was the policeman from Kenya. Treading gingerly on the frozen snow, he got halfway across, crumpled in a trembling heap astride the ridge and burst into tears.

The blood drained from our faces and silent tears of terror coursed down every cheek. My legs would hardly support me. I thought they'd buckle, and I would plunge into the reality of a "falling dream." Even Jenerwein was worried.

"Kommen zie hier," he commanded, shouting, as he bodily dragged the paralytic Kenyan to the far side.

Dazed with fear, I have no memory how I, nor the rest of us, made it across, but we did. Jenerwein tramped out a flat area in the centre of the snow-covered summit on which we sat facing inwards, huddled together away from the edge and trying to compose ourselves. In an attempt to cheer us and show us we had nothing to fear, Jenerwein walked round the outside edge yodeling at the top of his voice. It was entirely thanks to his flask of plum brandy we found the courage to brave the descent.

Once at the base, desperate, relieved, we scrabbled at the frozen knots of the rope to separate ourselves. From nowhere a severe blizzard suddenly enveloped us in a whiteout and we still had to climb 4,000 feet to reach the rest hut. At last the faint glow of a lit window guided us to safety. Thankfully the hut was manned, and we were welcomed with a proper hot meal. I was alive. We ate in silence, then collapsed.

Nightmarish flashbacks disturbed our sleep. I heard the Kenyan call out. A woman screamed. I woke drenched, sweating. Next morning, all six of us decided to continue.

"It better be an easy climb, Jenerwein," we warned him.

We put on our skins, and almost skated up the gentle slope of the beautiful Wildespitze, one of Austria's highest mountains. We stood somberly below the silver cross on the summit. Reading the names of the Austrians killed in the war, mortality became real.

Back in Ober Gurgl, I found a telegram waiting for me from the India office. "Report. Consulate Meshed. Appointment Vice-Consul." I had no inkling where Meshed was, nor had the village schoolmaster. He fetched his school atlas. We eventually found a tiny dot in northeast Persia near both the Russian and Afghanistan borders.

Two months furlough before I reported for duty. Vienna, Kitzbuhel, nightclubs, lonely widows, hungry women, "hostesses," I enjoyed them all. Then one day I'd had enough. It was time to see my family in England.

I returned via Budapest, Prague and Berlin, spending a few nights in each place.

The Palace Hotel in Budapest was built over natural thermal springs. Guests were offered a hostess with their room if they chose. I did choose and stayed a full week. Rosa came to my room and warmed my bed at night, took me to her favorite clubs, and rubbed my naked back in the hotel's Turkish baths where all the bathers, male and female, were nude. Group nudity. I felt curiously exposed. Then aping my confident naked sock-darning Colonel back in the Isle of Wight, I straightened my back, removed my hands and uncovered my crotch.

Rosa introduced me to the Madame of one of the most famous, or infamous, brothels in Europe. Rosa giggled when I asked, "What do you mean, sex on skates?" But she'd only answer, "You'll see. You'll see."

Rosa took me there early next evening. The front door opened directly from the street into the brothel's richly furnished salon. Parading, naked, a bevy of gorgeous women confidently displayed their attributes. Clients sat around on cushioned couches drinking champagne and eyeing the selection. Though Rosa swore she had never worked there herself, I had my doubts. The girls called her by name, and Madame obviously knew her very well.

"I've put you in Honeysuckle, Rosa, dear," she said.

Rosa led me by the hand up a marble staircase into a carpeted corridor hung with pornographic pictures, past rows of womb-like rooms, each overlooking the ballroom through cleverly concealed windows. Our "Honeysuckle" had a table ready laid with an appetizing supper and bottle of champagne cooling in an ice bucket. Below us through the window, I saw a solitary red plush settee in the middle of the ballroom, spot-lit by a bright chandelier. Rosa handed me a glass of champagne while we waited for the show to begin. Waltz music was playing. A naked girl roller skated languorously into the ballroom, draped herself provocatively on the settee and began caressing her body. After a few moments, in teetered her client on his skates, naked and aroused. Seeing him, the girl stood up, curtsied, then skated slowly backwards, beckoning him to follow. The client was fat and pot-bellied, and skating was obviously not his best skill. The chase was short, as was his sexual performance on the settee. The next to enter the arena was as good a skater as the girl, resulting in a very amusing chase and eventual conquest. Rosa and I, the other voyeurs too, I imagine, laughed at their antics, fed each other champagne before succumbing. Rosa taught me some new tricks that evening. The maroon velvet flock covering the walls, the down-filled double bed, the gilt sconce candelabra—the illusion of entering a womb was complete.

I left for Berlin the next day. While I was enjoying a coffee at an outside café, three Brown Shirts *Heil-Hitlered* me with raised arms, demanding a subscription for "winter help." They became abusive when I refused, and only left me alone when they realized I was British. It was 1934, the year Hitler ordered the Austrian monarchist, Englebert Doilfuss, murdered.

It was time to go to London. Visit Mother and Kathy. Less than three weeks remained before the Orient Express would whisk me back for another two years' absence.

I knocked on the door of Mother's and Kathy's London flat. They greeted me with worrisome news.

"Father is in Brussels living with..." Kathy hesitated. "A housekeeper, and has fallen gravely ill with an attack of tropical sprue."

I caught the next plane to Brussels, packed his things, put him on a stretcher, and flew him to London's Hospital for Tropical Diseases. Familiar with sprue, a nasty condition of the intestine rife in India, their doctors soon had him on the mend.

I settled him in a flat under the doting care of his mistress, his...umm... "housekeeper," Mrs. Ball, a no-nonsense divorcee whom I and my siblings grew to accept and like.

46

THE ORIENT EXPRESS

London To Meshed

Victoria Station. Platform 5. There she stood the train of my dreams, the legendary Orient Express.

"London–Istanbul," it proclaimed in gold and red lettering on every wagon-lit and Pullman car. The name conjured opulence. Liveried servants stood on the platform at every door. One stepped forward and escorted me to my cabin with its crisp linen sheets, mahogany furniture and attached bathroom.

"Will there be anything else, Sir? Your table in the dining car is reserved for eight."

I took the copy of the London *Times* from the attendant's gloved hand and handed him a sixpence.

"For your good self," I nodded.

The train lurched forward. Mother and Kathy waved, mouthing goodbyes through the window. A hoot, a puff of steam, one final wave, and they evaporated.

My last long train ride to Abbotabad. Smiling, I swiveled the armchair in my compartment to face the window. Round and round I spun—joyous I was on the move, heading to the sun.

Drizzle. Drizzle obscured my last view of England's bedraggled countryside. I saw nothing of the grey seas as we tossed across the Channel. Next morning I woke in Paris.

Riveted to the glass most days just looking, I savored my journey, my time alone, exquisite cordon-bleu meals and fine wines in the Pullman car. Apart from a brief nod to fellow travelers as I took my seat, I kept myself to myself, preferring my own thoughts.

"The journey…not the destination…is the thing…is the thing." The dictum I'd read in some book long ago rattled rhythmically with the wheels. *"It's the journey, it's the journey, not the getting there,"* the train seemed to sing. The very thing I was doing, I recognized with a smile—no home, no roots, a traveler, traveling to… it mattered not where.

I called the waiter over for a glass of port and idly watched the lights of some unknown town appear, then disappear into the darkness. The flickering reflection of candelabra in the darkened window illuminated a face distorted by the train's vibration. It was myself twenty years into the future, my face aged, lined as Mother's.

How she had changed. Poor Mother. I shook my head. Her thick black hair streaked with grey. Worse, Kathy. The dulling of my sister's sparkle, her resignation to spinsterhood and caring for our aging mother. Kathy was too young and beautiful for such a sacrificial role. Another worry—Mother becoming a religious fanatic.

"It's awfully embarrassing," Kathy had confided. "Mother has taken to driving around Hyde Park in a horse and carriage, hurling religious tracts at pedestrians she passes, with the admonition, 'Repent. God loves you'. She insists on my accompanying her."

Then there was their pokey, two-roomed flat in a depressing neighborhood, an uncomfortable reminder of the poverty and the homes of my childhood, and that my debonair persona was a fraud. My God. I realized with guilty horror I had become like Father who could never wait to get away, who couldn't stand being home with his family for long. Though I'd given Kathleen a sizable check with the promise to help out any time, the discrepancy between our lives still niggled my conscience.

I crushed out my cigar and staggered down the swaying corridor to my carriage.

The train sped smooth as a ribbon through France, Switzerland, Austria, and the nothing of the long dark tunnel of the Brenner Pass, before exploding into Italy.

I broke my journey in Venice to wander the canals, marvel at the frescos and absorb the serenity of its many churches. St. Anthony, St. Francis, the Virgin Mary. I knelt before each statue and lit a candle.

Ice-encrusted windows, flashing images, jumbled, disordered memories are all that remain of Belgrade, Sophia and the vast snow-covered Balkan plain. Constantinople, renamed Istanbul, was a culture shock after my days of relative solitude. Stylish women, as modern and smartly dressed as Parisiennes, walked the bazaars unchaperoned, unveiled, and sat in cafes chatting over coffee with their women friends. The crowded harbor, domes, minarets, the blue of the Bosporus, Constantinople lived up to its fairy-tale image. Too little time, too much to absorb.

I rejoined the train, impatient for the journey to end. Two hot days later, I, and a bunch of other travel-weary travelers were off-loaded in Nisbin's dusty terminus in the Syrian Desert and transferred to a Rolls Royce for the drive to a rest house in Mosul for the night. Nothing cosmopolitan there, after so many months of luxury, lying angled to avoid the worst lumps in the mattress, I stared in shock at the flies circling above me. This was work, I reminded myself. I was a uniformed soldier on duty not the pampered, moneyed traveler I aped. I had the unsettling realization I'd come to think of my career as one long pleasure trip and luxury was my right.

"Better change your attitude, Hugh," I resolved. "Better drum up some enthusiasm before presenting yourself to the Consul in Meshed."

If I'd known my future, I'd have seen my journey from "Gay Paree" to Mosul's grime as symbolic of the slippery road my career was traveling.

A newspaper correspondent, two missionaries, a rough American oil-driller on his way to Bahrain, and me, confined together in a Rolls, made for an ill-assorted group. However, by playing Gin Rummy and sharing our life histories, we found ways to rub along during the interminable drive across featureless plains to Kirkuk in Iraq.

Next stop, Baghdad. An Arabian Nights paradise on the road to the golden Samarkand, sadly it was not. Not even the idyllic palm trees planted along the banks of the gentle Tigris River could disguise its squalor. Whisky saved the three less holy of us from Bahgdad-belly. They and I drank nothing but. Not so lucky the missionaries who spent the following twelve hours to Khanakin squatting over the hole in the floor that passed for the train's toilet.

Dirty and hot, we dragged ourselves into another Rolls. Dirty and hot, we swayed and lurched along dirt roads so pot-holed, we joked they'd not been repaired since 1917, when first built by the Russians in their attempt to claim Baghdad. It was the newspaper guy who knew the country and its history. His stories of tiger, pig and deer in Persia's lower jungle and of good skiing in the Kurdistan Mountains kept our minds from skidding over 2,000-foot precipices on the countless narrow, hairpin bends. We clutched the sides, each other's knees, holding on. The missionaries threw up.

We took a short break at a roadside teahouse to strap chains onto the tires.

Slowly, inching upward, we made it over three snow-covered passes into Hamadan before nightfall. Much to the astonishment of the villagers, before settling into the rest house, I grabbed my skis from the luggage rack and took a couple of short runs in the powder to de-cramp my legs. Snow, mountains, and rarified air erased the last days' trials. Only beauty remained.

Kermanshah, Kazin, flashes of their prosperous terraced vineyards, fields and clusters of mud dwellings nestled among orchards and gardens are folded forever in my mind.

Teheran. As was normal practice for British travelers on Government business, I presented myself to the British Legation for a few days respite. Unsuspecting an ulterior motive, with dirt and dust ingrained in every pore and orifice, I was surprised to be invited in so enthusiastically.

"Just in time to help me out, old boy. My third secretary, Buss, has been struck low with a bug, and I have the devil of a job to finish, if you've no objection to being waylaid. I've already telegraphed Meshed." The Ambassador, Sir Reginald Hoare, beamed.

"Delighted, Sir. Absolutely delighted to oblige." Taking in their ten acres, their lovely house built beside a lake's sparkling waters, I hoped I hadn't sounded too eager.

One of those intrepid British women who scorned the fragile-woman role, Lady Hoare had recently bought herself a Moth and learned to fly. Taunting the Shah's no-fly order, she often buzzed the royal palace to make a point.

"Nonsense, dear. I have diplomatic privilege. I'll fly anywhere I please," she'd argued to her husband.

Sir Reginald refused to discuss the Shah when I questioned him.

"Shah Reza Khan?" he evaded, jokingly denying any knowledge of him. "Who's that?"

In truth, Sir Reginald greatly respected the Shah's attempts to modernize Iran without technical aid from any one country, Britain included. During informal social calls, he and the Shah had developed a genuine friendship, and thanks to his softly-softly approach, Britain retained her foothold in Persia. In the twenties, the Shah had sent the power-seeking Soviets packing. Britain escaped their fate.

Perhaps because Sir Reginald was an oddball, we got on well. One afternoon during my stay I came across him in his garden shooting squirrels. Handing me his air gun, he pointed to his children's backsides as they bent over their dinghy at the edge of the lake.

"Take a pot shot at one of those frogs," he joked. Taking back the gun, he popped off a couple of pellets, splashing the water beside the children and laughing as they jumped.

The hot weather arrived, and as in India, most of the Legation's staff migrated to the hills, in this case Gula Hek, a delightful resort at 7,000 feet in the foothills of the Elburtz Mountains. Before I could join them, Buzz rose from his sick bed to take back his job.

Sir Reginald and Lady Hoare were away skiing. With no time to say goodbye, I left on the final leg of my journey. The prospect of five hundred miles in the front seat of a truck filled me with dread.

Persia was now plainly named Iran; her ancient name rang with beauty. A country of spectacular contrasts, Iran ranged from the snow-covered 18,000-foot Demavend to the shifting sands of the Lut desert and salt marshes. Driving across its lush southern 4,000-foot plateau, I was surprised to find it so thickly treed.

Ah, such Persian gardens. True to idyllic images from Omar Khayyam, soothing water bubbled into shaded lily-ponds between beds of scented roses beneath the dark, spreading cedar, poplar, and mulberry trees. Gardens where nightingales sang, gardens where I could almost hear the pearls falling from the lips of poets, and the earnest discourse of philosophers and their friends. Head lolled against the lorry's juddering frame, my imagination ran. Well, a man could dream, and I had three days to fill.

Skinny Dipping.

Vice Consul Evvie Gastrell and his wife Dishie.

Consulate General Staff. Meshed.

Spies? Party. Meshed

47
SPY GAMES
Meshed, Persia

I crossed the Robat Pass on a cold March evening, 1935. The golden dome of Meshed glowed in the wintry sun below me, five hundred weary miles from Teheran behind us.

The jolting ceased. The lorry rode Meshed's level cobbled stones. Wide poplar- lined boulevards, lighted cafes, modern buildings and grand villas set back from the road floated, welcomed. Watching idly, for I was tired, I saw my driver turn past a kebab shop into the pitch-blackness of a narrow, walled street of maybe half a mile. The lorry braked to a stop. Lost? A hold-up? Suddenly I was fully awake. How the devil to escape? My thoughts ran.

"Arrive, *Sahib*. Arrive now."

Our headlights caught the Royal Arms and a sign reading "H.B.M. Consul-General" hanging on a massive pair of wrought-iron gates.

I took a deep breath, and crossed my fingers. The gates swung open and a turbaned servant ushered me inside.

"Welcome. Welcome. You must be Rose. Come on in. You must be dying for a cup of tea." My hosts' towering silhouettes filled a lighted doorway.

"Perhaps you'd like me to give you an enema later?" the Consul's wife added. "Parasites. Flush them out, I say."

The Vice-Consul and his wife had lived in Meshed close to the Afghan and Turkestan border since the Agency first opened in 1922. From our first meeting, we knew we would be lifelong friends. Free from Britain's conformist grip, ex-pats pushed boundaries to their limit. Like my naked colonel in the greenhouse, like the mad Mitch judge in India, Evvie and Dishie, like fat drops of rain, revived what they touched. I aped their fierce, independent ways.

Six foot plus, Evvie and Dishie Gastrell were hard to miss, their children too. Four naked giants striding down a mountain, clothes balanced on their heads with their hands before their faces, "so we won't be recognized," they giggled. Hiking naked after rolling in an icy stream. They enjoyed the feel of the sun on their skin and the freedom of their nakedness.

"We'll show you polo, proper polo as it should be played," Evvie and Dishie announced one day, and smiled. "Two Afghani teams are playing in a village on the Chinese border."

We joined the jostling crowd peering at a bare-patch of earth. Two rough circles marked either end. We didn't have long to wait. Rifle fire and whooping war cries startled me, and two wild groups of turbaned men galloped onto the ground at opposing ends. Cracking whips, their horses fretting, the ten-man teams arranged themselves, derisive, threatening. An elder led a goat between the lines. Bleating, fearful, it made to escape. With one slice of the elder's saber, its head went flying in a splatter of blood. The game began. Scooping, ripping, kicking, stabbing, both teams used whatever foul means they could to wrench the headless carcass from the other's possession and pitch it into the "goal."

"Noted and understood." I acknowledged." OK. So that's proper Polo."

Impossible to take seriously, my career became a farce, a clandestine game of espionage where each country stole carefully planted disinformation and out-of-date ciphers from one another's safes. Russian, German, French, Turkish, British—each embassy robbed the others. Ridiculous, but a game we all enjoyed despite its underlying serious side: issuing passports, helping White Russian Refugees, and aiding Russian Jews in their escape from Russia. One dark night, a sudden scuffle and a cry for help woke me as some poor devil was kidnapped and dragged back across the frontier. We were powerless to act—to interfere would cause a diplomatic incident.

Every country had its covert agenda for being in Meshed, though from the weekly fraternizing you'd never know any differences existed. At my first Embassy party I watched a Russian Secret Policeman lop off the head of our MI-6-man in a wild version of Oranges and Lemons. Clutched tightly to a German bank clerk's bosom, our ambassador's wife spun an Austrian waltz. Arms locked, hands touching, secretaries, clerks, grand officials, and junior staff alike, danced the Highland Fling, drank, ate and played the fool at parties hosted by Consuls, Embassies and Official Residencies.

"*Ya Vas.* To you. To friendship between nations."

The Russians drank to get drunk. They burst into song, danced and wept without ever becoming belligerent. Throughout dinner, our Russian hosts filled our glasses, insisting we down their fiery contents in a single gulp; they were hoping to worm non-existent secrets from their intoxicated guests. We used the same tactic. "Bottoms up," we challenged, handing the Russians a stirrup of ale, but not the smallest military detail let slip.

The only course served was soup, usually borsch. Informally seated guests helped themselves. Iranian wine, vodka, paté de foie gras, and fresh caviar from the Caspian flowed. I lived like a millionaire, or how I imagined a millionaire lived. Evenings faded in cigar and cigarette haze as I watched Russian folk dances, or swooned to the soaring notes of a master violinist, once leader of St. Petersburg's Imperial Orchestra.

For fear social contact with local Iranians and Meshed's multi-cultural population might be misconstrued, politically, I was stuck with the Embassy crowd. Then I discovered The Continental, a half-Iranian, half-European hotel. I'd slip into the upper auditorium to attend musical events and colorful folkloric performances—Katak, Cossack, ballet, Chinese acrobats, jugglers, and stylized three-hour Indian Epics. Eyes watched my every move. I watched them back, gleaning what I could of their culture. Differing national dress and mannerisms, the audience represented the World.

During the month of Ramadan, nights vibrated with the muffled beat of drums, first fading, then drawing so close they seemed outside the Consul's walls, only to recede again. On and on, always the same, now louder, now fading, their low, insistent thumpety-thump had a strangely menacing sound often lasting until daybreak. I'd imagine the procession wending its way to the tomb of the Imam Reza, so holy no infidel could enter it and live.

Life in Meshed was paradise. After a sudden late snowfall, I wangled a ski-trip in the Nisharpur Hills, the birthplace of Omar Khayyam, just as the daffodils, snowdrops, hyacinths and delicate primroses burst through the melt to announce the spring. May arrived with the drowsy scent of blossom heavy in the air, as the orchards and gardens burst into a fairyland surpassing even those of Japan. Mountain torrents tumbled through Meshed's flower-filled valleys and bluebell woods. Willow, poplar, larch and pine grew from springy turf and colorful blooms. I laid my head against a moss-covered mulberry root in the most beautiful place on earth.

Little did I know I was soon to leave Meshed's heaven for an arid hell in the desert plateau, and my days with the Foreign Service were numbered.

Hugh. Kuh-i-Taftan.

Kuh-i-Taftan Volcano.

Hugh with Rebel Leader. Ladis.

Nomads Shearing Sheep.

48

ZAHIDAN

Iranian Baluchistan

"Think of it as a promotion," Evvie tried to soften my obvious shock."Robber's Well," the literal translation of Zahidan's original name, Duzdap, suited. Devoid of incentive, I twiddled my thumbs and wondered what the hell I was doing. Despitethe empty, endless hours on my hands, not one poetic line welled—my mind, barren as the treeless desert.

I'd been posted four hundred miles south to replace The Vice Consul at Zahidan, a trade crossing in Iranian Baluchistan. He'd scarpered for home on six months' sick leave. When I arrived I could understand why. Why Britain or any country maintained a consulate in such a God-forsaken place, escaped me. Trade. Politics. Power. What else? Only the month before I arrived, our Confidential Clerk had been robbed at knifepoint by bandits.

If ever an area could be described as blasted, Iranian Baluchistan deserves such an adjective. The only signs of life on the salt-encrusted plateau, apart from scanty cultivation, were camel-thorn and tamarisk. Nomads wandered the arid uplands and rocky hills in search of pasture, quenched their thirst from brackish mud holes. Eroded low mountain ranges rose a few thousand feet and trapped the plateau in their bare brown arms. Intense cold alternated with fierce heat, and for four interminable months, every orifice and surface of my body stung with scorching sands blown by the "Wind-of-one-hundred-and-twenty-days."

The Vice Resident's grim, mud bungalow half a mile outside Zahidan's ramshackle town, lay close to the Iranian barracks and derelict buildings of the defunct railhead. With the exception of two official buildings built since the war, Zahidan's downtown consisted of three shops run by Sikhs. A scattering of houses constructed with earth and wooden railway sleepers withered unseen behind by high mud walls to keep the desert out. Repair garages abounded to service the grinding motor traffic passing through Zahidan day and night in ballooning dust-clouds.

Leafing through Consulate files in the safe, I uncovered a cache of money in the secret service fund where it had lain untouched for twenty years. Spend. Spend. Spend. My idle fingers twitched as I counted ways to use every penny. An idea festered.

"Create an oasis in Zahidan's hellhole as I'd created in Aden."

Telegraphs boomeranged to Meshed. With Evvie's go-ahead for what I called "improvements," the drab bungalow and guardroom transformed to gleaming white. Next "improvement," a garden. Six salt- resistant palms and pink flowering oleander later, my haven began taking shape. To make it worthy of a British Consulate, I added a squash court and small swimming pool, and hired two men and a bullock to draw water from the garden well and keep it filled. My oasis was ready. My three and only friends and I splashed happily in the pool and sipped cool drinks from a floating bar laden with bottles and glasses. "The Desert Resort," locals named it.

"Outlandish...wanton...flagrant misuse...Government funds..." Colonel Daly, the Consul, was not amused and made to scurry back from leave. He circled my name with black. But before Colonel Daly returned, life dragged, and I had weeks and weeks to fill.

I made a particular friend of MacDonald, one of the few European inhabitants in Zahidan besides myself. Then, there was the American sub-manager of the Anglo-Iranian Oil Company and his charming wife, and.... That was it—Zahidan society. But I had company at least, unlike the solitary bachelors of the Indo-Persian Telegraph Company, forced to stick out years alone in some small bungalow buried in desolate outposts without ever seeing another European. I thought back to my crystal set and my dreams of choosing that career. I must have been crazy.

I made myself take trips just for the change of scene. My reward, after journeying for seven hours; Ad-i-Dawa's cooler elevation, with its spring, tank, greenery, and good shooting of *oorial*, a wild, bearded sheep, and ibex. Or drive through Sistan's hot and low-lying rice fields just to catch sight of their green and to dig for "finds" in the great ruined cities half-buried in the sand of a once fertile plain watered by the great River Helmand from Afghanistan. I shipped boxes of pottery shards and colored glass vessels to the British Museum. I measured a tomb I'd discovered, and made detailed sketches of the painted hunting scenes on its walls. One onyx oval bead, I pocketed—a memento I treasure still.

I drove to spend ten-day leave in Quetta, choosing the shorter three-hundred-mile route through Lut's shifting sands in central Iran—preferable, I thought, to the safer thousand-mile detour via Isfahan, Teheran and Meshed, until taking a breath in the desert's burning air became a life and death struggle. I understood why people chose the longer route.

Was I hallucinating? As I drove the three hundred miles across Lut's burning desert from Quetta, I saw bursts of smoke spark red from twin snow-capped cones floating 13,000 feet above the bare, brown hills in the rays of the setting sun. Kuh-i-Taftan, a beacon, She beckoned me. I was hers. Obsessed. I desired to climb her. Problem. Semi-active, the volcano lay near the South Baluchistan Iranian military stronghold on the Indo-Iranian border. I needed a pass from the Iranians.

With an eye on the coveted pass, I engineered weekly calls on the local Iranian Governor with the feeblest of trumped up pretexts: I needed his advice... an extradition warrant... settle some dispute... discuss damaged crops...compensation. Well aware of my agenda, he always greeted me courteously, and over many cups of Russian Tea, exchanging banalities through a haze of Isfahani cigarettes. I knew he knew and he knew I knew he knew. When etiquette finally allowed me to mention the purpose of my visit, each time he shook his head and refuse me permission under a cloak of vague excuses... concern for my safety...strict no-trespass rule... a military area.

"Perhaps when the tribal uprising was over it might become possible," he would conclude.

"Kuh-i-Taftan, such a beautiful mountain. Shame only a foreigner, an Englishman, not an Iranian, had ever conquered her." I'd press my point. "The prestige of Persia is at stake. Now, if an Iranian expedition should achieve the summit, then ... perhaps, if such an Iranian expedition were arranged, I could accompany it?"

Only a madman wanted to climb "the Place of Heat," Kuh-i-Taftan, the mountain of fire belching poisonous, sulfurous fumes, where the air was so rare a man might scarcely breathe. I must be a spy fishing for military secrets—a spy to be humored. I could read his mind.

To be rid of me I, the Governor gave me permission to shoot black partridge.

"But–you must be accompanied by a guard, and travel no farther beyond the border than Ladis." No mention of Kuh-i-Taftan.

I arrived at the border post above Mirjawa without incident, only to find the local governor had secret orders to restrict my pass to Ladis. "Yes," he had heard from the Governor of Zahidan, "…but the area near Ladis was very unsettled." He did his utmost to dissuade me. I remained politely insistent. It took many cups of tea before my host mentioned a certain "X" was on his way to Khash. Perhaps if he agreed to meet me, matters could be arranged.

"X, Patriach of the Nomads," a member of an old Iranian family, couldn't have been more helpful. I found him camped just beyond Ladis, sharpening a wickedly curved knife on a whetstone, and surrounded by armed brigands swathed in indigo and rust-dyed turbans. "X," a tall man in homespun clothes and heavily armed with both a rifle and a knife, remained seated, his eyes glinting from what little I could see of his face. He waved, indicating a saddlebag.

"Sit," he commanded, "I invite you to my humble supper."

Three black partridge dripped invitingly from a spit over the embers. The tribesmen sat on their haunches in a half-circle on the far side of the fire, poised like hawks to defend their leader to the death should I make one wrong move. But I was no threat. I was in my element, relaxed, smiling, free as I was in India's Himalayas. Forbidden, I knew, but I'd crossed the border to scale Kuh-i-Taftan, the volcano climbed only once before.

We talked far into the night, sipping sweet mint tea, swapping tales of mountains conquered, dangers we had overcome and of the peace we found in nature's timeless beauty, and its wild. Two cultures melded. Two faces glowing in the firelight, we dined beneath the stars. I was home.

"I'll accompany you part way in the morning," my new friend, the "Patriach of the Nomads," offered as I departed for my own camp.

Just after daybreak, he clambered beside me into my Standard Fourteen and guided me a short way along an goat track leading southwards towards Khwash and the Indian Ocean.

"Me here," he said, leaping out. "You there. Up." One embrace, and he was gone.

Distances were deceptive in that pristine atmosphere. Kuh-i-Taftan's peaks remained as remote as a picture postcard despite my two-hour scramble over her boulder strewn lower slopes.

1:00 p.m. The incline steepened into a cliff-like slope skirting the base.

My Baluchi guard squatted, lowered his rifle and refused to take another step. "Bad spirits. I not go. Wait here for *Sahib*."

I left him in a shady ravine squatting by a muddy pool telling his "worry beads." Anxious.

Kuh-i-Taftan's twin peaks loomed high above, wreathed in smoke. Wading through soft volcanic powder, tortoise-slow, I inched over ash-covered, sun-baked granite to eleven thousand feet, my teeth filmed with grit.

4:00 p.m.. At last I reached the sulphur-encrusted rubble, when a low rumble, a slight tremor beneath my feet, a puff of smoke, and a shower of ashes made me bound for safety. A cold breeze whistled eerily in the rocks. Looking back, I suddenly shivered, half expecting a tenuous form to materialize from the vapor. Kuh-i-Taftan. The volcano. The only living being, I floated far above the world. The legends and superstitious fears surrounding Kuh-i-Taftan gnawed, reminding me I was alone and day was fading fast. Reaching for my pocket flask, I took a swig of brandy and turned my back on her foul-smelling form. Slithering and slipping until I reached her base.

7:00 p.m.. My guard touched my feet, greeting me as an apparition returned from the dead. He cranked the Standard's start handle. Five hours later, we lurched into Zahidan.

I was in trouble. The grapevine hummed red. News of my deeds already preceded my arrival. Not only was I half a day late, worse, I had shared a meal with the rebel leader, a bandit heading Britain's most-wanted list. So that's who he was—my hospitable "Patriach of the Nomands."

I read the cipher telegram addressed to me.

"Explain action. Bandit Leader 'X.' Indo-Iranian border infraction."

Within the month, Colonel Daly had me transferred out of Iran and posted to South Waziristan on the North West Frontier of India as Assistant Political Agent.

"Count yourself lucky, Rose, you've not been dismissed," he concluded.

There were worse places than Waziristan in my book. I took one last defiant swim in my desert resort, emptied the dust from my boots, and exited Zahidan a happy man.

Three weeks later, a fuming Consul General, Colonel Daly, relieved Evvie Gastrell of his post, sending the Gastrells home on leave. Evvie never held a grudge against me. I think he rather admired my guts, my adventurous spirit. For years he related the story to my children. "Your father was entertained by a dangerous, wanted man…around a fire, shared his supper…." He embroidered, stitching in ever more fanciful details—ballgames played with goats' heads, contests between barefooted men jousting from the rumps of galloping ponies, and of gold and silver coins won and lost.

I was ordered to call on the Foreign Secretary, Sir Aubrey Metcalfe, on my way through Delhi on route to Waziristan. While he worked himself into a rage, I worked on preventing a smile from spreading across my face as I thought back to my idyllic evening with the Patriarch of the Nomads, how the corners of his eyes had crinkled as we laughed together in the flickering firelight. Apoplectic, words exploded from Sir Aubrey's throat, bloating his cheeks, "absolute disgrace…

diplomatic incident...embarrassment...unconscionable behavior."

Downstairs at the Maiden's Hotel, sipping a consolatory gin, seeing a stream of partygoers, I joined them crashing the Queen Alexandra's Rose Day Ball and made for a pretty girl watching the dancers from the sweeping staircase. I spotted Metcalfe watching. He glanced quickly away without acknowledging me.

"May I have the pleasure...?" I took Elizabeth by the hand.

I slipped the other around her waist. Her gloved fingers pressed lightly on my shoulder. Elizabeth wrote my name beside every waltz, polka, two-step and foxtrot on her dance card. If I was persona non grata before, I was doubly so by the evening's end. Ignoring Sir Aubrey's dirty looks, we vanished into "Kali Jagah," literally a "black place," where couples could flirt unseen. By evening's end, we were engaged. Next day I left for Tank in South Waziristan and Elizabeth faded to a pleasant memory.

Hugh. Desert Oasis. Zahidan.

49
SOUTH WAZIRISTAN
Banishment

"Rotten luck, old chap," and "Watch yourself. Mahsuds and Wazirs greet with a smile, next moment shoot you in the back.

Colleagues commiserated, believing I'd been banished to a place of penance, a savage country of rugged mountains and waterless valleys, inhabited by fierce tribesmen as unpredictable as rabid dogs. South Waziristan's description boded adventure.

Both previous Assistant Political Agents were murdered in the villages between Razmak and Wana, the same territory I covered, while "paying out" the Khassadars–frontier police. I swear Colonel Daly hoped I'd meet the same fate. He nearly got his wish I was shot at so many times. During intelligence-gathering and monthly pay-out trips, I quickly discovered which villages were hostile.

On one such trip, transporting bags of silver coins on a regular pay-out run towards a distant Khassadar's village, I'd gone about ten miles when a hail of fire trapped me and my two armed escorts in a narrow canyon. Clearly tipped off, a band of about a dozen tribesmen leapt from the Shahur Tangi hills, antiquated muskets blazing. The Ford V-8's sluggish acceleration prevented escape. Leaving the engine running, we leapt out, streaking for cover. From behind a rock pile, we fended off our attackers, me with my pistol, my escorts with their rifles. Outnumbered, outmaneuvered, it was merely a matter of time till we were overpowered. Bravely, we kept up our fire. Then—a miracle—salvation. Marching towards us appeared a squadron of the South Waziristan Scouts returning from an Exercise. A quick skirmish killed one robber, and the others fled, scrambling up the canyon walls with their wounded.

"Close shave, there, Rose. Only two months ago we lost two convoys in this very spot. Completely annihilated. Their boots and weapons looted, their bodies mutilated," The Scout's C.O. comforted.

Lesson learned. To avoid the same fate, I chose random, wildly differing dates and times of day to pay the Khassadars. Keeping to a regular schedule on the North West Frontier was as stupid as walking unarmed into a terrorist's camp.

As Assistant Political Agent my job was to bribe and keep the tribes loyal to Britain. I paid the Khassadars, the Khassadars paid the tribal *maliks*—village warlords—who in turn paid their tribesmen to muzzle their guns and allow our Army convoys safe passage through their section. Too tempting a target, convoys rarely escaped sniper fire as they rumbled along British Government roads, though every pot shot cost a fine of guns or money. Without fail, infuriated tribesmen claimed innocence and denied responsibility. Only threat of military action persuaded them to pay. As the P.A.'s watchdog, it was my turn to see his orders carried out, my turn to give the punitive order should they disobey. Unpleasant memories from four years earlier replayed, memories of harsh Punitive Columns I'd taken part in, with orders to burn a rebellious village to the ground.

Newly arrived and not yet fit, I got caught up in a fierce battle while accompanying the Razmak on Punitive Column to a remote village in the wilds beyond Rogan Regza. Sniper bullets hailed down, pinning us down. Finally we drove the snipers off into the snow, allowing us to scamper for the Sharwangi Narai Post in the bitter cold of night.

It was past nine o'clock by the time camp was set safely secured within its protective, barbed-wire apron, and supper served. The combination of heat from the Canadian stove, stress of the long battle, and one too many "Rogan Regza Macs," a lethal cocktail concocted from equal measures of rum, gin, and whisky, made jelly of my legs. Roused by the dinner bugle-call, I wove unsteadily through the snow to the Brigade Mess. The soup course nearly over, I apologized to the Brigadier for being late, then hastily ladled a generous helping into the bowl set before me. A titter rippled. The Brigadier's bushy eyebrows rose in astonishment.

"Hugh," he admonished, "are you aware, that's the fish sauce you are devouring?"

My very post as Assistant P.A. branded me an outsider, despite the fact we slept and ate together behind double barbed-wire aprons and suffered equally the hail of rebel fire. Embedded, I spread my time between two Brigade Headquarters—Wana, on the Afghan Frontier, and the high-altitude camp at Razmak. With them, I endured their strenuous marches on Column, some twenty, some fifty miles, and accompanied their every grueling maneuver and exercise. Attempts at comradeship and good working relationship failed. Influenced, perhaps, by Daly's report from Meshed of my misdeeds in Zahidan, the Colonel of the Scouts, the Brigadier, and others in command, disliked me on sight, and resented my power over them—that I, as P.A., held the trump card. I could see suspicion blazing in their eyes.

"A man seconding from a Gurkha Regiment for the soft Foreign Service—must be damned odd."

Like one another or no, we were stuck. Four years out of the Army, I was fit, but not as fighting fit as the wiry South Waziristan Scouts and the Brigades of British, Indian and Gurkha Battalions posted there. Regardless of the terrain, the Columns swept the Afghan Frontier in lines stretching twenty miles or more without losing breath. *"Gashting,"* they called it.

"I hope you're a 'Tough Sucker,' Rose. I fully expect to see you on *Gasht* with us." Colonel Crosby, Commander of the 1st Royal Battalion of The 5th Gurkha Riffles and the South Waziristan Scouts introduced himself. On sight he disliked me as I did him.

"Tough Sucker. Tough Sucker."

I bridled every time he used the epithet—and he used it often. Whatever a "Tough Sucker" was, I clearly never made the grade.

"Forget your boots, Rose. *Chuplies.*'Men wear *chuplies*–Pathan sandals, out here in Frontier country. Better suited to these hills." He eyed my leather army boots and thick socks.

I studied his thonged *chuplies* and broken toenails. I firmly kept my boots on much to his disdain.

I added his name to a growing list of enemies I'd made since arriving in Waziristan. But for my immediate boss Barney, the Political Agent, and his wife, Waziristan was hell. Clinging to their friendship like a drowning man, I jumped at every invitation to spend weekends at their bungalow in Tank. Playing gin rummy or quietly reading, we talked our dreams, drank and laughed.

One night Barney roused me from my sleep in a towering rage.

"Hugh. Get dressed at once. It's the Mahsuds. The mad dogs. I'll turn out the Razmak Column and burn down their blasted village—fine the bastards five hundred rifles."

It took me a little time to whittle out what dreadful deed, and which "mad dogs" had so enraged him.

"A group of Mahsuds killed two of our men at the Rogan Ragza post near Razmak. Jump in, Hugh. No time to call an Escort. You and I, we'll show those murdering bastards."

Headlights blazing, lighting up the flat plain and mountains ahead, visible for miles, sitting ducks, the two of us roared towards the tribal border. Grinding gears, twisting, turning, we inched up the tortuous Shahur Tangi road. I jumped at every shadow, imagining a trigger-happy tribesman crouched, ready to knock us off before we reached the safety of Sarwekai's small post. There we roused a group South Waziristan Scouts to escort us for the remaining miles.

The closer we got to Rogan Regza, the less the curses rained, the fewer the oaths of revengeful pillage. Barney calmed and so relented, that by the time we arrived he decided to let the Mahsuds off with a fine of five hundred rifles and a warning to the tribal warlords.

"If any of you tribesman, Mahsud, Wazir, or Afridi, dare shoot up the post again or kill any of my men, I, personally will burn your villages to the ground."

Too softhearted, too lenient, I was right to fear for him. When Barney left Waziristan for Baluchistan at the end of the year, a tribesman shot him dead rather than pay a fine.

Colonel Daly, the Consulate General back in Meshed; Aubrey Metcalf, the Foreign Secretary in Delhi; the Colonel and Brigadier of the Scouts Colonel Crosby, the "tough sucker," and now the Resident of North and South Waziristan–My enemies hovered, waiting to pounce.

I gathered another enemy. Colonel "Butch" Parsons, an austere bachelor with work his only focus. Bulldog, we called him. We spoke once only, but long enough to have him "pfwhapfwahing" with rage. It was after dinner one night in the Brigade Mess.

"What do you think of my latest idea? . . . Scrap manned pickets and blockhouses along the North West Frontier. Rustle up a couple of aircraft. Bomb every village to smithereens. That should keep our Columns and convoys safe."

"Bad idea, Sir. Essential to have our men on the ground." I argued my point.

True to his bulldog nickname he snarled, nostrils flared. Thereafter, he lay in wait, gathering evidence of any infraction. He wanted rid of me.

The evidence was not long in coming: I had the effrontery to lure men away from "legitimate" work to play weekend polo in a club I formed. I had the effrontery to disagree with him. A few months later, he moved in for the kill.

I knew I was breaking international law and it was strictly forbidden to venture anywhere near the Frontier border and of course I should have followed my orderly's advice and curbed my impulse. But what glory, what fame if I succeeded, if I was who captured the fanatical national hero long hunted by the British for his bloody raids. Like me, the Fakir of Ipi crossed and re-crossed borders at will. Like the sun and shadow, he recognized no lines across his land.

"Big danger. Not safe to go, *Sahib*," the orderly pleaded.

But I was determined. Foolish. I dragged my unwilling Orderly and a couple of heavily bribed Khassadars as Escort. Evading sniper fire, we reached the policed Frontier. Offering extra silver bribes for information, I asked the Fakir's exact whereabouts using the Khassadars as my spokesmen, without any way of checking what they actually said.

"Who? The Fakir of where? Ipi? Mmm, no." The trans-border tribesmen shook their heads in mock innocence. "We'll tell you, *Sahib*, should we hear of such a person," they assured me, pocketing my bribe. How stupid I was—assuming they'd denounce their hero to me, their enemy, and jeopardize their lives for a silver coin.

"We don't care a damn if you'd been killed," Command ranted. "The political repercussions you could have caused—and you could have shattered Britain's good relations with the Afghan Government."

"But...but…," I blustered in explanation. "It was a calculated risk, Sir. My intention was to capture The Fakir of Ipi. Rumor was he'd crossed into British-governed tribal territory from Afghanistan. Too temptingly close to pass up such a chance. I take full responsibility."

Next day, the Foreign and Political Department of the Government of India politely and firmly "invited" me to rejoin my old Regiment.

Not sure whether to laugh or feel ashamed at being so ignominiously dismissed, I chose laughter. Not out loud of course. What did I care? Nothing held me to this desolate place, no mountains to climb, no snow, no polo, not even a friend after Barney left. I'd become as much an enemy to be rid of as the rebellious tribesmen. But I'd beaten my predecessor, beaten the odds. I was still alive.

I packed my tin trunk, clambered into the old V-8 and headed for the hills.

Squeezed into my by-then-too-tight uniform, metaphorically as rumpled as my career, I presented myself to the new C.O. of my old regiment, the Third Gurkhas in H.Q. Bareilly.

"Good to have you back, Rose," he lied. "Hear you had a spot of bother."

50
FLOTSAM

My drill rusty, I'd forgotten how to play soldier. The C.O. didn't quite know what to do with me. Though my fellow officers were friendly and welcoming, our interests were as from different planets. I no longer belonged.

To my relief and theirs, the Colonel shunted me out of sight to an isolated desk as Compensation Officer, Bareilly. Thanks to my probation year with Mickey and our month on horseback Riding on Circuit, the countryside was familiar. I knew the unspoken social rule of delaying mention the purpose of any visit, and chatted endless hours, sitting cross-legged, sipping buffalo-milk *chai* with the *thulsidars* of villages I visited. Many villagers remembered me and asked fondly after Mickey-*Sahib*. Using his model of settling villagers' complaints before they happened, I inspected rice and alfalfa fields and tapioca and other crops trampled useless by our troops on maneuvers. I paid for fences destroyed, and cows and buffalos injured, and goats terrified into miscarriage. Touring the countryside with a Garhwali Major at my side, I eased myself back into uniform. India became "my India" once more—but the regular Army…? I'd never last. Aden, Meshed, Zahidan, and Tank in South Waziristan, their hardships smudged.

Their isolation, barren deserts and dangers glowed attractive against the suffocating familiar routine—down to the Plains for cold weather, up to Lansdowne for hot, and drills and training.

How to become my own man? I was lost. I heard Harry Garland's voice.

"Power. Promotion, Hugh. Be the one in charge." Yes, conformity kills, I muttered...Reilly. I buried myself in a Promotional Correspondence Course.

1937. I sat and passed the Staff College Exam. "Major Hugh Vincent Rose."

"I believe a reward is in order," I congratulated myself, revving my Ford V-8 into life. "A fortnight's skiing in Gulmarg, Kashmir would be appropriate."

I called for my bearer. "Pack my bags and skis."

As I chugged Dal's sparkling lakeshore to Srinagar at the head of the Kashmir valley, my spirits rose with each liberating mile. I rented a houseboat for the night. From a rattan lounger on the aft deck, *burra* peg of whisky in hand, while the houseboat staff rustled up a Kashmiri curry, I watched the lake craft busying by, each punted by a man so skillful with his pole, he skimmed the crimson-gold surface scarcely creating any eddies.

Next morning, as I stepped ashore, a hive of *syces* swarmed me.

"Mine. *Sahib*. Mine big strong," each clamored, wanting me to choose their horse.

Using both Urdu and Hindi, I fixed a price and mounted the least bony of the hire ponies. Gripping the pommel to keep from sliding to the valley, my poor nag, "Chine," labored my six-foot body up the near vertical mountain through pine and birch forest. We stopped every hour to catch our breath, dismounting in open grass clearings. Time gentled to dappled leaf-light.

Gulmarg, a small hamlet of log cabins built below the snow line, welcomed with burning pine wisping from its chimneys. Ahmed, the smiling host of the Nedous Hotel, in truth a modest guesthouse, kept a constant ire blazing in my room, filled my tin tub with scalding bathwater and had prepared and ready when I returned exhausted after a day's skiing. Sipping a peg of whisky, my aching muscles soaking in a tub before a roaring fire, warm water rising over and off my belly with each breath, I rehydrated to who I was.

For ten days, a "ski-coolie" carried my ash-wood skis and Kandahar bindings, and his pony, my ski-lift, plodded me up the 2,000 feet run to Killanmarg. Twisting in my saddle, first one direction, then another, sideways, looking up, down and across the Kashmir Valley to Nanga Parbat's 20,000-ft. Sunset Peak, I let nature's pristine beauty wrap me in her silence. Absorb me. I was her vastness, her snow-laden branches, the blueness of her sky. The only sounds my breathing and the crunch-squeak of the pony's hooves biting the frozen snow in an ethereal world.

Two weeks later, stitched back in uniform on the plains of Bareilly, living only for my nine-month furlough in October two months away, I jumped onto a train to Bombay and boarded the Rajputana for home.

A long-time regimental friend, Freddy, hailed me in the first-class lounge. Both sex-starved, we homed in on two good-looking women and danced our way across the sea. Mary was my honey, and I hers–till we docked, gave one last clinch, and bade farewell. Freddy's girl was married to another. Both vowed, however, nothing would keep them apart. Although she divorced her husband a year later, the Regiment forbade their marriage. Freddy killed himself. I was a pallbearer at his funeral, and wept for my friend.

Stepping onto England's "*green and pleasant land*," I wondered why I'd ever left—briefly, until rain held me trapped in Kathleen and Mother's London flat for six days in a row. I could only ask, "How have you been?" so many times. I could only answer their "Did you? Were you? What?' questions so many times before the pleasure of being together after so long apart wore thin. Uncomfortable in the grey, pokey lodgings, a reminder of my childhood, I promised to remove them from those grim surroundings for good.

"Come, we're going house hunting." Kathy and I scoured the country round Sandhurst College, southwest of London. It was autumn. The beech and sweet chestnut woods had already turned to russet-red and yellow. Their branches arched across the lanes, blotting out the sky and evoking memories of smoking leaf-piles, the bitter taste of beechnuts, and the smell of damp, long forgotten.

Kathy and me—closeted together in a car, brother and sister reacquainted. Over a Ploughman's Lunch of Cheddar and Stilton cheese served with globs of farmhouse butter, slabs of crusty bread, a large pickled onion, and a pint of brown ale, we talked of duty, and the sacrifices Kathy made for Mother.

"I'm dating," Kathy told me shyly. "A Polish soldier." But his wife lived in Poland so they could never marry. Not until her Karol became a widower. They waited forty-two more years.

"His wife is strictly Roman Catholic, you see," Kathy told me sadly. "Divorce isn't possible."

Fifty guineas deposit and five hundred more bought a three-bedroomed house and pretty garden in Camberley for five hundred more. I helped them move and saw them settled before I flew the coop. I could only stand so much mothering-brothering. I had dreams to dream, and women to chase. But top of the list, I would learn to fly.

Ever since riding tandem behind my pilot friend on our weekly mail drops between Aden and Socotra, I relived those flights, gliding, swooping up, down, rolling and plunging. Easy. Flying was no more than pulling a joystick. Kitted in leather helmet and jacket, I presented myself at the local flying club only nine miles from Mother's new house.

"I want to fly," I said.

Within as many weeks, I had clocked the requisite six hours solo, won my pilot's license and splashed my accumulated pay on a single-engine plane. England from the air...perhaps a trapeze artist feels the same thrill. The same wild sense of what it must be to be a bird–to fold your wings and skim above the trees. It was a toy I couldn't afford to keep. I sold it eight months later at the end of my leave, before returning to India.

For three months I was in love with Cecile. She and I spent weekends at a County Manor House where the host's only rule was that guests must be back in their own beds by the time maids knocked on their doors with trays of early-morning tea. When I caught her with her face pressed between the Master of the Hunt's thighs, it was, "Tally-Ho. Cecile."

I packed my bags, left her to the horsey crowd, and made for the snows of Murren in the Swiss Alps and the arms of another beautiful woman. For five months we skied the runs by day and my bed by night. Warm in our feather bed one night, Angeline told me two of her friends had admired my skiing.

"If you would like to be put up for membership in the Kandahar Club," she breathed into my ear, "they will 'first' and 'second' you, darling. I'll introduce you to Sir Arnold Lunn tomorrow."

Was I interested? My hand paused on the soft skin of her belly. An entrée to the world-famed Club headquartered up the road in the Palace Hotel? Arnold Lynn, the great skier, and founder of the select club, inviting me? Skiing and dining with the best of the best of its erudite members. It was an honor I had never dreamed of.

There were stiff tests to pass, social and on skis; a steep downhill schuss and slalom, free heel telemark, stem christies, full christies and a three-mile cross-country tour in differing snow conditions. Over the next few days Sir Arnold stayed glued to my side while I performed. He oversaw every test. In the evening, his hawk's eyes watched my interactions with his friends. At last, one test was left for me to pass.

"Ready, Hugh?" From behind, "Arnie" gave me a mighty push towards and over a two-hundred-foot drop.

"No crouching. Upright. Keep upright. Skis touching. Parallel. You must stand the entire run. Remember...Skis together...." His words faded, abruptly silenced by the swish, swish of wood slicing through the crisp snow.

Ramrod straight, skis tight, sticks held pointing back, I disappeared in a spume of powder.

I passed my Silver K. I became one of the elite—a member of the prized Kandahar. For the next month, I breathed snow before returning to my plane in England.

Hugh Skiing. Mürren.

Hugh Rose and Barbara Allcard. Claygate Church. 1937.

Hugh and Barbara with Elizabeth. Lansdowne. April 1938.

51
I FIND A WIFE IN THE BASEMENT

Peter Norton, the same cousin who had opened her Chelsea home to me and every bachelor short of a bed when I was a cadet at Sandhurst, owned a contemporary gallery on Cork Street. I dropped by often, but not to see the strange work on the walls.

Peter was in love and seized every opportunity to flee to the arms of her betrothed. Three-hour lunches for her were the norm.

"Be a dear, Hugh. Sit the gallery for me. Nothing to it, anyone coming in, just show them around," and she'd be gone, leaving me in charge with an airy wave.

Picasso, Henry Moore, Bayer, Man Ray, Miro, Mondrian, I tried to get my head around the awkward angles of square fruit, and people with no semblance to a human. I prayed for no visitors, and no questions about the work. One room of her gallery displayed a collection of mechanical toys and musical boxes. Clonk, my heart sank—footsteps on the stairs. The door swung open. Before me, stood Queen Mary with her lady-in-waiting. Jumping to my feet, I attempted a Royal bow. Maybe she found me improperly dressed, maybe my bow not deep enough, for Queen Mary wagged her finger mockingly.

"You naughty, naughty man," she said, then asked me to activate a particular musical box for her, one that required a ha'penny.

Royalty never carry money. I fumbled through my pocket change for a coin, dropped it in the slot, and set the tiny figures dancing to a rendition of *"Home, Sweet Home."* Queen Mary tapped her parasol in perfect time and accompanied the tune in a clear soprano voice before sweeping away. Green. On her return from lunch, Peter turned green when she learned she had missed the royal visitor.

Peter introduced me to Barbara, a young woman working in the building's bowels archiving Peter's collection. It was her crooked upper tooth when she smiled that I noticed first. It wasn't her beauty that attracted me, for in truth her face was too strong and boyish, and her body a little too short and wiry, but from the moment of our meeting that sudden flash told us we were in love. In her eyes I was a handsome man in uniform, well traveled, an adventurer who could lead her to pastures overseas she'd only ever dreamed.

Lying with her in her mother's bed one night, in a state of post-coital bliss—her mother was away—we discovered, apart from sex, we shared a love of snow sports and outdoor adventure. Barbara told me she'd been the "frontman" of a luge team in Switzerland and once been thrown from the luge against and over the ice walls and knocked unconscious.

"And," she continued, "I was the youngest ever archery champion of Surrey County. Here, look."

In a photograph stood a schoolgirl in a pinafore dress, with a thick pigtail hanging below her waist, the string of a massive bow pulled confidently against her cheek as she aimed an arrow.

"Mummy wanted me to be a boy," she confided, "not another dratted girl." Her mother had pushed her newborn girl away. Barbara acted boyish all her childhood to compensate for the accident of her birth. The exception was music. There, she was wholly feminine. She was so gifted a violinist that her father, an accomplished musician himself, gave her one of his two Stradivari and sent her to study under a sixty-five-year-old master violinist in Switzerland when she was barely sixteen.

"You are a gifted, brilliant musician–technically," the master said, adding cruelly, "but you have no passion. Here, I'll teach you passion." The dirty old man fondled her breasts and, surprising her between her legs with a sudden force, took her virginity. She abandoned her Stradivarius forever and turned to skiing. I never heard her play.

I confessed my nightly visits to Louise, of losing mine to a housemaid. Too many affairs to recount, we ran our fingers over each other's bodies and buried our past in folds and hollows.

Horror. My seed latched to her uterus wall and fertilized an egg. We had known each other for three short months. Post-haste, before her pregnancy "showed," the Banns were read, and we were married in Claygate Parish Church. Beaming, proudly handsome in my military uniform, I led my bride down the aisle. Stunning in her satin, body-hugging dress and virginal veil, our wedding picture shows her smile and crooked tooth. It was naturally assumed our hasty wedding was so she could travel with me to India at the end of my leave. Nobody suspected. Appearances mattered. I feared my Regiment's reaction to a birth too early, one that advertised pre-marital relations. We toyed with a "termination." The Indian gynecologist in Bombay dissuaded us and persuaded us to keep our baby.

Two days before Barbara gave birth, she stayed home while I attended an official dinner. Contented, she sat toasting her toes by the fire knitting a baby shawl, when footsteps, accompanied by the familiar jingle of spurs, tramped along the verandah.

"You're home early, Hugh," she said as the door opened, holding up the hurricane lamp to greet me.

It wasn't me. Nobody entered, nobody there but dancing shadows.

Elizabeth Penelope was born on April 12, 1938 on the dining room table by the light of a *hurricane butti* in the Simpkins Bungalow in the Himalayan foothills of Lansdowne's Hill Station.

Fifty years later, my daughter went on a recce to discover her birthplace. Elizabeth and the Gharwal Officer's wife billeted in the Simkin's Bungalow were sipping Darjeeling tea and nibbling silver-leafed pastries, when the windows began rattling. The front door banged shut and open two–three–four times. It was a windless afternoon.

"To greet me," Elizabeth confided. "The ghost welcomed me back."

The first years had happy moments as well as difficult ones. Too close for comfort, hugger-mugger living had limitations neither of us expected. A new baby didn't make marriage any easier despite the white-haired English nanny who loved our baby for us, and reduced my father-role to snapshots—me, awkward, the tiny creature wriggling in my arms. We were rarely alone. Nanny, servants, the Army constantly peered over our shoulders. Barbara liked order and keeping precise time. I threw my clothes on the floor and wore no watch. Our differences separated us. The honey that had first attracted us, lost sweetness.

We never left Elizabeth to play alone in the garden, not from fear of injury, but to prevent panther and leopards dragging her into the jungle to be eaten like many children, women, and young men were each year. One night an unusual noise disturbed my sleep. Investigating, I saw the silhouette of a black panther framed in her bedroom window, eyes shining beacons in the moonlight, poised to snatch Elizabeth's tender human flesh. Grabbing my shotgun, I fired off a round, saving her. With a growl he was gone. As a child, Elizabeth loved that story.

"Tell me Daddy," she'd plead, "tell how you saved me from the panther."

One of our happiest times was a trek to the Valley of the Gods in the Kulu Valley. Leaving Elizabeth and her *ayah* swinging gently in a Duli, a litter swung between two poles, we raced ahead—free. Barbara and I alone in the Himalayas, alone in pastures where huddles of silver birch stood shimmering with the delight of being alive. Underfoot, gentian, crocus and primula splashed color along the edges of the snow drifts. Hand in hand we walked in beauty—

fingers gently part the green
expose rubies dangling clustered
beside a Kashmiri snow-fed brook
surprise my tongue with the sweetness of wild strawberries
in those same woods of rhododendron and pine
nestled at their mossy feet, poke tiny trefoils—
I nibble wood sorrel between my front teeth tasting lemon
above the treeline but below the snow
a solitary birch shreds pale parchment—
one hundred pages for raven to scribe his story
deeper between the forest firs
scarlet-red and white spotted toadstools
lure me to take a bite promising eternal rest
but I am not tempted
stepping into knee-high carpets of gentians and columbine
I come across a snowdrift pitted with sparkling imprints
where a yeti passed last winter on his quest towards the sun

One early morning as we approached the isolated game reserve of Spiti, we startled three white geese swimming in the sky-reflecting waters of a lake where rare blue poppies sprinkled its grey-rock shores—a vision fixed forever. Barbara picked and pressed a bloom between two pages of our guidebook. *Macanopsis Bayleyii*, she knew the Latin name. Flora was her subject.

On another day's trek making for our destination, a Dak rest house at the base of a glacier, the gold glitter of a distant mountain blinded us with make-believe riches manifested as from a genie's lamp—fool's gold of course, but we could dream.

Next day involved the hardest climb. Our goal, Manali, lay at the base of the 15,000-foot Rotang Pass to Ladakh. Staying just long enough to say we would made it to the Pass, we slipped and slithered downhill, fleeing from the biting cold to join *ayah* and baby Elizabeth in Sunshine Orchards, a lodge run by Major Banon and his Kulu wife. The Major had forsaken his Army career for love. His father too, he told me—a General, who had also married a local woman after he'd retired. It was he who'd built the lodge and planted an apricot and apple orchard. I tried picturing my stiff father as liberal. I pictured myself on the mountainside isolated with Barbara and a young family. Neither picture worked.

It was late September when the Battalion disappeared down the hill to Bareilly, leaving me in command of a skeleton staff. The Hill Station in Lansdowne reverted to a place of ghosts–Barbara and I the only European occupants of the Garhwal Station. A baby, a wife, the early onset of night, and copious *chota* pegs of whisky could not fill the empty hours, for by then we had both uncovered our mismatch. Our nearest neighbors lived a snowbound mile distant along the ridge.

I made a weekly uphill trek to my friend Philip Mason's isolated winter aerie in Puri five miles above Lansdowne, often staying overnight. "It was too dangerous, too dark to ski back, Barbara," I excused my absence. "

Huddled before the fire, I told him of my boredom and hinted at my troubles. Philip understood my frustration and sense of confinement on the arrow-straight path mapped for me, first by my father, then the Army and marriage. He and I had shared a bungalow one time in Bareilly, hiking and tracking jungle fowl when we weren't in serious discussions. From the moment we had met in Bareilly four years before, our un-conventional attitudes had bonded us instantly as lifelong friends. How he laughed when I told him about my naked colonel darning his socks in the nursing home's conservatory when I was recovering from malaria. and his declaration, "Conformity kills, compromise castrates."

"Write your stories, your poems down my friend, " he advised so I took up my pen.

"I never knew I was a writer until I wrote," Philip told me. "Think of writing as skiing across a pristine snowfield. The marks you make are yours."

I strapped on my skis to return home.

"Ski for your life, Hugh, before life's avalanche swamps you," he called after me.

I turned to wave. Parallel ski tracks marked the snow.

Philip did put marks on paper. Discovering a talent he never suspected, he made his name with *Founders and Guardians*, then wrote numerous books about the Indian Civil Service and British India. With him as my mentor, I wrote articles, poems and short stories that winter, many of which were published in various journals, including *The Calcutta Statesman* and *Blackwood's Magazine.*

52
WORLD WAR II DECLARED

Sunday, September 3rd, 1939

War. England is at war. Peace and our marriage, like the glittering mountain we had seen in Manali, crumbled to fool's gold. Personal ambitions crumpled, unimportant overnight—victory, fighting for king and country became my new goals. Pulled from the Himalayan hills, our Gurkha Battalions were deployed to Quetta's earthquake-prone plain. I saw a city flattened by the 1935 quake. Quetta's memorial to a quarter of a million people emphasized how suddenly life could be cut short. Barbara packed our first home into a dozen trunks and followed me to Quetta with Elizabeth.

The initial rush to take up arms and join the fray fizzled. War had not yet impacted Quetta. Mock attacks, drilling, monotonous routine, the location apart, life in India changed little. When I thought of Europe's rationing, its bombings and loss of life, our luxurious lifestyle turned suddenly obscene. Recognition changed nothing. Food was plentiful. Tailors stitched our clothes. Ration cards were issued. Inexplicably, the only things rationed were sheets..

Quetta's vibrant social band-aid patched our marriage with champagne and vintage claret at the Club. Hugh Michael was born on January 5, 1940 in the safety of the military hospital, an heir, a Rose to follow in my footsteps. Proud, I dreamed his dreams, watched him greedy at Barbara's breast unknowing of his future military fame, and of the General he would become and the Knighthood in his destiny.

Splashes of red ink across my Staff College exam papers, the lowly posting with Quetta Air Defense following the course, told me "Staff" was not a choice and I was returned to my Regiment. Excited, my orders were to accompany them to Iraq which the Germans planned to invade. Leaving Barbara with the babies, I rejoined my Battalion camped in far-away Ambala, in Haryana State, bordering the Punjab, readying for deployment to Iraq.

To my disgust, after two weeks Command reposted me to Quetta to plan Quetta's defense. "Invaluable, your knowledge of the Persian Frontier... Mirajawa... Zahidan," they told me.

"I knew the area all right," I cursed under my breath. "Too damn, bloody well." I sulked for a week. Domestic battle was not the kind of War I wanted to fight. It was the first of many blows to come.

There were plenty of excuses to escape the brick wall growing between Barbara and me, and abandon my desk in Quetta...reconnoiter the area...rebuild roads...check whether the railway can be restored.

"Have to leave again, Barbara," I'd say, trying to hide my glee. I recalled the abandoned railhead near the residency I'd "improved" and wondered how and if my "Desert Resort" had survived. The three-hundred-mile journey was still as hot and bumpy. "The Place of Heat," Kuh-i-Taftan, the mountain of fire, still belched poisonous, sulfurous fumes, but my pool was empty and the squash court cracked. The man who'd taken my place focused only on his work.

Putting my mapping and surveying skills to good use, I forgot my desire to fight. The travel, I loved. I rode the railway to the limits of its railhead at Nokundi, mapped the disused track beyond to Zahidan, went on *recce*, reconnaissance, to Kandahar, and plotted a route over the Chapman Pass suitable for a military advance. Baluchistan, Persia, Afghanistan. I drew up plans to defend their borders. High Command awarded me a Commendation.

Back from Zahidan, I had hardly settled back into so-called domestic bliss, when I was off on an undercover mission to Gwadar, the strategically important flying-boat refueling station for Karachi. London wanted the Government of India to investigate rumor of a subversive plot to blow up Imperial Airways. Getting to Gwadar involved a long drive through the bandit-ridden desert of Kalat State. I broke my journey in Kalat, staying with a friend from Foreign Service days, Louie Pinhey, the Political Agent and advisor to the Nawal. Next morning before taking to the road with my *sepoy* escorts, Louie warned, "Keep your eye out for sudden spates when crossing dry *nullahs*. Heavy rain storms in the mountains a hundred miles away have already made many impassable."

Hearing, but not heeding his words, I settled into the jeep's backseat to enjoy the journey. Sure enough, fifteen miles from Kalat City, we came to a *nullah* swirling with floodwater, a hundred feet wide. After checking the horizon and testing the water's depth, we nosed the jeep gingerly down the bank and into the water, making for the far side. We were almost there when a rumbling roar made us turn to see a ten-foot wall of water bearing toward us at great speed. There was nothing we could do to reach safety. The spate whammed us full on knocking us sideways, overturning the jeep, and tossed us like twigs into its raging waters. I remember the brown force, the mud, the singing in my ears, my struggle for breath. Then, flash, it passed. Gulping air, half-drowned, soaked and badly bruised, I clawed a handhold and somehow managed to crawl up the bank. The water level sank as quickly as it had risen, leaving the half-buried jeep's wheels spinning in the air, and our stores and water tank gone, swept away. Miraculously, all three of us survived. No transport, miles from anywhere, we were marooned. One *sepoy* volunteered to set off on foot to Kalat for help. It was after dark when he returned with both a lorry and a jeep. Our attempt to winch our jeep failed. Trapped and useless, it would lie there until the mud dried. Back in Kalat, safe in my friend's bungalow, Louie never once voiced the "I told you so" he was thinking.

Jeepless and wiser, I continued my spy mission to the refueling station by train and coastal steamer via Karachi. It turned out there was no plot, no dangerous plan in Gwadar. Whisperings and mutterings of disgruntled staff were the only problems I uncovered, those, and an acrimonious relationship with management, distant in their London Headquarters. After a couple of the staff had been transferred and better working conditions had been implemented, peace reigned. Imperial Airways was in no danger. My spy mission was at an end.

For once I was truly glad to be anchored at home with Barbara for a while. She smiled, pleased to see me back. Together after dinner in the moonlight, feet propped on the verandah's balustrade, the snow-capped summit of Merdah and distant peaks perched balanced on our very toes. Like that illusion, our companionship wasn't real.

Among the Staff College students we entertained, a frequent visitor was John Masters, THE John Masters who became a well-published author in the 1950s, with *Bhowani Junction, The Deceivers, Bugles and Tiger,* to name a few. I suspected nothing. Nothing, until it was too late to stem Barbara's and his affair, an affair leading to a pregnancy, an affair ending in a tangled divorce of "he-said-she-said," and a desperate tug-of-war over which child to keep, which child to use as checkmate in the ugly game we played. I never really understood why Barbara hated me, why her hatred never abated. I only know she did.

Partly for appearances, partly for convenience when work kept me in Quetta, we still lived under the same roof. Besides, I loved her, or thought I did. Though another man's child swelled her belly, I refused her the divorce she begged for. Even after their lovechild Susan was born, I hoped our marriage could be saved. Strange, fate, I now played the role my mother's first husband, William, played. Like him, I offered to bring up another man's child as my own. Like my mother Emma, Barbara determined to abandon marriage vows to live with her lover. Was it karmic justice that I pay for my mother's adulterous sin?

I grabbed at the chance to leave when my time in Quetta District Headquarters came to an end, and I was posted back to our Regimental Depot in Dehra Dun in the Himalayan foothills prior to going overseas with the Second Battalion as second-in-command, and finally taking part in the war. Perhaps distance would end Barbara's affair. Isolated, cloistered together in new surroundings, mountain air, our children, snow, my hopes were high.

Packed into my Bentley, Barbara and I left Quetta with the children and nurse on the long drive across the Sind desert to Murree, a 6,000-foot high Hill Station between Pindi and Islamabad in one direction, and Kashmir in the other. Barbara and the children would stay in Murree while I took up my new post in Dehra Dun.

The Indus had overflowed its banks and flooded the high plain to form a shallow lake spreading for hundreds of watery miles. A temporary road of loose wooden planks barely wide enough to take the car was the only way to cross. Elizabeth still remembers her childhood terror, inching along the flimsy structure suspended inches over the murky floodwater, and her fear of imaginary crocodiles lurking unseen to eat us should we make one slip.

But the only crocodile was Barbara's lover, who unbeknownst to me had an assignation to slip into my bed the minute I left for Dehra Dun. When I discovered he'd followed us to Murree and lurked close by to pounce, I knew then I had lost, I knew our marriage was over and the fire of her hatred towards me would never be extinguished.

Once Barbara thought me safely out of the way in Dehra Dun, she took the children to Gulmarg in nearby Kashmir for a week to meet her Jack, as she called John Masters. Warned, I spiked her gun. I tracked her and claimed my bed. Her rendezvous interrupted, she cursed me, mad with rage. That first night, disturbed by something, I awoke to find her standing over me, a spiked stiletto heel poised to strike me in the temples.

"I wanted you dead. I wanted to kill you," she'd screamed. "But you opened your eyes. I couldn't do it with you staring."

My sunglasses forgotten, my mind roiling, I broke my arm skiing, became snow-blind, and spent the week in a darkened room weeping. I was in hell.

It was a relief to be back in Dehra Dun and busy. Detailed, with eight officers, to join the Second Battalion in the Western Desert as part of the Eighth Army under General Sir Claude Auchlineck, I was impatient to be gone, to leave my domestic cesspool, and fight a real war.

I boarded the newly converted *Cap St. Jacques* in Deolali, and sailed for Suez—my appointment, "O.C., Troops." Though only a Major, I was the most senior officer available. Finally, I was off to war.

Mid-journey in Suez, as I was preparing my men to ship out, a telegram arrived and split me in two.

"DEMAND DIVORCE. MOVED. BOMBAY WITH CHILDREN."

Fight for my children? Fight for my country? I chose war. My children would have to wait. I assembled my draft of men and transported them to a reinforcement camp outside Cairo to await further orders.

Nanny Comport and Elizabeth.

53
WAR

Divorce And The Collapse Of My Career

London
November 1943

Darling Hughey,

I've left Penang and am back home in London with Anne. I've heard Bill is still alive, though no letters of course. I worry dreadfully. It's been three years now. Rumor is the Japs have our P.O.W.s building a railway somewhere in the jungle. I saw Mother and Kathy a week ago. They begged us to move in with them for as long as this blasted war lasts, but you know me, I'd go stark staring mad. The W.A.C.S. keep me busy, so I've placed Anne as a boarder in a small ballet school. Chin up. This must end soon and you'll be home to share a pint.

Fondest love,
your sister,
Aileen.

War turned suddenly personal. More news arrived. Three good friends, Charles Boucher, Harry Garland and Charles Grey languished behind wire in some Italian Internment Camp after being captured during a fierce battle at El Alamein. I half-wished to be with them. Instead, I was to join the Battalion at their base-camp north of Nicosia in Cyprus. The Battalion, suffering heavy casualties, was forced to retreat to Mena, Northeast Africa, and regrouped as the Tenth Army, were deployed from there to Cyprus via Haifa.

The situation in Cyprus was critical. Short of men, Lt. Col. T.N. Smith from High Command hatched a madcap plan to deceive the Germans into believing an entire Army Corps was encamped in Cyprus instead of one small division. Each of us officers sported fake badges one rank above our actual rank, with orders to strut purposefully back and forth as though intent on urgent business. If the situation hadn't been so dire, our play-acting would have been amusing. Simulating maps and charts, with rolls of paper under our arms, peering through binoculars, our canes pointing ostentatiously to the mainland, we hoped to fool spies watching. Mimicking Monty's inspired ploy, Colonel Smith disguised our jeeps as tanks using wood and cardboard for sides, and protruding drainage pipes simulating guns. Keeping our lorries and other vehicles constantly on the move, our bustling camp gave the impression we were preparing for an important and imminent mission. The ruse worked. The Germans never attacked.

Several months after my arrival, Colonel Smith left Cyprus to command a tactical advance party to Italy, and handed over his command of the 9th Battalion to me. Acting Lieutenant Colonel, bumped up a rank by the accident of War, was the chance I'd waited for—a Command. War my focus, planning and more planning. Family, England, my children, poetry and personal goals, even Barbara, faded.

January 1944, the call came at last for the Battalion to ship out to Lebanon to await orders to sail for Italy. My first important mission. Sleep was impossible. This would be the first action for most of us. The Officers Mess buzzed, excited with talk of victory, of routing "those kraut-eating Huns." Two days later, we boarded a mine-laying destroyer headed for Beirut.

Dropped overnight into a playboys' make-believe world of ice-cream vendors, golden sun and sea, children, sandcastles, pretty women sheltering beneath their parasols, I struggled to remember we were at war and war would soon take me to the Front. Was I awake? Sipping lemonade, a beer, I stared at the newspaper's unreal photographs of coiled barbed wire, broken bodies clawing at the earth, houses reduced to rubble and tear-streaked faces of the bereaved. What if they were Mother, my sisters, my bother or my niece, would I so casually turn the page to another article?

No orders arrived. Three weeks passed as if there was no war. I spent them lazing in the palm-fringed pool of the French Officers Club, dining and gambling at the Georges Cinq Hotel, playing polo at the club close to our tented seashore city. Illusion. My mind keyed for action, I couldn't relax. I took my position seriously. Commander of the Battalion, I summoned every planning skill to be the best I could be. My kitbag packed and ready, my rifle gleaming, the call came. In two days, we would sail for Italy.

"A telegram for you from Army Headquarters in New Delhi." The Colonel, solemn, wordlessly handed me the small paper rectangle with its ticker-taped message.

"Posting cancelled." I stiffened. Words faded in and out. I read and reread the grey print. I could not believe what I was reading.

An officer...beginning divorce proceedings against his wife...no fit state...to command a Battalion in times of war...Proceed to Aden. G.S.O. The telegraph's words held no meaning.

Action, command of my battalion, the Front, sideswiped into a backwater, cast onto the rubbish heap, my new order could have been to hell for all I cared.

Damn that man. Damn that thief, John Masters. Not only my wife, but my career too. Stolen. I cursed him with every foul expletive I could summon. Bitterly, I handed over the Command to Major Minchinton–the Command that was rightfully mine

Worse followed. Arriving in Aden, Brigade Headquarters informed, because of policy change, State Force Units were no longer to be used on active service. I was to take my Battalion to Kassassin, Egypt, in the desert between Ismailia and Cairo. Demoralized by the pointlessness of my role, I gave up. An automaton, a wind-up toy, I became a strutting, wooden soldier. I thought back and wondered how my naked colonel would escape the dead-end trap where I was caged? No answer came.

A tented camp should have been ready for us, but Brigade H.Q. had done nothing beyond providing a water tanker, forcing us to bivouac in the desert's stinging Shamal-blown sands for days until the tents arrived. A week later, everything but small arms were requisitioned. Stripped of our vehicles, weapons, equipment, the Battalion was defenceless. My command was in name only.

Previous orders rescinded, the Battalion was ordered to sail back. No ship. With nothing to do but wait, most weekends I fled to Cairo to drown my sorrows. Finally, a troop ship arrived and removed us from that hellhole. We sailed from Suez for Bombay under frigate escort.

Breathing fire and murderous vengeance, I sued the bloody thief, Masters, for damages in Lahore's High Court and was awarded custody of my Elizabeth and Michael. They could keep their Susan, though she carried my name.

My war escalated to farcical. The State of Udaipur welcomed our Battalion as conquering heroes for its bravery in having "crossed the Black Water," the seas, and for our valiant action. "Action?" I sneered sarcastically under my breath. "Bravery? What, for almost seeing action?" Almost. Almost—my whole career could be described by almost.

"Rule Britannia..." the Maharaja's and our own Gurkha Soldiers banged and bugled across the Palace grounds, bringing me back to the present. I turned to watch the *Durbar.* Elephants, fully caparisoned in scarlet and gold, lead His Highness The Maharaja and Maharani's private army, the Mewar State Forces, in the welcome parade. Lengthy speeches later, the Maharaja granted our Battalion two months' leave, and invited me to spend three weeks in his luxurious State guesthouse with two polo ponies at my disposal, an elephant to take me *ghooming,* and a personal *shikari* as guide. Polo, shooting, dinners and picnics, my life relaxed back on track. Downing too many *burra* pegs of whisky, I soothed my wounds.

I don't know what possessed Barbara. Perhaps she thought immediate severance kindest. She dumped five year old Elizabeth and Michael, barely three, with a Warrant Officer and his wife at Jhansi. Elizabeth has since shared her memories of that unhappy time, and her terror at often waking alone. One night, Michael woke wanting potty. No one was around. The house hovered dark. Empty. Fearful of being punished if she allowed Michael to break the house rule and "go" without permission, she pulled a sweater over her baby brother's pyjamas, wound a woolen scarf about his neck, dropped him to the ground from the bathroom window, before jumping out herself.

"Landing hurt my ankles," she said shaking her head. "Then we walked in the dark to a neighboring house and banged to be let in. I see it still—the startling blaze of light, happy children eating supper, the neighbors' startled looks finding us huddled on their doorstep in our nightclothes, and their warm hugs as they ushered us inside. Our "carers," tracked down finally at a party in the Officers Mess, unashamed, arrived to collect us, their faces black as thunder."

Hastily taking a weekend's compassionate leave, I found the children pale and pinched, the happy innocence of childhood sucked from them. A bachelor in Bachelor's Quarters, I had no home. Good friends in Dehra Dun, Margaret and Tom Hurst of the Seventh Gurkhas, came to my rescue and took the children to live with them for the weeks it took to arrange for a Court official to collect and deliver them by train to me hundreds of miles away in Quetta. A date was set. The Hursts gathered my children and took them to the station for their handover.

Uninvited, Barbara and a friend appeared on the platform for one last hug farewell. Elizabeth remembers—burning sun...bare legs...the stifling, dusty station…narrow stripe of shade…confusion…struggling for her mother's arms… desperate to stay…not wanting to leave.

"Why aren't you coming with us, Mummy? Why are you crying, Mummy? Promise Mummy, promise. You'll come in two weeks won't you? Promise?"

"Say goodbye to your mother. That's the last you'll be seeing of her." The Court-appointed escort gripped the children firmly by their wrists and forcibly lifted them, fighting, into the compartment, screaming for their weeping mother.

Skinny-legged and solemn, my two children had no smiles for me when they arrived. "When is Mummy coming?" my daughter asked again and again. My son stared, unspeaking, sucking his thumb. I signed for their delivery as I would for two packages. Stored them till I was free to take possession.

I had no choice. I had to leave them, parcel them onto a stranger until a ship's passage came available to take my children home to England, a country neither knew. Strange, I was following tradition, the pattern of the Raj, sending my children "home," and make them Raj Orphans.

"It's only for a little while," I tried to comfort them as I dropped them off at Mrs. K.'s small bungalow.

Just one living thing, one dusty tree stood in the dreary dirt compound abutting the Army base's perimeter fence. Separated from her husband, Mrs. K., desperate to return to England, agreed to take in Elizabeth and Michael in exchange for her passage home. Another stranger, another sordid home, but what to do, they couldn't live with me in the Mess. Poor children, expressionless, huddled, clasped together hand-in-hand, dry-eyed, blankly staring. They had long given up crying.

"It's not for long. We'll be together every two weekends," I consoled. "Soon, we'll sail away to live in England." But it was months. Ships were few and far between. Families were bottom of the list.

Chapman, a cantonment on the Afghan border about forty miles beyond Quetta, was close enough to visit my children. Shameful to admit, it was a relief to escape back to friends and fun. I did spend some weekends with them, but only whenever there was nothing better on. To appease my guilt, I arrived with small presents—a few coins, a purse, a brush set, and once an Arthur Rackman-illustrated copy of *The Water Babies*. Elizabeth and Michael safe in the front seat of my Alfa Romeo, I headed directly to a lonely grass widow's bungalow. One weekend, the dry river swelled full spate and swept the bridge downstream. Smiling, I wheeled the car about for another night of love.

"Goody. Goody. We can't go back to Mrs. K," the children sang.

While my grass widow and I sipped cocktails, the moon rose full, spreading her silver mirror across the foot-deep floodwater covering her garden. The vision of her child's and my children's glistening bodies dipping, leaping as minnows is imprinted forever on my mind. Elizabeth remembers that evening—one happy highlight of those long months.

Some weekends I booked into a modest hotel. Cuddled beneath the whirring fan, a child in each arm, I told tales of princesses locked inside mountain-tops weeping frozen tears, of wicked ogres tramping across snows, of a fairy paradise where wild strawberries and sugar-cakes grew. *"Through the Night of Doubt and Sorrow," "De Camp Town Races,"* and *"Oh, My Darling, Clementine,"* I sang till their eyelids drooped. Those melodies, my baritone voice, hold poignant meaning for Elizabeth.

I made excuses—true, barracks were no place for children; true, I lacked parenting skills, but what of their needs? I could have rented a place, hired a nurse, and even taken them with me while I treated myself to ski-weekends in Gulmarg, a month's leave with the Ski Club of India, short breaks with my friends, Philip and Mary Mason, in their Official Defense Secretary's residence in New Delhi, with time to swim in their palm-fringed pool, and time to flirt with an attractive woman guest sunbathing on their lawn.

"Mind if I join you?" I asked, ordering the Bearer to bring us both a Tom Collins.

Philip appeared in a grey topper and morning coat on his way to a meeting with Wavell interrupting our *tête-à-tête.*

"Oh, I see you have already met. Hugh Rose, Edwina Mountbatten." He formally introduced us.

Battalion Headquarters in Chapman, my camp perched strategically, straddling the mountain summit controlling the Afghan border. A cave-dwelling mullah also lived there. Crazed, he wandered the ridge day and night, his arms skyward, imploring Allah with shrieks more bloodcurdling than any jackal's howls. The first time I heard his agonized cries I leapt up brandishing my pistol thinking we were under attack.

Apart from patrolling the border and interrogating unfamiliar travelers, we had little to do but wait for war to grind to its end. In the last days of April—news: Hitler and Mussolini both dead. Peace in Europe was in sight.

"May 9th 1945. V.E declared. Treaty signed."

Messages poured in by ticker-tape, signal, and by "Helio." Strange coincidence, May 9th, 1857 was the day before the Indian Mutiny broke out.

"Have you heard? Victory. V.E. has been declared." We shouted at everyone we met. War in Europe was over—not so in Asia, not for another three months.

August 15th 1945. Peace. World War II was over. Beacons to glory, strings of bonfires blazed from hill and mountain, visible from Quetta's plains. The

North West Frontier, the entire Indian continent rang with victory cheers.

"Hip-Hip Hurrah. Hurrah. Hurrah." I cheered. In my hand I waved a telegraph, a personal reprieve.

"August 15th, 1945. Compassionate leave. Three months." Time enough to take my children back to "Blighty." We could go home.

I collected my children and Mrs. K. from Quetta and jumped aboard the next train to a holding camp in Karachi. After days of endless medical checks, vaccinations and bureaucratic paperwork, I tucked our exit documents under my arm and scrambled up the gangplank. Neither child had seen a ship. No description or picture had prepared them for trembling engines beneath their feet. They clutched me, calling, "Earthquake. We got to get off."

Michael and I shared one cabin in the men's quarters, while Mrs. K. whisked Elizabeth below decks to the ladies' cabins. I rarely saw her during the five-week voyage. She spent her time below decks throwing up every day of the voyage but five. Elizabeth never told me during the crossing Mrs. K. slapped her "to cure your sea-sickness." And when she sank dizzy down to her knees, Mrs. K. yanked her roughly upright.

"Stand, you brat. Keep your back against the cabin wall," she'd yell, her face close. "I'll throw your little brother and precious Daddy overboard if you tell... and let sharks eat them."

Impetigo spread across Elizabeth's face, forcing her to spend ten days in the ship's hospital.

Mrs. K. vanished before the gangplank touched the shore of Liverpool Dock. With her vanished the tin of Yardley talcum powder I had given my daughter, and the strap of our bedding-roll. Elizabeth remembers those details, not I.

As we pulled into London's Paddington Station, a roar of laughter erupted from the troops as Elizabeth, her head out of the carriage window, called for a horse taxi.

"*Tonga-Hai.*"

My eldest sister, Rita, took us refugees to stay in her house at 49, De Vere Gardens, just off Kensington High Street across from Hyde Park. For the first few nights, Anne, my sister Aileen's sixteen year-old daughter slept beside them in the guest room double bed. I popped my head around the door. Anne in the middle, Elizabeth curled on one side, Michael the other, they looked so peaceful sleeping there, So happy.

With Anne's help, they adjusted to the strangeness of a country where grass grew green and thick, a country with no turbaned or *saree*-clad servants to bathe and rub them dry, or hand them a dropped hanky or toy, a country where people weren't brown, and where nobody understood their Hindi.

Easing into my father role, I pushed paper boats across the Serpentine in Hyde Park, threw breadcrumbs to mallards and swans, played hide-and-seek in the rhododendron grove, and made-believe Peter Pan's flute called the children to never-neverland from his statue. Children's imaginary worlds blended indistinguishable from reality. Not fully understanding a child's mind, I took them to see *The Red Witch*, a film of pirates, sinking ships and giant man-eating clams. Their terrified screams brought the usherettes running. We fled into the bright lights of Piccadilly Circus. Though we got to know each other better, I couldn't reach them, couldn't touch their wooden hearts. They'd forgotten how to cry. They never mentioned their mother. Not once. It was later I learned Mrs. K. forbade it, slapped them.

"Don't you ever, ever say Mummy again. She's gone." Slap. Slap. She emphasized she meant it.

My Compassionate Leave ended. I left them in the wilds of Dartmoor at what in truth was a paying orphanage, a Holiday Home for Children, and took the Imperial Flying Boat back to India. Two years there, two months furlough, occasional letters, I was more like the absentee father of my own childhood than I cared to admit.

Elizabeth and Michael.

54

LAST DAYS OF THE RAJ

"Leave India to God. If that is too much,
then leave her to anarchy."

-Gandhi, May 1942.

World War II over, Partition, my severance from India and my role of British Officer in sight, I reported to the Regimental depot at Dehra Dun to find I was to proceed immediately to Malaya to take command of the 4th/1st Gurkha Rifles stationed at Kuala Kangsar.

My C.O. was vague as to the reason. "Report to Brigadier Cobb. He'll fill you in." His evasive answers should have warned me of difficulties ahead.

My task was to reshape their wildly frayed edges to fit the Army's square peacetime box. Brigadier Eddie Cobb and his Adjutant welcomed me enthusiastically—a little too enthusiastically.

"Hell of a job ahead, Hugh. The men are furious one of their unit was not appointed."

The 4th/1st, formed in 1940 when war raged across Asia, had never experienced peacetime soldiering and its confining rules and regimentation. They survived the terrors and deprivations of jungle warfare against the Japanese not by following, but throwing out the Army's rulebook. Wild, a bunch of men turned feral with no war left to fight running the Japanese P.O.W. Camp housing their hated enemies, many of whom had surrendered, was the last thing they wanted. Rifles useless in their hands, they slopped around, despondent.

My appointment, I, was the final insult; a C.O. who wasn't one of them, a C.O. who'd never seen action, put in command of their first-class fighting unit. Strange irony, that I, a "disrespector" of time, a misfit with my own regiment, be appointed for the job of instilling Army discipline. I ordered adherence to the Army's dress code and regulatory distinctions between ranks forbidding fraternizing. I reinstated daily drills and strict time-keeping, They made sure I knew I wasn't welcome and what they thought of my interference.

They housed me in a haunted room where continual crash-banging open-shutting of windows and the door made sleep impossible. "I trust you slept well?" They smiled at breakfast. Their sneers confirmed I'd been set up. Not to be beaten, I looked my second-in-command straight in the eye.

"As Senior Officer, I am requisitioning your larger room," I told him pleasantly. "You'll take mine."

All but openly disobeying my orders, men and officers slouched late to morning parade, uniforms crumpled, boots unshined. Shuffling to an untidy formation they performed as mockingly as they dared. It took a week of heavy repetitious drilling before realizing the faster they complied, the faster drill was over.

One major in particular challenged me. At first I ignored his rudeness. He turned his back every time I entered the Mess. Not only did he stroll late to parade, he appeared unshaved and disheveled. He overstepped the officer/other rank boundary by being too familiar with his men. When he refused outright to obey an order to prepare his Company for a daily kit inspection I threatened to clap him under guard and ship him back to India. It was the tipping point. He folded and obeyed.

Not only the men, the camp itself was in "shit order" without guardhouse or emergency gong. I corrected the worst oversights my first day and established a Guardroom set within a neat square of whitewashed stones such as "Fort Tent" sported on the North West Frontier. I had every cracked mug thrown out from the Officers Mess, ordered china and glass from Regimental H.Q. India, and allowed no officer to appear at dinner wearing parade-ground fatigues. Slowly, slowly, despite universal opposition, I gained their respect, and they regained their pride. "Spit 'n polish" restored, we turned our attention to the internment camp housing of the five thousand Japanese P.O.W.s at Kuala Kangsar—cleanliness, better food, and medical care. Orderly, their camp, like ours, lifted both prisoners' and guards' morale. Many Japanese surrendered the moment Japan declared defeat.

I'd been in Kuala Kangsar about three months when Brigadier Cobb left for the Imperial Defence College, England. I grabbed his spacious bungalow and offered my Second-in-Command his old room. The Regiment ran smoothly, allowing me to relax my iron grip. R&R was restored, sports and a polo club introduced. Tentatively, truce was declared. I made a couple of friends.

Villages sprawling the coastline were suspected of illegally importing arms for the Chinese terrorists. Our 4th/1st Regiment received orders to seize their weapons and destroy any arms dumps. United by the prospect of battle, for once we worked together planning the operation. "Mudlark." My Sikh Brigade Major came up with the code name. Faces blackened, bayonets sharpened, camouflaged in battle fatigues, we put silently out to sea.

Dawn. From the Brigade H.Q. I established in one of the landing craft, I gave the order to land. The bow gates of the landing craft opened, spilling two battalions of Indian infantry out onto the beaches and into the jungle. Surrounding the villages, they cut off escape. Arms were seized, dumps destroyed, and villagers captured. Perfectly executed, without loss of life, Mudlark was quickly over. Hardly the frontline, Mudlark was the closest I made to planning and commanding a battle.

I could feel my India coming to a close, smell it in the air. Independence came at a price—incomes, jobs. I caught the fleeting regret in people's eyes. The Battalion I escorted back to Dharamsala felt little pride in the task assigned—disposing mounds of surplus military equipment lying around Chittagong. It was as though we threw out three hundred years of what Britain had struggled so hard to amass.

Create a Muslim Pakistan or not? Was Ghandi, Nehru, Jinnah, or Mountbatten right or wrong? India struggled.

Mountbatten, intent on a speedy transfer of Britain's power to India, ordered regiments disbanded and repatriated. A bare skeleton of British troops remained to oversee India's birth to independence.

Jinnah succeeded in creating his Pakistan. He succeeded in splitting a nation.

Muslims and Hindus turned on one another like mad dogs loosened from chains. Calcutta erupted—strikes, riots, looting. Friend knifed friend and family burned family. Streets became rivers of blood. Illegal sales of surplus American arms and ammunition abandoned by "Vinegar Joe" Stilwell's troops ensured violence escalated.

Ghandi, close to death, lay tragically limp, refusing food in protest of the violence erupting in his beloved India. Next, he was up rousing his supporters to peaceful demonstration, demanding India remain one nation. I glimpsed his actual person once. Bespectacled, bare-chested, in only a homespun *dhoti,* the frail man walked with the aid of a cane at the head of a crowd accompanied by a tall western woman in a white *saree.* India's hero. I was ashamed I had once referred to him as "that half-naked fakir."

Gandhi lost his hold. Emergency was declared. Regiments not already disbanded were ordered immediately to retake control of Calcutta. Delhi H.Q. appointed me C.O. of my father's old regiment, the Third Gurkha Rifles, and sent me into Action. August 16th, 1946 marked "the week of the long knives."

Bloated corpses, unburied in the streets, became food for rats and roaming packs of pie dogs. Bodies of children, babies, women trailing blood-spattered *sarees*, and shirtless men, eyes staring, floated down canals and rivers with the fish. Trams, abandoned, spilt corpses. Torched, houses flamed. Burning tires spewed black...sporadic rifle fire...overflowing mortuaries...the all-pervading stench—recurrent nightmares I'm unable to erase.

I set up the "Third's" main H.Q. in the Calcutta Museum alongside the Second Gurkha Regiment, a second H.Q. in a Ladies Seminary, and a third near the Sealdah Railway station. A museum room displaying bottles of gruesome medical, formalin-preserved specimens served as Officers Mess. Eating and sleeping within sight and smell of floating body parts only compounded the dreadful scenes outside.

Command posts were under constant terrorist attack. Caught in violent battle, our troops were forced to retaliate and attack their strongholds. For the first time, I killed a man. Coming at me with a knife, his hatred blazed, spanning the ten feet separating us. I pulled the trigger. Seeing his life force fade, something within me died.

Though civilian Europeans were spared, the "week of the long knives" lived up to its name. Rioters as well as Indian and British troops died. It took our two Gurkha Regiments, five British, five Indian Regiments and the local police, to partially restore order. Why? Why? Why? Who was fighting whom, and why were Indians killing Indians when previously they lived in tolerance of each other's religions? The Raj, British Rule—was that in vain? Had Britain failed so utterly? In a grim mood, we asked these questions.

As cold weather approached, the situation simmered under control, and, like the sun's heat, the violence abated. Ordered to leave, we dispersed to Fort William for final disbandment. All but our uniforms and memories became India's to keep. Reminders of a century shared, we handed them our Colors, funds, silver, our hard-won battle trophies—our Regimental history.

On August 15th, 1947, mirror images of one another, Lieutenant Colonel P.O. Dunn, and I, nose-to-nose, sword-to-sword, backs rigid, stood frozen in salute as the Regimental Band played Britain's, *"God Save Our Gracious King, long live our noble King...happy and glorious...long to reign over us...God save the King."* Our Union Jack slid slowly down the flagpole for the final time. India's tri-colored stripes rose to take its place, and unfurl fluttering to the crowd's mighty roar, drowning the sound of India's new national anthem. I handed over our Colors and made them his, the first Indian Commanding Officer of our regiment, Lieutenant Colonel P.O. Dunn. Neither he nor I could see one another's faces for tears. We shook hands. India became India's. I no longer belonged.

"Britain could hold India if she had a heart to do so," Lord Wavell declared before he resigned. "But to leave India peacefully as a single state would take at least five years of continued British Rule."

Britain had no heart to do so, and let her hold on India go. Atlee's Labor Party under Attlee ignored Wavell and appointed Lord Mountbatten, who, true to his promise, scuttled hastily from India, leaving behind his shameful legacy of civil war.

Did Attlee, by then Prime Minister, forget his very own words, the words spoken so vehemently to me after lunch one day during the Simon Commission meeting at Ratan Tala House when I was recuperating from malaria? I remembered. His every word.

"Partition will happen only over my dead body."

Did he feel remorse Partition happened not over one, but over half a million, some say one million, dead bodies? Did the acrid smoke swirl from those million funeral pyres to penetrate his dreams and stick in his throat?

So garlanded, hardly able to breathe, so blinded by tears, barely able to see, I rode the train as if in a dream to Bombay's Ballard Pier to embark from the same quayside where the lowly Subaltern, Second Lieutenant Hugh Vincent Rose, first stepped onto India's soil twenty-seven years before.

Imperial Lament

remember also on Armistice Day
the dead still potent to inspire
scattered lonely in sun-baked graves
forgotten
silent hosts of a lost Empire
waiting for the muted trumpets' reminder
to think of them on Armistice Day
and thank them.

EPILOGUE
THE UNTURNED PAGE

Partition liberated me along with India that August 15th, in 1947. With a pension of 700 pounds sterling a year and a 4,000-pound golden bowler, I became a free man. Borneo, Eritrea, Malaya, my path led me to their mountains and jungles, to the European snows, and to the wild places of a pen and paper. I dreamed madcap dreams of flying bedsteads, and plots of groundnuts spread beneath coconut groves. I found true love again at last. I remarried and bore another child.

I look into my future, to the last day of my eighty-six years. I see my striped pajama legs slip below the cuffs of the grey trousers I've pulled on over my sleepwear after my pre-dinner bath. Presentable, I descend the stairs and take both her hands, my wife of forty years, my Susan's hands. I say,

"Before we have our drink, let's say our private mantra."

She takes mine, and as we look into each other's eyes, we repeat together,

"I love you more and more each day."

I see her turn towards the Georgian decanter to pour my evening's *burra* peg of whisky, for I am feeling tired that day. I wait for her. I see her pouring hers. I gasp and allow my glass to shatter on the floor. My head slumps forward and I am gone to become an explorer in another world.

the end was us
and the beginning
only to have loved
was to light a star
in the nameless chaos

OBITUARIES

Lt-Col Hugh Rose

LIEUTENANT-COLONEL HUGH ROSE, an intrepid soldier and explorer, who has died aged 86, was the first European to climb the Kuh-i-Taftan, an active volcano in Persian Baluchistan.

Rose enjoyed a remarkably adventurous life, in which he saw service on the North-West Frontier, in Tibet, Aden, Persia, Egypt, Malaya and Borneo. Many of his experiences verged on the bizarre.

Hugh Vincent Rose was born on April 11 1905 and educated at Aldenham and Sandhurst. He had his first sight of military action at the age of nine in 1914, for his family were then living at Knocke-le-Zoute, where the Belgian infantry confronted the German Uhlans.

His family was evacuated from Zeebrugge by destroyer. Soon afterwards he told the whole exciting story to an old lady he met in the grounds of Farnborough Convent. Subsequently he learned that she was the Empress Eugenie.

Rose was commissioned in 1924 and was posted to the 3rd QAO Gurkha Rifles who were then in the Khyber and saw active service against the Afridis and Orakzais.

In 1931, with two companions, he crossed the main Himalayan range by four dangerous and little used passes — each more than 18,000 ft — to explore and sketch, for the Survey of India, an unmapped area called Hoti, on the British border land of Western Tibet.

There he discovered an unknown pass across the Zaskar Range into Tibet but heavy snowfalls trapped his party, one of whom had a badly poisoned knee, at 14,000 ft. As the only skier in the expedition, Rose then crossed into Upper Kumaon, covered 18 miles by moonlight to the village of Gonsali and returned the next night with food and stores carried by two Kamet porters.

Thus fortified, the party crossed into Tibet and thence home by the Niti pass. All three were then severely reprimanded for overstaying their leave and for crossing into Tibet without official passes.

In 1932 Rose was seconded to be personal assistant to the Resident and Chief Commissioner of Aden. Shortly after his arrival the Emperor Haile Selassie and King Alfonso of Spain turned up at the same time to stay at the Residency.

At the subsequent banquet Rose had to decide whom to place on the Resident's right, a ruling Emperor or a non-reigning King married to a British princess. He decided in favour of the Lion of Judah and as a result was made a Chevalier of the Ethiopian Order of Menelik II.

Although Socotra was part of the Aden Protectorate it had never been visited until reports were received that the Sultan was flying the Italian flag. The Resident, the political agent and Rose thereupon sailed for Temerida, the capital, in HMS *Penzance* which, on arrival, trained its guns on the palace and invited the Sultan on board.

The Sultan was received with due ceremony before being ordered to entertain the ship's company ashore for a week and to provide 30 camels and guides for the exploration of the interior. Although the coastal Arabs were prosperous merchant traders, the Aboriginals in the interior were given to witchcraft and cannibalism.

Rose: intrepid trouble-shooter

The party then went on to Mukalla, where the Sultan laid on a Guard of Honour. Although dressed as Boy Scouts this guard turned out to be the Sultan's slaves.

The party's next assignment was to fly in three Wapiti aircraft to Shibam in the Hadramaut, which had also never been visited. The object was to stop a civil war between the Fahdli Sultan of Shibam and the Seyyids of Tarim and to rescue an English peer's son who was feared lost in those parts.

On their return journey, having ended the war and found the peer's peregrinating son, Rose had to share the rear cockpit of his Wapiti with a wild Arabian Oryx destined for London Zoo.

Shortly afterwards, when spending 10 days leave in British Somaliland, Rose suddenly came face to face with a black-maned lion and its mate. Both were on the point of charging him when his life was saved by a village marriage procession which suddenly emerged from the bush with ululations and drum beating.

Rose's next appointment was at Meshed, in north-east Persia, as Vice-Consul. There his chief task was to organise the escape of White Russians across the border, 70 miles away.

He also helped to organise espionage, which included the robbing of a safe in the Soviet Embassy. Subsequently he was appointed Vice-Consul at Zahidan in the south, where he collected numerous archaeological specimens.

Here he discovered that the 12,000ft-high Kuh-i-Taftan, though an active volcano, was blanketed in snow, and also lay in a prohibited military zone where the new Shah was fighting rebel tribesmen. As he descended, Rose encountered some black-tented nomads whose white-bearded patriarch had a goat killed in his honour.

On returning to Zahidan, however, Rose learned that his hirsute host was the chief rebel and that in consequence questions were being asked about Rose in both the *Majlis* (Persian Parliament) and the House of Commons.

Rose was then transferred to South Waziristan, on the North-West Frontier of India, as assistant political agent. Rose's predecessor — and indeed his successor — were murdered, a fate which Rose only narrowly escaped, being shot at several times.

On another occasion, when trying to discover the whereabouts of the elusive Fakir of Ipi, Rose's small party was ambushed and nearly wiped out.

The headquarters of the agency was at Tank, where, assisted by the Nawab who provided the horses, Rose founded a tent club, as pig-sticking associations were known.

In 1935 Rose attended the Staff College at Quetta. Subsequently he held various staff appointments, but during the Second World War he served with his battalion in the Middle East, at one time as acting CO.

After this he became GSO1 in Aden and then Commander of the Mewar Infantry in Egypt. After the war he commanded the 4th/1st Gurkha Rifles in Malaya and also took over 33 Brigade.

His last active service command was with the 1st/3rd Gurkha Rifles in Calcutta during the traumatic period of Partition.

In 1950 Rose came out of retirement to act as deputy director of operations against Coptic and Muslim terrorists in Eritrea. There he introduced the "Ferret Force" system, later adopted by Gen Templer in Malaya.

In 1952 Rose obtained a Colonial Office appointment as State Home Guard Officer, Perak, Malaya, and from there, in 1954 went to Singapore to work with the Joint Intelligence Committee, Far East. His final appointment was Deputy Defence Secretary, North Borneo.

At the end of this contract he returned to England and floated a property company in South Kensington and a firewood business in Devon.

Apart from his polo, pig-sticking, shooting and ski-ing (which he continued into his eighties), Rose was a competent squash player who represented the United Services and Army and Navy clubs, and an enthusiastic yachtsman.

Rose published a book of poems and contributed to various journals, including *Blackwood's Magazine* and *The Times*. He was a Fellow of the Royal Geographical Society.

His first marriage, to Barbara Allcard, was dissolved. They had a son (Maj-Gen Michael Rose) and a daughter. Rose married secondly, in 1954, Susan Sclater; they had a son.

Daily Telegraph, 13/09/1991

NOT A SAINT

Tribute by Philip Mason OBE CIE, English civil servant and author. Known for his two-volume book on the British Raj, The Men Who Ruled India.

I closed my eyes and saw clearly a Himalayan blue poppy, like a fragment of the noonday sky dropped to earth, growing just where I had found it, half a century ago, in a sheltered place below an outcrop of rock, near the summit of a little peak of nine or ten thousand feet in the foothills near Simla. increasingly often in old age - a feeling of awed wonder at my own identity. 'What on earth am I doing here, in this body, with these memories? Who am I really?' That is what one wonders. It is a feeling hard to convey to anyone else but quite unmistakable., It does not last long when it comes.

It is not surprising, of course, that a questioning of one's own identity should arise in old age when one lives with the knowledge that the physical link with this body the personality must before long be interrupted. The point is brought home - if that were needed - by the loss of friends. I have lost four in the last few months - and I mean friends, not just acquaintances. I wonder what has become of them. One in particular has been much in my thoughts, perhaps just because he was so different in character from myself.

He was a soldier, always in hot water when I first knew him sixty years ago, usually for some impulsive action carried out on the spur of the moment. He sought and enjoyed danger; he was generous and loyal to his friends, often unwisely outspoken in their defence. He was a man who said yes to life and took it with both hands as it came, seldom stopping to think. He enjoyed food, drink and the company of women. There was a mountain in Persia that was forbidden to foreigners - but it was a mountain and it was there so he had to climb it - and there was trouble. He said he would go ski-ing till he was eighty and he did........ He wrote some poetry, not very good, which he was reluctant to inflict on others; he loved sea and sky and air and rapid motion. He was kind and merry and brave. I think St.Peter would have liked him.

Peter who keeps the gate - he would have liked my friend.

He was not a saint, any more than I am, but I think the part of me that loved him and enjoyed his company was not the worst part.

PHILIP MASON

Hugh at his 80th Birthday Party

GLOSSARY

Angreezi . . . . English
ayah . . . . nanny
badmash . . . . robber, bandit
bagh . . . . tiger
baksheesh . . . . money
barasti . . . . dwelling made of woven palm
bearer . . . . personal servant, valet
bhisti . . . . water boy/wallah
box-wallah . . . . civilian
burra . . . . large
burtza bush . . . . kind of thorny vegetation
butti . . . . oil hurricane lamp
chai masala . . . . spicy, sweetened tea often made with buffalo milk
chappati . . . . flat bread
charpoy . . . . wooden bed strung with choir or jute
chital . . . . kind of spotted deer
chota peg . . . . small, one-finger measure of whisky
chowkidar . . . . night watchman
chuplies . . . . thonged, open footwear
dacoit . . . . member of a band of armed robbers
dastur . . . . graft, bribe, commission
decco . . . . common english slang for "a look"
dhal . . . . dish made of lentils
dhobi . . . . laundry
dhoti . . . . male sarong worn pulled between the legs
dish-dash . . . . ankle-length shirt worn by men in arabia
dood . . . . milk
droshki . . . . horse-drawn or motorized taxi
Durbar . . . . official welcoming procession
felus . . . . Arabic for money
ferengi . . . . foreigner
ghar . . . . temple, holy building, church
gharri . . . . taxi
ghooming . . . . strolling, walking
grass widow . . . . . . a wife left alone while her husband is at sea or away on business
groundsheet . . . . a waterproof ground cloth placed under camp bedding
gurkhali . . . . adjective for gurkha
jadughar . . . . holy house, temple
jheel . . . . swamp

kunji . . . . .curved knife in decorative silver scabbard worn by sheikhs, etc
kakar. . . . . .kind of deer
khud . . . . steep slope
lathi. . . . . metal-tipped cane
laghan . . . . .tithe
limu-pani . . . . lime water
lingam. . . . . phallic symbol of shiva
machan . . . . platform erected as a hiding place, used for hunting large animals
mahout . . . . elephant trainer, groom
majlis. . . . . .formal reception room
malik. . . . . .tribal headsman
munshi . . . . .teacher
murti. . . . . statue or shrine imbued with holy energy
namaskar . . . . .hindu greeting
nullah . . . . dry river bed
oorial. . . . . wild bearded sheep
pani. . . . . water
picket . . . . fortification
pie dog . . . . stray, half-wild mongrel dog
plimsoll. . . . . .canvas footwear
political agent. representative of the foreign political service
puggri . . . . turban made of length of wound cloth
punka . . . . wetted mats hanging from the ceiling, used to cool rooms
quaich . . . . .charcoal holder
raga . . . . devotional classical Indian musical composition
raj . . . . sanskrit meaning reign
R.M.C. . . . . Royal Marine Corps
roti . . . . bread
salaam. . . . . .greeting
sambhar . . . . .kind of deer
samosa. . . . . triangular deep-fried, savory-filled pastry
sangar . . . . small temporary fortified position made of loose stones
sepoy. . . . . shikh regiment; or indian soldier serving under british command
shandy. . . . . beverage consisting of beer and lemonade
shikari. . . . . guide
"six of the best" . . . . euphemism for a beating
Subedar-Major . . . . senior rank of an indian officer in british india
syce . . . . groom
Tannoy . . . . .brand name for a sound-amplifying system
thulsidar. . . . . village headman
tonga. . . . . .horse-drawn transport
topee . . . . straw-stuffed helmet
wallah . . . . .man, person
van. . . . . .last, rear

The Rani Jhansi. The Warrior Queen.
One of India's most beloved heroines, rides from her besieged fort with her baby strapped to her back. Before I had any idea of writing my father's biography, I discovered this sculpture in the Santa Fe flea market not knowing its identity or connection to my family. Commonly known as Lakshmibai she was captured and killed during my great uncle, Sir Hugh Rose's campaign in June 1858.
See pages 99–100.

Lightning Source UK Ltd.
Milton Keynes UK
UKHW01n1352300518
323461UK00002B/66/P

9 780986 118821